THE LAW FOR A WOMAN

THE *Law* FOR A *Woman*

REAL CASES AND WHAT HAPPENED

BY *Ellen Switzer*

IN ASSOCIATION WITH

Wendy W. Susco, J.D.

CHARLES SCRIBNER'S SONS
New York

Library of Congress Cataloging in Publication Data

Switzer, Ellen Eichenwald.
    The law for a woman.

    Bibliography: p.
    Includes index.
    1. Women—Legal status, laws, etc.—United States.
I. Susco, Wendy W. II. Title.
KF478.S95   346'.73'013   75–12722
ISBN 0-684-14379-8 (cloth)
ISBN 0-684-14694-0 (paper)

3 5 7 9 11 13 15 17 19 C/C 20 18 16 14 12 10 8 6 4 2
1 3 5 7 9 11 13 15 17 19 C/P 20 18 16 14 12 10 8 6 4 2

Printed in the United States of America

CONTENTS

PREFACE

Since the first edition of *The Law for a Woman* was published, two important new laws affecting our rights to obtain and maintain credit have been passed. There has also been a clarification by the U.S. Supreme Court of the 1973 abortion decision. We have added this preface in order to include these recent developments.

The Equal Credit Opportunity Law went into effect in October 1975. Credit grantors (i.e., banks, loan companies, credit card companies and retailers offering charge accounts) will no longer be able to practice any form of sex or marital status discrimination. The only criteria for a decision to grant or not to grant credit must be the individual's reliability and credit-worthiness.

The new law literally affects millions of women throughout the United States. It means that no bank or other lending institution may refuse to consider a mortgage application of a single woman who is employed or who has some other form of steady income. Banks may no longer discount the earnings of wives when deciding on the amount of a mortgage or a loan to be allocated to a family. Married women must be granted charge accounts in their own names — if they are credit-worthy individuals. Many retailers insisted in the past that accounts be carried in the husband's name, even when the wife had an income of her own (usually because she held a job) and cancelled the accounts arbitrarily when the woman became widowed or divorced, just when she needed credit most.

Credit grantors may no longer interrogate married women about their birth control practices and intentions to bear children, nor may they charge higher interest rates because of sex or marital status. If a woman is asked questions (either verbally or on a written form) which seem to her to be unrelated to her individual credit-worthiness (i.e., a charge account application that insists on knowing not only *her* salary or other income but her husband's as well), she may refuse to answer such a question, and her refusal cannot be used to deny her credit. If she can prove discrimination, she may sue for actual damages, plus in some instances $10,000 in punitive damages. What this means to women is that now more than ever before, they should establish their credit-worthiness as early as possible. Lawyers advise that any young woman who goes to work should open her own charge accounts as soon as possible, instead of continuing to use her parents' accounts. Married women should insist on credit in their own names (i.e., Mrs. Eileen Smith instead of Mrs. Joe Smith or even worse, Mr. and Mrs. Joe Smith), and any woman who is planning a legal separation or divorce should have all charge accounts she plans to keep changed to her own name if they have previously been listed in her husband's name.

Recently widowed women have often found that all their charge accounts were cancelled as soon as their husbands' death notices appeared in the local paper. (Credit managers seem to be avid readers of obituary pages.) This practice is also no longer legal. If the widow has an income, from Social Security, pension funds, life insurance, a job, or any other source, she can demand that her credit be restored immediately.

The Fair Credit Billing Act which went into effect on January 1, 1976, applies to both men and women. But since a woman frequently pays department store, utility, and other regular monthly bills, she should beware of the nature and implications of this law.

The act requires that all credit grantors *must* acknowledge all letters pointing out possible billing errors within thirty days of receipt. On the other hand, the debtor has to notify the credit-granting agency by letter (a telephone call or writing objections on the bill itself is not enough) that an error has apparently been made. Within ninety days of receiving the letter, the credit grantor must either correct the error or explain why, in his opinion, the bill was correct. While this procedure is underway the credit giver may not write dunning letters to the debtor or turn the disputed matter over to a collection agency or attorney. If you, as the debtor, are not satisfied with the explanation you get from the credit giver, and you notify him in writing within ten days of receiving the explanation, the normal collection process may be initiated. If, however, it turns out that you were right all along, the credit giver must make this known to every individual or agency to which he has reported your overdue bill. Also, when making the initial report, the credit giver has to tell the collection agency or attorney that the amount of the bill is still in dispute and that the debtor is not making the payment because the matter has not been cleared up.

All of this may seem like nit-picking to many women. But anyone who has ever tried to correspond with a computer owned by a credit card company, a department store, or, worst of all, a hospital will greet this new law with a sigh of relief.

The other important purpose of the act is to protect the consumer from having to pay for defective merchandise or incompetent services. If the debtor has a problem with property or services purchased on credit, he or she may have the right to refuse to pay the billed amount, if he or she has tried in good faith to return the merchandise or to give the person rendering the service a chance to correct the problem. Again, this may seem like complicated legal jargon, but anyone who has ever accepted delivery of a defective TV set or washing machine, or received a plumber's bill of $100 when the shower still leaks or the sink is still stopped up, will be delighted with this new protection.

Unfortunately, this part of the act is limited to merchandise purchased in your home state, within 100 miles of your current mailing address, and costing more than $50. This means that unfortunately you are not protected from unscrupulous mail-order houses and other organizations that sell merchandise or services nationwide and that are not in your immediate area. To protect yourself from this kind of problem, you should check with your Better Business Bureau before sending money or a check through the mails. The Bureau may already have received many complaints about the organization; on the other hand, it may know that you are dealing with an honest business and have little need to worry. If you have been swindled by a mail-order firm, you might complain to your local post office. You may not get your money back, but the U.S. Postal Service investigates all alleged mail frauds and may be able to put the perpetrator out of business.

Two court decisions clarify the Supreme Court's abortion decision of 1973. Early in 1976 the Supreme Court, by letting stand a decision by a lower court, ruled that private hospitals, including those run by religious organizations, may refuse to admit a patient for an abortion even if she and her physician agree she should have one. On the other hand, public hospitals (i.e., hospitals that are designated as community facilities or are run by state or local governments) are probably bound by the 1973 decision and must admit such women for abortions.

Also, no woman may be denied Medicaid funds to pay for an abortion if she is otherwise eligible for this program, according to an Appeals Court decision. Several states had banned the use of public funds for abortions; they must now obey the Court's decision, unless they are willing to lose all federal health grants. So far, no state government has been willing to go that far. This matter may still reach the United States Supreme Court but most lawyers feel that the Court will uphold the lower court's decision.

On looking over the record, both in legislation and in court decisions; it seems that, in spite of some setbacks, the legal fight for the rights of women is moving ahead — but we still have a long way to go in terms of enforcement, as well as in terms of legislative and judicial action.

THE LAW FOR A WOMAN

INTRODUCTION

> It certainly cannot be affirmed, as an historical fact, that this [the right to pursue any lawful occupation] has ever been established as one of the fundamental privileges and immunities of the sex. On the contrary, the civil law, as well as nature herself, has always recognized a wide difference in the respective spheres and destinies of man and woman. Man is, or should be, woman's protector and defender. The natural and proper timidity and delicacy which belongs to the female sex evidently unfits it for many of the occupations of civil life. ... The paramount destiny and mission of woman are to fulfill the noble and benign offices of wife and mother. This is the law of the Creator.

The above paragraph is not contained, as many of us might think, in a tract of an antifeminist religious sect or a Victorian book on manners and morals. It's part of a U.S. Supreme Court's *majority* decision, in the case of *Bradwell* v. *Illinois*, decided almost one hundred years ago. Myra Bradwell wanted to become a lawyer. She had fulfilled all the prerequisites that would admit her to the bar of her state. She was refused on the sole grounds that she was a woman. The U.S. Supreme Court sustained that refusal, quietly but firmly, with the implied contention that under the Fourteenth Amendment to the U.S. Constitution, women were not "persons."

Section I of that amendment reads: "All persons born or naturalized in the United States, and subject to the jurisdiction thereof, are citizens of the United States and of the state in which they reside. No state shall make or enforce any law which shall abridge the privileges and immunities of Citizens of the United States, nor shall any state deprive any person of life, liberty or property, without due process of law, nor deny any person within its jurisdiction the equal protection of the law." The amendment was passed, of course, as a sort of corollary to the Thirteenth Amendment, which freed the slaves. Apparently it did not occur to the honorable Court that its provisions might be applied to a woman as well, since under this amendment a black *man* could not be denied admission to the bar, if he were otherwise qualified.

The idea of women as legally different from men eventually became so deeply imbedded in case law throughout the United States' jurisdictions that it took a special amendment to allow them to vote. The year after the *Bradwell* case, in 1874, the Supreme Court denied women the right to vote under the *Bradwell* precedent. It was not until 1919 that women gained "personhood" for purposes of suffrage: the Nineteenth Amendment specifically states, "The right of citizens to vote shall not be denied because of sex," and this was adopted only after a fierce struggle. Courageous women throughout this country had to fight for their personhood even though every important national document had declared all citizens equal under the law, from the Declaration of Independence to the Bill of Rights.

Women had great hopes for themselves after the Nineteenth Amendment was passed. Many of these hopes were disappointed. The struggle for equality under the law had to continue into the 1970s and continues still. The Equal Rights Amendment, which passed both Houses of Congress overwhelmingly, still has not passed the required number of state legislatures to become the law of the land. Until it does, women will be regarded as different and unequal in many legal cases.

There are women who are not only willing, but eager, to accept these inequalities, because they feel that they provide them with certain advantages. There were also women in 1919 who did not want to vote, because they felt that politics was essentially a masculine activity, conducted in the indelicate and raw atmosphere of smoke-filled rooms. They agreed with Justice Bradley that "man is, or should be, woman's protector and defender."

But the vast majority of women are changing, and they are changing rapidly. In the first years that women had the vote few laws were passed to adjust some of the inequalities that existed in both statutory and case law in the United States. In the past five years, more laws that truly guarantee women equal rights and equal protection under the law have been passed on the state and federal levels than in the previous fifty years.

The probable reason for this is that male legislators have come to realize that, on some issues, a great many women vote as a bloc, just as other minorities have used bloc votes to gain necessary legal, political, social, and economic clout.

Certainly Myra Bradwell would be pleased if she could have lived to see the present legal scene. During 1974, more women entered law school than in any previous year. Some schools report that almost one-third of their students are women. They also are entering other previously male-dominated professions in unprecedented numbers. There are more women physicians, architects, engineers, plumbers, carpenters, jockeys, reporters, and business executives in 1974 than ever before in our history.

What's more, women are entering politics. It's likely that former President Richard M. Nixon never really considered naming a woman as Vice-President when Spiro Agnew departed in disgrace, but at least he mentioned it as a possibility. Ten years ago such a suggestion would have been greeted as a joke. In 1974 almost fifty women ran for Congress, several for the U.S. Senate, two for governor of their states, and countless others for positions in state legislatures, as mayors, and for membership in city councils. In a number of primaries, in which they were considered hopeless underdogs, they have won, often spending a small percentage of the campaign funds generously doled out by their male opponents.

In the past few years, Equal Employment Opportunity laws at both federal and state levels have been passed. Of course they are being enforced through the courts and economic pressures from federal and state governments are being applied. Equal Educational Opportunity laws were passed in 1974 at the federal level, and even stronger laws are before several state legislatures. Housing laws include nondiscrimination codes, and public accommodation laws have been made applicable to women, as well as to racial minorities.

There is, of course, a question of whether women are a "minority" in the technical sense of the word. Numerically, there are more women than men in the United States, and what's more, women seem to hold in their own names more of the wealth of this country than men.

But as Helen Mayer Hacker, in her introduction to *Sex Roles in Law and Society*, has pointed out, "In defining the term 'minority group' the presence of discrimination is the identifying factor. As Louis Wirth has pointed out, 'minority group' is not a statistical concept, nor need it designate an alien group. Indeed, for the present discussion, I have adopted his definition: 'A minority group is any group of people, who because of physical or cultural characteristics, are singled out from others in the society in which they live for differential and unequal treatment, and therefore, regard themselves as objects of collective discrimination.' It is apparent that this definition includes both objective and subjective characteristics of a minority group: the fact of discrimination and the awareness of discrimination with attendant reactions to that awareness."

Ms. Hacker continues to explain that often the person who experiences group discrimination may be "unaware of the extent to which his group membership influences the way others treat him. . . . Consequently, he interprets their behavior towards him solely in terms of his individual characteristics. Or, less likely, he may be conscious of his membership in a certain group but not be aware of the general disesteem with which the group is regarded."

Ms. Hacker's analysis may be an explanation for two kinds of women who consciously disassociate themselves from the feminist movement: (a) those who tell themselves and others that they have not experienced discrimination because they, themselves, have attained a superior position in the working world (the "Queen Bee"), or (b) those who say that they are willing to accept certain kinds of discrimination, such as refusal of certain jobs, lower pay for equal work, unequal marriage and divorce laws, and so on, in order to maintain privileges in other areas of their lives, most notably the privilege of allowing a man to take care of them.

Women have another quality in common with other minority groups. Because they may be held in lower regard, they often tend to suffer from a certain amount of self-contempt. Some of the harshest judgments on "unfeminine women" who "try to be like men" have come from other women. As psychologist Matina Horner, president of Radcliffe College, has pointed out so graphically in some of her research, "Many women fear success as much as they fear failure. They tend to have a deep conflict which equates success in work and intellectual achievement, with loss of feminity."

Women's perception of themselves as weak and somehow inferior may account for the fact that, for centuries, they have allowed unjust laws and customs to deprive them of their rightful place. It also may explain why so many women are *unaware of the legal rights* that have been won for them by their sisters in alliance with fair-minded male legislators and judges, and their hesitancy in using legal channels to gain these rights for themselves, even when they are aware of their existence.

In this book, through case histories, we hope to help women understand what their legal rights are in the fields of marriage and the family, work, education, housing, credit, and many other areas of their lives in which they have been treated as a "minority." We also have included a chapter on the rights of children, who are frequently discriminated against by law and custom even more vigorously than women.

We hope that this book will help women understand that the millennium is not yet here, nor will it arrive the day the Equal Rights Amendment passes the last legislature to become law. Women will have to continue to fight, in the courts and in their communities, to gain the status of "persons," which, according to Judge Bradley, they lacked under both the U.S. Constitution and the Divine Law.

Chapter I

SOME IMPORTANT FACTS ABOUT THE LAW AND LAWYERS

We live in this country under a fairly complex set of laws, some written and some unwritten. The written ones, the Constitution of the United States and those of the individual states, along with legislation passed by the federal and state legislatures, are called statutes. The unwritten law is called the common law and is derived from the traditions we have inherited from the European colonists who settled this nation. Whether written or unwritten, the law governs our daily behavior and virtually all our relationships, be they business, governmental, or social. Law is, after all, society's way of regulating behavior—encouraging some forms, discouraging others, and forbidding still others—through the mechanism of reward and punishment.

Because few laws are self-enforcing and because it is believed that the parties themselves should not be the final arbiters of their own legal disputes, we have developed a system of courts to decide what the law means in a particular set of circumstances and on whose side the law may be in a dispute, whether the dispute be between individuals, corporations, or even between governments. In the United States, each state has its own court system, consisting of at least one level of trial courts where a judge (and jury) hear each side of a dispute and decide what the facts are (the jury's role) and what law applies (the judge's role). In addition, each state has at least one appellate court to review the decisions of the trial court. The appellate courts, however, do not take testimony or hear witnesses. They make no judgments about the facts. Rather their job is to review the application of the law to the facts found in the trial court.

In addition to the state court systems, which usually hear

disputes arising under state law, we also have a federal court system consisting of trial courts (U.S. district courts) and two levels of appellate courts (the circuit court of appeal and the U.S. Supreme Court). The federal courts hear cases involving federal law (those passed by the Congress), questions raised under the U.S. Constitution, and disputes between citizens of different states involving more than $10,000. State courts are not bound by the federal courts' application of state laws, but only by the appellate decisions of its own state courts. They *are* bound by the decisions of the U.S. Supreme Court and by federal decisions on federal law and constitutional questions.

For example, let's say a woman has been denied an abortion by her local hospital. The prohibition might have been upheld by a local court even though federal courts have been very explicit that abortions on demand cannot be denied. The appellate division of the state court could then overturn the lower court's decision and the woman would be entitled to her abortion. Actually, she is entitled to the abortion in any case, because the U.S. Supreme Court has eliminated all state abortion laws, and if she applies to a federal court, the Supreme Court decision will come into play. Various states have tried to pass their own antiabortion laws in direct contradiction to the Supreme Court's decision and have always been overruled at the federal level.

Laws are generally broken down into two broad categories, criminal and civil. Criminal law is generally statutory, or written in law books, and consists of "thou shalt nots." The government is the accuser and the law-enforcer against alleged offenders. The accused may challenge the governmental right to make certain behavior illegal by raising the questions of whether the law is constitutional (e.g., A sells birth-control pills in state X. The legislature of state X has made it illegal to sell birth-control pills. There is no question that A has done so, but she can challenge state X's right to make her behavior illegal as a violation of her constitutional rights—those guaranteed her by the federal, and perhaps state, Constitution). In addition, the Constitution imposes on the government the burden of proving that the alleged wrongdoer did, in fact, do something wrong that constitutes a crime.

Once an appeal has been won, it probably constitutes a precedent for other, similar cases. For instance, the seller of birth-control pills probably would not even be arrested, even though technically there still might be a law on the books of her state prohibiting the transaction. The U.S. Supreme Court, in the case of *Griswold* v. *Connecticut* decided that the prescription, sale, and use of contraceptives could not be prohibited by a state, since it infringed on the rights of a woman's privacy guaranteed under the U.S. Constitution. Some states have been slow in removing anti-birth-control laws from the books, but they are simply not enforced, since any judge would throw such a case out of court, even if a police officer decided to make an arrest.

Civil law, on the other hand, involves disputes between individuals. It regulates behavior in a variety of ways by allowing access to the courts when one individual in some way either does something "wrong" to another (e.g., smashes into her car) or fails to meet rightfully held expectations. Civil law, in turn, is divided into special areas, such as torts (civil wrongs), contracts, and real property, each of which has its own rules. Much of the law in these areas is unwritten common law. When the legislature decides that the common law is inadequate to deal with modern conditions, it can change the law by passing a statute. The field of labor relations today is one example of statutory influence through change in the common law of contract. "No-fault" legislation has changed part of the law of torts. The law of torts used to say that only one who, through no fault of his/her own, is damaged by the negligence of another is entitled to be made whole for his/her damage by the negligent party. No-fault automobile laws have changed that rule so it does not apply to auto accidents.

Marriage and divorce laws fall into a special category by themselves, neither under torts nor under criminal laws. Only rarely does a marital case get into criminal court, even if the action the plaintiff is claiming as a reason for wishing to dissolve the marriage might be considered a crime. For instance, if a wife claims "cruel and inhuman treatment" (her husband beats her regularly when he is drunk) in a divorce case, she is not seeking to have him jailed, but just to have the marriage legally dissolved. If she wanted him jailed, she would have to call the police right after a beating and bring criminal charges against him. That would refer the case to *criminal* court, where the husband might be jailed or fined, but it would not get the wife a divorce. She would have to sue for that separately.

As you will see in the appendix on divorce laws in the various states, in many jurisdictions "no-fault" divorces now can be granted. They work similarly to the no-fault automobile accident laws. The partners just agree to disagree, and the marriage is dissolved, with neither taking the blame. Most courts require that a property settlement, including such factors as alimony, child support, and so on, be reached by the couple before a no-fault divorce is granted. In some states (Connecticut, for instance) there is a suggestion in the law that any minor children have their own attorney in a no-fault action. When it passed the statute in 1973, the Connecticut legislature apparently feared that couples might be so eager to split up that the rights of these children to support, inheritance, and so on might be ignored.

In reading this book, bear in mind that laws vary from state to state. When we are not talking about constitutional rights or federal laws, it is wise to check your own state's laws before proceeding. Remember, too, that laws are not static. Legislation is passed every day and court interpretations of the law change. It is best, therefore, to seek the advice of an attorney if you need to know how the law specifically affects you.

Finding the right lawyer is often difficult, particularly for women. To date, the vast majority of lawyers, including divorce lawyers, have been men. Although many are very sympathetic toward the rights of women, others tend to identify, consciously or unconsciously, with male litigants. Too many women filing for divorce on legally incontrovertible grounds still hear the attorney, who is supposedly representing *them,* say something like this: "Why do you need alimony (or such a large property settlement or a lump sum to help you get job training)? You will probably be married again within a year . . . you're so attractive." Or the lawyer may try to persuade a woman who does not want alimony because she knows that she is perfectly capable of earning her own living and considers taking money from her husband demeaning, that she should try to "get every penny we can squeeze out of him," because, after all, "you may decide that you don't *want* to work after all."

Lawyers with such attitudes also may regard a woman's suit against a company that has denied her equal employment opportunities as frivolous. "Your husband supports you very well. Do you really want to make all this trouble for your employer, when you don't really need the money?" he may ask.

Finding a compatible lawyer is as important as finding a compatible physician. Women, particularly, might want to make sure that the attorney they have picked respects them as individuals, and doesn't regard them "as the little woman who has been wronged" or "as one of these feminist troublemakers." Either attitude can be very harmful to one's morale when one is trying to win a difficult court case and can persuade the unwary to settle for less than is rightfully hers.

It's considered perfectly ethical to talk to several lawyers before deciding on whom to use in a given case. However, the attorney will probably charge for the initial interview (just as a physician will charge for an initial consultation, even if the patient decides to use another doctor to perform whatever procedure is necessary).

If a woman does not know any attorney in her own community she might ask friends who have been through divorces, similar litigation, or antidiscrimination suits whom they retained and whether they were satisfied with the service they received. Some communities now have women's centers, which try to keep up-to-date lists of attorneys who specialize in representing women fairly. In other communi-

ties there are now women's-law collectives, which take only
cases in which feminist issues are involved.

If you feel that a lawyer is not representing you adequately, it's considered entirely ethical to change lawyers.
However, you formally will have to dismiss one lawyer from
your case before you can engage another one. It would be
unethical for the second lawyer to accept a client who is still
represented by a colleague.

If one lawyer tells you that you just don't have a case, you
might wish to consult a second one. Law is not a precise
science and interpretation of case materials may differ.

It's generally advisable to engage an attorney in any case
(criminal or civil), even if the issues seem entirely clear-cut.
You may have noticed in recent court cases that defendants
who are lawyers themselves are represented by a different
attorney in court. (Almost all the Watergate defendants were
attorneys, for instance.) It's very difficult to be objective
about matters that affect oneself and one's own emotions,
and an outside adviser, who can look at the situation objec-
tively, is usually essential.

This book is not meant to turn you into an instant amateur
legal expert. It can, however, serve as a guide in deciding
whether or not you wish to pursue a matter in court and can
give you some indication of what your legal rights are and
how you can make sure that they are observed and enforced.

Chapter II

YOUR BASIC CONSTITUTIONAL RIGHTS AS A CITIZEN

Case Histories

1. You are sitting in your home reading the newspaper when the doorbell rings. A police officer apologetically tells you that one of your children has been accused by a neighbor of pilfering several small items. He says he understands that the neighbor who complained is considered rather peculiar by many people, but since she keeps "bothering" the police department, would you mind if he just checked around your daughter's room? That would be the end of the whole incident, he assures you. Do you have to let him in?

2. You are standing on a street near city hall, minding your own business, just as a picket line opposing one of the mayor's most recent policies gets a little out of hand. The marchers are told that they must break up the demonstration promptly, or they will be arrested. Five minutes later the police proceed to arrest everyone in sight, including you. Do you have a legal right to resist this arrest, since you were not a part of the picket line and have no connection with the organization that is disobeying police instructions?

3. You are the editor of an underground college newspaper, and the dean tells you he doesn't like your latest editorial. You are ordered to change the editorial immediately or the college will confiscate all copies of your paper. Would this be legal?

4. You are separated from your husband, and he is living at a different address. However, the house in which you live is in his name, and telephone bills, utility bills, and so on are still being paid by him. During a recent conversation he has let you know that he thinks you are seeing another man.

Since you actually have not *seen* the man to whom he has referred, but have talked to him a few times on the telephone, you accuse your husband of having your phone tapped. You indignantly call the telephone company to put a stop to this spying. They point out to you that, since the telephone is in your husband's name, he has every right to tap his own phone, even if he is living at another address and has another phone number as well. Are they correct?

5. You accidentally run your car through a red light. The police officer issues a ticket for a traffic violation. After he has checked your license and your car registration, he indicates that he would like to search the car. He indicates that there have been complaints that a car matching the description of yours was used in a crime. He is not accusing you of anything and he doesn't have a warrant. Must you allow him to search your automobile?

6. Your daughter writes to you that she is visiting friends in a commune. Ostensibly, they are supporting themselves and the farm by growing organic vegetables. But your daughter indicates that she has found a large cultivated bed of marijuana among the radishes, tomatoes, and cabbages. She assures you that she had nothing to do with planting the crop and does not intend to use it or to participate in its harvesting or sale. She is having a marvelous time, and really doesn't want to come home. But she is worried that her friends might be arrested. She asks if under these circumstances she might be legally implicated in a drug charge. Would she?

7. Some years ago you were doing research for the League of Women Voters on third parties in your state. You heard a candidate from an extreme left-wing group offering pamphlets for his organization on a radio program. To assist your research you wrote for the material. Ever since that time you have apparently been investigated. Friends have told you that men who identified themselves as FBI agents have been asking questions about you. You have a feeling that some of your mail may be watched. It turns out you are right. During the time when you wrote to that political organization it was

on the Attorney General's list of subversive organizations (the list no longer exists). Your name is on file at the local FBI office as someone who has been associated with that group. Did the FBI have a right to have you watched? Can you make them destroy whatever record they have gathered on you and destroy your file, since you feel that the information might somehow leak out and damage your career?

8. You are in a park and see the police evicting some long-haired protesters with, in your opinion, unnecessary force. One of the young men already has a bloody head. Is it your legal right to intervene and to tell the policemen to stop roughing up the protesters?

9. You have been called for jury duty, and the dates that have been set conflict with the dates on which your company prepares for its annual meeting. As far as you are concerned, the court could not have picked a more inconvenient time for your appearance. Must you appear on the date set by the court, can you be eliminated from the jury list, or can you ask to have the whole matter postponed to a more convenient time?

Each one of the above examples is based on a recent court case, with some of the facts slightly disguised to avoid identification of specific individuals. Each case also involves personal and legal rights and responsibilities, and the final disposition of the problem probably would be the same whether it happened in a small town in Utah or in New York City.

In the United States you have the same basic legal rights no matter where you live. Most are spelled out in the first ten amendments to the United States Constitution, known as the Bill of Rights. Some of these rights have been amplified by additional federal laws or their application has been broadened by recent federal court decisions.

However, having a legal right and making sure that it is respected are two different problems. That is why, should you get into any trouble with the law, *you must have an attorney.* There is an apocryphal saying, "Anyone who acts as his own lawyer has a fool for a client." In the press you

occasionally may find a situation in which a layman successfully defends himself or herself and wins. If you read carefully between the lines, you will usually notice that there was
a well-qualified attorney in the background. Judges frequently (and correctly, in the opinion of most legal experts)
have turned down requests from a defendant in a criminal
case to act as his own counsel. Of course, in civil (as opposed
to criminal) cases, especially those involving small sums of
money, people often represent themselves. There's hardly
any point in taking a lawyer with you into small-claims court
—his bill might amount to more than the disputed claim.
However, when there is any danger that anyone might go to
jail, a lawyer is essential, no matter how innocent you may
consider yourself of the charges brought against you and how
grievously you may feel your legal rights have been tram-
pled.

Case Solutions

CASE 1. This example (the officer who asked to search your
apartment) involved the Fourth Amendment to the U.S.
Constitution, which secures persons and houses "against unreasonable searches and seizures. . . ." No law officer, except
under emergency conditions (someone is threatening someone else with a gun, for instance) may enter anyone's home
without a warrant or permission to enter. This warrant will
have to be obtained from a judge "upon probable cause."
The law officer will have to convince the judge that he has
"reliable information" a crime has been committed. Therefore, if the police ask to enter your home "just to check
something out," you should ask to see a warrant. If none has
been issued, you have every right to refuse to let the officer
in.

If the police officer has a warrant to arrest someone in the
apartment, but no separate warrant to search, he may look
for evidence in the immediate vicinity of the arrested person. For instance, he may pick up drugs or other contraband
that is lying openly on the living-room table. He may *not* go

through bureau drawers or kitchen cabinets without a separate search warrant.

However, the Fourth Amendment has been interpreted to apply *only* to police and other official agents of the government, not to landlords, friends, parents, and others who have keys to your apartment or who may have a legal right to enter it. For instance, your landlord, if he has a passkey, may search your apartment if he is suspicious of your behavior. If he finds drugs or other contraband, he may turn this over to the police and it may be used as evidence against you. Your present or past roommate, a former husband, lover, or anyone else to whom you have given a key doesn't need a warrant to search through your belongings. If evidence is found, it too may be taken to the police and used against you. However, if the searcher does *not* have a key (and therefore, presumably does not have the legal right to enter your home without your permission), you can bring charges of trespassing or breaking and entering against him.

Parents and guardians have the right to search your apartment even if they have to break down the door to do so, unless you are of legal age or "an emancipated minor." The definition of "legal age" varies from state to state, but it now usually means eighteen, although some states have maintained the age of twenty-one. The definition of "emancipated minor" also varies somewhat, but usually means over eighteen and self-supporting in those states in which the age of majority is twenty-one. A married woman is considered "emancipated" no matter who supports her or what her age is. In a college dormitory the housemother or other college officials have the right to go through rooms, lockers, and so on without a warrant, although the police must have a warrant to do so. Courts have considered college officials to be "in loco parentis" (i.e., taking the place of parents) and have given them the same legal rights as parents in cases of search and seizure. The rationale is that these areas are not "zones of privacy," since one should know that college officials have access to these areas.

It may seem strange that a warning about friends, ex-hus-

bands, lovers, and parents has to be included in this chapter
about your legal rights. However, there are literally thousands of cases (usually drug-related) cluttering up already
overcrowded court calendars because of complaints brought
by friends and relatives of the defendants. Parents worry.
Lovers get jealous. Roommates get angry. And sometimes
they are prompted by these feelings to try to get you into
trouble with the law. The police, prosecutors, and judges
detest such cases. For one thing, it's exceedingly difficult to
obtain a conviction, because the person who brought the
accusation has to *prove* that he or she actually found incrimi-
nating evidence in your possession. So this kind of charge is
a nuisance for everyone concerned. For the defendant, however, it's often more than a nuisance—it can be a serious
crisis. Therefore, as a matter of policy, give keys to your
apartment only to those in whom you have complete faith.
If you ever feel that your confidence has been misplaced, ask
for your key back, or better still, change the lock.

Since some state and city laws require you to give the
landlord a key, it's just best not to arouse his suspicion, or else
to find a congenial landlord.

CASE 2. This case deals with arrest. Unfortunately, the
police have the right to arrest you without a warrant, if, in
the arresting officer's opinion, you have been involved in a
crime, such as a public disturbance or riot, even if you know
that you are a totally innocent bystander. You can bring suit
for false arrest later, but that's usually a fairly hopeless procedure. Meanwhile, go along quietly, and as soon as you get to
the police station, demand to call your lawyer. If you have no
lawyer, call a friend to call his attorney or call Legal Aid. If
you have no friends, you can ask that a public defender be
appointed to represent you. Do not resist arrest in any way.
Resisting arrest (which includes going limp and being
dragged to the police van) is considered a crime in itself and
may get you a fine or a jail sentence, even if the arrest itself
was totally unjustified.

CASE 3. Your right to publish an underground or regular
newspaper, magazine, or proclamation involves the First
Amendment to the U.S. Constitution, which concerns "free-

dom of religion, speech, press, assembly, and petition." It states, "Congress shall make no law respecting an establishment of religion, or prohibiting the free exercise thereof; or abridging the freedom of speech, or of the press; or the right of the people peaceably to assemble, and to petition the government for a redress of grievances." This means that you are free to publish almost anything as long as it is not libelous, does not incite to riot (which usually means giving instructions on how the riot is to be carried out), does not urge someone to commit a specific crime and tell him how to do it, or is not considered by law to be pornographic or obscene.

However, whoever holds the purse strings for your publication does have the right to censor its content, unless you have a legal agreement to the contrary. This means that if the college pays for your paper, the dean can stop you from publishing an editorial attacking him. A private college also has the right to tell you where you can and cannot distribute your publication on its property. Therefore, if the college administration finds your publication objectionable, you may have to finance it yourself through sales, advertisements, and contributions, and print and distribute it off college grounds, unless you are at a state university. Then the same rules that apply to public places also apply.

In some localities you need a permit to sell anything (including your paper) on a public street. If this is the case, ask for the permit. You cannot be turned down just because the chief of police doesn't like either your ideas or your vocabulary, or both. It may take the intervention of a friendly attorney, but unofficial police censorship usually ceases promptly when the city administration understands that the publisher is aware of his legal rights and intends to see them respected.

If you wish to mail your newspaper, you have a right to apply for a third-class mailing permit. Such a permit must be issued to you if you meet all the qualifications, even if your local postmaster doesn't like what you say or how you say it. However, keep in mind laws against pornography and obscenity, especially in publications addressed to minors. When in doubt, ask a lawyer.

Case 4. Your husband does indeed have the right to have

the phone tapped. It's listed in his name and billed to his account. The telephone company often puts a tap on a phone at the request of the subscriber if he or she has been receiving obscene telephone calls, for instance. The police also can be requested by a family if they have received extortion, blackmail, or kidnap threats, for instance. Even if the telephone is listed in your name as well as your husband's, he would be able to give permission for a tap. If you want to preserve your privacy, you will have to get a new phone, in your own name exclusively, and pay your own phone bill.

The police or FBI can tap a telephone legally only if they have a warrant issued by a judge who is convinced that there is cause to believe a crime is being committed, and that the telephone is used as part of that crime. Recently, thousands of criminal cases against gamblers, pimps, and drug sellers were thrown out of court throughout the United States because law-enforcement agencies, under the direction of the U.S. Department of Justice, had obtained evidence through warrantless wire taps. Apparently, former Attorney General John Mitchell believed that these tapes were legal—and they were not.

Occasionally, a case is discovered in which a business hires an undercover agent to tap the phone of a competitor. If this is proven in court, the agent and the person who hired him are both guilty of a crime. The whole issue of telephone taps comes under the Fourth Amendment of the U.S. Constitution, which maintains the "right of the people to be secure in their persons, houses, papers and effects against unreasonable searches and seizures. . . ."

The problem in Case 4 is that legally, since the husband was presumably tapping his *own* phone, no outside party was invading that right.

CASE 5. Several years ago, if you had run your car through a red light, the police only could have given you a ticket, even if they suspected that your car might have been used in the commission of a crime. They would have been obliged to get a warrant to search the car later, in your garage perhaps. In 1974, however, the U.S. Supreme Court changed the ground rules. Now any car that is stopped by the police for a violation may be searched. So, if you are requested to leave your auto for a search, you must comply, even if the officer has no warrant.

The same reasoning, however, does not apply to your person. In other words, the police can search your car, but only pat you down. They cannot open your purse, force you to take off your jacket, go through your pockets, or in any other way conduct a thorough search. You cannot be searched either if you should be arrested for crossing against a red light on foot. You may be given a ticket, asked for identification, and if the officer finds anything suspicious about you, patted down. But that is all.

CASE 6. Any attorney would tell you to advise your daughter to leave that commune with all deliberate speed. If her friends are arrested for possession of drugs for sale, she would be implicated whether she had anything to do with planting the marijuana or not. She might be accused of being an accessory "before and after the fact," and unless she can convince the judge and jury that she cannot distinguish a marijuana plant from a geranium (an unlikely possibility), she probably would be convicted. The same would be true if she were caught in an apartment where drugs were used, even if she herself was not one of the users.

A simple drug-possession charge can get a person into serious trouble. Sentences can range from seven days to life, depending on the state and the judge. As of the fall of 1974, New York State has the toughest drug laws in the United States, but sentences in other states, with less stiff laws, are sometimes tougher than those handed out by New York judges.

So, if anyone in your family is arrested on even a seemingly minor drug charge, immediately call an attorney. Be sure that no one makes a statement without a lawyer present (a right we all have under Article V of the U.S. Constitution).

Often in simple possession cases, lawyers advise their clients to plead guilty if they can get a well-substantiated charge reduced from a "felony" to a "misdemeanor." Conviction of a felony, even if one is only sentenced to probation, may have drastic effects on one's future. It may mean, for instance, that the convicted person can never teach in a public school, never hold a state or city job, never be admitted to law or medical school, and so on. All felony charges are exceedingly serious and should be treated as a definite threat to one's future.

CASE 7. A situation almost identical to this case happened quite recently to a New Jersey high school girl named Lori Paton. A dossier was compiled on her after she wrote for information from a political party that once had been included on the now defunct Attorney General's subversive list, as part of her research for a civics class.

Lori's mail came under surveillance in 1973 when she wrote to the Young Socialist Alliance, affiliated with the Socialist Worker's party. She became aware that her movements were being watched when FBI agents came calling in her neighborhood, asking questions about her character, her possible arrest record (she didn't have one), her father's credit rating, and other things. When the agent discovered, much to his embarrassment, that Lori was engaged in a high-school project, he dropped the case. But her file was kept active for "subversive connections" in FBI headquarters.

Lori sued, with the assistance of the American Civil Liberties Union, and her file was removed and destroyed. However, this was only a partial victory for Lori and the ACLU, which had filed a class action for her, as well as for other citizens who might seek information about unpopular minority parties or causes. The judge in the case rejected the argument that FBI mail-cover surveillance, in and of itself, violated any constitutional rights protecting the privacy of the mails. This decision probably will be appealed.

Meanwhile, if you know that you are being watched because of an innocent inquiry, you probably could complain to the FBI or the police and demand to have your file destroyed. To be sure this is done, you may need an attorney. Because the judge confined his opinion *only* to Lori Paton, your rights of privacy are still not safe.

CASE 8. No matter how brutal and unjustified the actions of the policemen seem to you, you must not interfere with an arrest. Such interference, in itself, is considered a crime, and you will probably be arrested without being able to help the young people. However, you can try to get the badge numbers of the policemen who seem to be exceeding their authority, and report them. Your unsupported word against that of a policeman probably will not receive much attention. So, it's a good idea to line up some other witnesses. If the officers are not wearing badges or have their badge numbers hidden, report that fact. There have been instances in recent years when officers deliberately have removed or concealed their badges in order to escape identification by citizens. This is always against police-department policy, and should be brought to the attention of the authorities.

CASE 9. You probably won't even have to mention to the court that the jury date is inconvenient because it's inventory time in your place of employment. In most states you can be excused from jury duty simply because you are a woman. Most state statutes exempt certain classes of people (the very old, the sick, policemen, firemen, etc.) from compulsory jury duty. One of the classes most frequently exempted, as a whole, is women. As a matter of fact, several states are so certain that women should not serve on juries that they ask any woman who wishes to serve to put her name on a special list. Only if she is on that list will she ever be asked to serve.

Most people find jury duty bothersome (it's badly paid, often comes at inconvenient times, and the prospective juror often finds herself sitting for endless hours in a drafty room waiting to be called to decide something as seemingly unimportant as an automobile injury case or a tenant/landlord dispute), and many women have considered this exemption from jury duty a privilege. It is one special exemption that would be wiped out if the Equal Rights Amendment passes the necessary number of state legislatures to become law.

When one thinks about the implications of this exemption, however, it may seem less like a privilege and more like an insult. What the legislators who wrote the exemption into the statutes were saying is that a woman is really not a full-fledged citizen with all the rights and obligations that citizenship entails. Her place is in the home and in the kitchen. Important business (such as the business of the courts) can best be carried out by men.

Not having a woman on the jury can be particularly damaging to women defendants or plaintiffs. Often a woman's motives and problems are better understood by other women than by a jury made up entirely of men. There have been several recent court cases in which the conviction of a woman by an all-male jury was appealed, in exactly the same way as the conviction of a black by an all-white jury was formerly appealed—and often won. The reasoning behind these appeals is identical. The U.S. Constitution guarantees us a trial by a jury of our peers. If the woman is in the dock, an all-male jury is definitely not made up of "peers."

If the ERA or other federal and state legislation wipe out laws and regulations that make it easier for women than for men to avoid jury duty, women would be covered by exactly the same rules as men: if an appearance would truly constitute a hardship on the person or the person's employer (e.g., the inventory week or the annual meeting), the prospective juror and/or the employer may ask to have jury duty postponed until the hardship period is over. If the prospective juror is the mother of a young child, she almost certainly will be excused if she cannot find appropriate care for the child for the duration of her jury period.

However, there seems little more reason to excuse a female secretary than a male electrician from taking part in a process without which the American judicial system would break down.

Chapter III

EDUCATIONAL RIGHTS

Case Histories

1. You have applied to your state university, which has an excellent academic reputation and charges only $200 a semester in tuition. Another college of similar standing would cost at least $2,000 a year in tuition. When you add costs of room, board, books, and so on to the bill, it would come to about $4,000, which is much more than you can afford.

Your high-school grades for the past two years have averaged about B plus. You are in the top ten percent nationally in your Scholastic Aptitude (SAT) score. So, judging by the university's previous acceptance records, you are almost certain to be admitted.

Three months after you have sent in your application you receive an unpleasant surprise. A letter from the dean of admissions informs you that, because of the extraordinarily large number of applicants from your home state, the university had to be extra selective this year. He regrets, but you are not among those who were admitted. He graciously wishes you luck with your future plans and indicates that with your excellent academic record you probably won't have any trouble gaining admission to another school.

You are, of course, very disappointed but accept the university's decision until you find out that Joe Jones, a member of your high-school English class, has been admitted at the state university. You happen to know that his SAT score was somewhat lower than yours, and that he has a B average at best. You begin to wonder why he managed to get accepted and you didn't. Your local newspaper gives you the answer

the next day. The dean of admissions, in an interview with
a reporter, says that the university had received many more
"potentially acceptable" applications from women than from
men. He further explains that "acceptable" means a grade-
point average of B or better and an SAT score in the top
fifteen percent of students taking the exam.

When the admissions office tabulated that huge pile of
potentially acceptables, they discovered that sixty percent
were women and only forty percent men. Committee members began to foresee the day when the college would "tilt"
in the direction of becoming an institution for women. This
was a possibility they wished to avoid. So, they decided to
slant their admissions standards slightly in favor of men, in
order to keep enrollment of both sexes about fifty-fifty,
which, the dean explained to the reporter, was "much more
desirable."

It might have been desirable for the university, but it certainly wasn't for *you*. Since you could not possibly afford to
go to an out-of-state college, and your local community college (the only other possibility) was clearly inferior to the
state university academically, you were being deprived of a
chance for a superior education simply because you were of
the wrong sex. Could the university legally discriminate
against you to keep its sex ratio even?

2. You have applied to a formerly all-male private university as an undergraduate student. The university informs you
that, although you meet all their qualifications, their "quota"
of women students for this year has already been filled. Is it
legal for the university to set such a quota?

3. You have been a champion swimmer in every division
for which you were eligible since you joined your Junior Y
swimming team. Now you hold a state championship for
diving. You have heard of a college that prides itself on its
excellent swimming team and has offered special scholarships to topnotch swimmers in your state. You apply—only to
find out that the swimming-scholarship program is for *men*,
although the school is coeducational. Is such a policy legal?

4. You have applied for a scholarship in your junior year at

the college you are currently attending. Your father recently
has suffered severe financial reverses in his business, and
indicates that he simply cannot afford your college bills any
longer. You have always helped to pay your expenses by
holding a part-time job, and you have also borrowed to stay
in school. It seems unwise (if not impossible) to go further
into debt, and you feel that your studies would suffer if you
spent many more hours on your outside job.

The college counselor indicates that you are certainly scho-
lastically eligible for financial aid. The college wants to make
sure, however, that your father's financial predicament is
real. Until this year, all that would have been required of him
was to fill out a financial statement, indicating income, the
number of dependents, and extraordinary expenses that
might make it difficult for him to pay your college bills. Now
the college administration has decided that, on a spot-check
basis, they want to see the income-tax returns of families that
apply for scholarships for their children. It seems that a great
many fathers have been understating their incomes on application forms and, as the college official puts it, "We used
to think simple trust was enough, but we found that we may
have been giving some of our scarce scholarship money to
students who really didn't need financial aid."

You tell your father that along with your scholarship application he will have to include a duplicate copy of his income-tax return. He is outraged and informs you that he
considers the college's request not only insulting but illegal.
"IRS returns are completely confidential," he says. "Nobody,
including your college financial office, has the right to see
them." Is he right?

5. You were in your first year of graduate study in social
work when you became pregnant for the first time. You
decided to wait to complete your education until your last
child was old enough to go to kindergarten. You now have
three children. The youngest is four years old, and there is
a good day-care center near your home where you plan to
enroll her. The other two children are in school, and a neighbor has promised to look after them (for a small fee) on those

days when you have late-afternoon classes. You go back to your old school of social work and apply for readmission.

The dean, a man whom you remember as a dedicated Freudian, tells you that academically you certainly won't have any problems. Your scholastic record was excellent. But he seems hesitant in promising you that you will be readmitted. When you ask some probing questions, it turns out that he wants to know a great deal more about the arrangements you have made for child care while you are a student. He also seems to be concerned that you may "neglect" your family responsibilities after you have graduated and taken the full-time job you have told him you plan to seek. He keeps hinting that there must be something wrong with your marriage —otherwise, why would you want to leave your wifely and motherly role to pursue a career?

You agree that this man has a right to his own opinions, but he also might recommend that you not be readmitted because, in his opinion, you are "temperamentally unsuitable" to be a social worker. Can you take legal precautions to keep this from happening? If it has happened already, is there any law to protect you from what seems a prejudicial decision on the part of one admissions officer?

6. You are the editor of your college newspaper. As part of an investigation into drug traffic on the campus you discover that cocaine can be obtained in a small luncheonette that is a campus hangout. You got your original information from a classmate who is an occasional drug user, and you have been to the luncheonette yourself to confirm the facts. A few days after your story appears, the district attorney's office calls you in and asks where you got your first tip. You refuse to divulge your friend's name, and claim that, as a reporter, you must protect your sources. The district attorney tells you that this is a dubious notion even if you *were* a reporter. However, according to him, you are not. You're a student, and if you don't tell him where you got your information he will put you on the stand at a grand-jury investigation of drug traffic in your county and ask you the same questions. If you refuse to answer, you can be held in contempt of court and jailed, he warns you. Is he right?

7. You have applied for admission at a well-known college. Your grades, SAT scores, and recommendations from teachers are excellent. You are turned down for admission, and when you question a member of the admissions committee who happens also to be a family friend, she tells you that "something" showed up in your high-school records that made the committee hesitate to accept you. You remember that in your junior year you were picked up, along with some of your friends, on a drug charge. The whole matter turned out to be a mistake, but you had to appear in court and missed several days of school in the process. You suspect that this whole episode, probably in a distorted fashion, got into your high-school record. You and your parents go to see the principal of the high school and ask to see your records. He tells you that these documents are "highly confidential." On further questioning, you learn that, as far as you and your family are concerned, they are not only confidential, but also secret (i.e., the principal won't let you look at them). However, material from these records obviously has been shared with college admissions offices. Can you force the school to let you look at the records and to straighten out any errors that may exist?

8. You are attending a community college while holding down a job. You are also an avid tennis player. Your college has tennis courts, and has been organizing a male tennis team. You would like to play some tennis in your spare time, but the courts are reserved for team players (all men), except for a few hours a week when they are open to anyone who has paid his or her athletic fees. Unfortunately, the times during which the college would let you play conflict with your working hours. As you calculate the amount of time that the courts are open to nonteam members (i.e., females) you realize that women can actually play only about one-tenth of the hours that are open to men. You think this is highly unfair, since you pay exactly the same athletic fees as your male fellow students. Incidentally, the college swimming pool has similar rules. Is the school acting *illegally,* as well as unfairly?

9. You are graduating from college this fall and are looking

for a job. You know that the job situation for recent college graduates is tight. On the bulletin board you see an announcement for a management-training program at your local bank. Since you are an economics major, you think this may be an ideal spot for you. When you talk to the counselor at the college employment office, he tells you that the bank has indicated they are interested only in men. "Of course, we know all about the Equal Employment Opportunity Act, and we are very careful not to discriminate against women in our own employment policies here at the college," he tells you. "But the bank is a very valuable placement resource for us. When they specifically ask for *men,* we feel we should not go against their wishes. After all, next year they may skip us entirely when it comes to recruiting new employees, and I'm sure you wouldn't want that to happen, would you?" The whole conversation makes you furious. What's the use of Equal Employment Opportunity laws if you can't even have an *interview* to establish that a company discriminates against women? On second thought, you feel that not only the bank, but also your college employment office may be breaking the law by refusing to recommend you for an interview. Is this true?

10. You have been out of college for ten years and have worked as a medical technician. Actually, you have always planned to go to medical school, but at the time of your graduation you simply could not afford such an expensive education. Your college grades were excellent, as were your medical-school aptitude tests. As a matter of fact, you had been accepted at a medical school, but not enough scholarship money was available, so you decided to work in a related field until you had saved enough money to complete your training. You reapply to the medical school that accepted you ten years ago, and they turn you down, because the admissions officer tells you you are *too old.* "We get so many applications that we accept only the most desirable candidates," he says. "We certainly don't discriminate against women. That would be illegal. But we prefer our candidates to come to us as soon as they have finished college, or cer-

tainly no later than two years after graduation. Actually, I notice that you are married. That's another reason why we would hesitate to accept you. You might get pregnant, and then you'd probably drop out. You know that the United States has a shortage of physicians. We want to be sure that our candidates complete their training, and that they spend as many years as possible in actual medical practice. After all, that's the only way we can help to solve the country's medical problems, isn't it?"

You know that the university cannot discriminate against you because you are a woman. If you could prove that your sex was the reason for the turndown, they might lose their federal funds. But can they legally discriminate against you because of your age or your marital status?

11. Your local vocational school gives an evening course in auto mechanics. You are a secretary in a large car-repair shop, but have always preferred engines to typewriters. You would like to qualify as a mechanic. The vocational school tells you that the course is meant for *men only*. "We're not in the business of training women to change automobile tires," the principal declares rather snippily. "When the taxpayers established this school, they intended to prepare young people for a lifetime profession. If you don't like typing, why don't you enroll in our beauty-culture program? You might find that very interesting." You assure the principal that you have even less interest in beauty culture as a career than you do in secretarial work, and that you really would like to pursue a career in auto mechanics. He still refuses to enroll you. Is he legally permitted to do this?

Several of these cases are covered by a new law specifically designed to prevent discrimination against women in education. Before the passage of the Amendments to the Elementry and Secondary Education Act, which were signed into law by President Gerald Ford on August 24, 1974, you probably would have had little legal recourse against college admission officers, athletic directors, and others who were clearly discriminating against you because you are a woman.

The new amendments have changed the situation drastically
—in your favor.

Except for a few specified limitations, the changes and
amendments apply to all aspects of educational programs or
activities of a school district, institution of higher learning, or
"other educational entity" that receives federal funds.

With respect to admissions, the new law applies to all public undergraduate colleges, all graduate schools, and all vocational schools (including those at the high-school level). It
does not apply to *private* undergraduate colleges. However,
even institutions whose admissions are exempt from coverage must treat all students without sexual bias, once they
have been enrolled.

Among the covered areas are admissions policies (as explained above); access and participation in all school activities, including athletics; access to all courses, even those that
were once reserved for one sex (i.e., home economics for
women and building-construction techniques for men); benefits; and services and financial aid and opportunity for employment, including employment for work-study students, as
well as regular employees of the university.

Case Solutions

CASE 1. With regard to the university that wished to keep
its enrollment "balanced," after the newspaper interview
appeared, the university's admission office was hit by a flood
of letters from indignant women applicants, alumnae, lawyers, and irate taxpayers who pointed out that the university
was breaking the law. Even before the Department of
Health, Education and Welfare, which administers the new
antidiscrimination law, could be heard from, the director of
admissions gave another interview admitting the university's
mistake. He promised to review the applications of all
women who had been turned down because their presence
on the campus might "tilt the sex ratio."

The university faced the possibility of an extra-large freshman class, since they obviously could not un-admit some of

the men to whom confirming letters had already been sent, and they prepared for a very difficult year. Actually, their fears did not turn into unpleasant realities. Many of the women who had applied had picked the university as a second or third choice. Most were qualified to go to private colleges with even higher academic standing than the state university and were able to obtain scholarships. So, the day after Labor Day, the university found, much to its relief, a normal-sized freshman class of about fifty percent males and fifty percent females. As the admissions director said to the reporter who came to cover opening-day ceremonies, "I guess the whole matter has turned out to be a tempest in a teapot." That's not how the women who originally had been denied admission because of their sex and who had picked the state university as their first choice, for financial or other reasons, felt about the matter.

CASE 2. This example falls into a different category. Under the new law, private universities, in their *undergraduate* programs, still may maintain any sex ratio they choose. So, if a formerly all-male college decides to enroll only ten or twenty percent females, they may do so. Also, colleges that traditionally have been all-male or all-female may maintain their present status at the undergraduate level. However, if these colleges also maintain a *graduate* school, they have to admit men and women to that facility without sex discrimination. This means that Smith College, for instance, can continue to admit only women as undergraduates, but in their Graduate School of Social Work, they have to admit men on an equal basis with women. Yale may decide to admit no more than 350 women in its new freshman class, but in all their graduate programs (including medical and law schools) they have to practice a sex-blind admissions policy.

CASE 3. The new amendments definitely cover this case. Any college that provides athletic scholarships for men *must* provide comparable scholarship money to women. This does not mean, of course, that a college that has a football-scholarship program for men has to establish a football team with scholarships for women. It does mean that if a certain amount of financial aid is set aside for a sport in which women generally do not participate, a similar amount of aid should be provided for women in some other form of athletic endeavor. Certainly a college that has a swimming team for men and provides special financial incentives to attract outstanding male swimmers will be expected to provide similar financial assistance to female swimmers. What's more, if a female swimming team is not presently in existence, the women are entitled to make sure that one is established, that coaching staff and equipment are provided on a comparable basis with that available to male students, and that competitive swimming is made part of the college's overall female athletic program.

If the student in Case 3 can prove that she is a champion swimmer and that no financial aid or opportunity for competition is provided for her at the college of her choice, similar to the opportunities and aid provided to male students, she can file a complaint with HEW. Usually, just an indication that she knows what her rights are, and that she will insist on having them respected, will be sufficient to make the financial-aid office change its mind. Women athletes have been gaining more athletic scholarships in the past few years, but the new law will really make a difference in acceptances and financial-aid programs in 1975.

CASE 4. This probably would not have happened five, or even two, years ago. It is not covered by any special law.

Colleges trusted parents of scholarship applicants to give them true answers on application forms. As a matter of fact, many institutions of higher learning did not even ask that the scholarship applications be notarized. In recent years, with the rising cost of education and the inflation squeeze on families, college officials have spotted more and more applications that were fraudulent. One admissions officer told of a student who had been attending school on a complete scholarship until the college found out, quite accidently, that the family lived in a $100,000 house and owned three cars and a boat. The father had stated that his income was $15,000 a year. With three children, that made the family eligible for financial assistance. Actually, it turned out that that particular family did indeed have $15,000 in *earned* income, but that, in addition, they were receiving about $175,000 a year from a family trust fund.

No admissions officer can force a family to produce income-tax returns. They are indeed, as the student's father indicated, confidential. However, if he refuses to produce them on request, the chances are that no scholarship will be provided.

Most admissions officers deeply regret that the former relationship of mutual trust no longer can operate. But scholarship funds are in short supply, and university officials feel that they are breaking faith with those alumni and other generous donors who provided the scholarship money in the first place if they don't make every effort to make sure that the funds go to those students who really need them.

CASE 5. The Freudian social-work school dean cannot decide whether or not to accept a *female* graduate student based on the kind of child-care plans she has made for her youngsters, unless he asks the same questions and applies the same standards to *male* students who are married and have children. He also cannot impose his own prejudices about the female role on a prospective student. He may not like the kind of role she has chosen, but he cannot allow himself to be influenced by his disapproval in deciding whether to admit her to a graduate program or not.

According to several lawyers interviewed on this point, just the fact that he asked the questions and made the disapproving remarks might give the woman reason to claim discrimination under the 1974 statute. If she is not admitted, although her grades, recommendations, and other qualifications make her an eligible candidate, she would have a prima facie court case—a fact she might well point out at the time of the interview. Again, the chances are that when the dean realizes that she knows her rights, they probably will be respected. Otherwise, she can complain to HEW.

CASE 6. The student editor unfortunately is not covered by any law. Even if the courts should decide that she is a bona fide newspaper reporter (not just a student writing for a paper in her spare time), she could be forced to reveal her sources or be held in contempt of court.

A great many student reporters and editors believe that they can protect their sources, just as an attorney can protect the private information given him by a client. This is not true, as many college newspaper editors have found out. Several have been subpoenaed, and occasionally one even spends some time in jail until he or she gives the court the requested information, or until the judge decides that the punishment has gone far enough.

Actually, well-known *professional* newsmen and women have been subpoenaed, not only to provide information about stories they have written, but also to give courts any additional notes, tapes, or films that they have not even used in the press, on the radio, or on TV when a controversial case they have covered went to court. Several state legislative bodies, as well as the U.S. Congress, now have so-called "shield laws" before them. This kind of legislation would allow a reporter to protect his sources. Most civil libertarians feel some kind of shield law is essential to protect a free press, since many news sources would dry up if reporters were constantly asked to testify about confidential information. Within the past year, several reporters have gone to jail rather than break faith with the men and women who gave them such information under the impression that they would be protected. This can happen in all states except those that already have shield laws.

Even if federal shield laws are passed, and none has so far,* there still would be a question whether a student reporter writing for a college newspaper would qualify as a professional newsman or newswoman. Therefore, student editors should be careful not to intimate that they have secret information on criminal or other controversial stories, even if they have some facts that could blow the local political machine,

---

*Bills establishing one have been introduced in both houses of Congress but not yet passed.

police department, or college administration right out of their seats. The student writer or editor might very well find himself or herself in the uncomfortable position of having to testify in court and hurting friends and associates who were involved in providing the damaging facts.

CASE 7. The parents and student are now protected by a new law, HR 69, The Elementary and Secondary Education Bill, which was amended in August 1974 with the Family Educational Rights and Privacy Section. This amendment went into effect on November 1, 1974. It gives students and parents the right to see all personal and education files kept on the student and the family by the school. What's more, the student and his family have the right to a hearing to challenge the contents of the records. The information in the student's file cannot be revealed to anyone without the student's and/or the parents' (if the student is a minor) written consent, except to other teachers in the school or university and designated federal officials. If a school or college refuses to let a student see his or her file, or refuses to let him or her petition to change inaccurate facts in that file, federal funds can be withheld from that school. Since almost every school or university in the United States receives some federal funding, this law probably would apply across the board. If the family in Case 7 is refused access to a student's files, they should remind the high-school principal of the existence of this law, and if necessary, notify the Department of Education in their state.

CASE 8. This is covered by the 1974 amendments, just as Case 3 was. The school is required not only to make time on the tennis courts available to you on an equal basis with the male team, but you also can insist that a mixed tennis team or a special female team be started. The women who wished to play tennis have to be provided with the same equipment, the same quality of coaching, and the same access to the courts and locker room as the men.

CASE 9. The employment counselor of your college is acting as an *agent* for the prospective employer who wishes to interview only men. The counselor therefore is involved in a conspiracy to discriminate against female students—and can be held just as liable under the Equal Employment Opportunity statutes as the bank that is trying sneakily to get around its obligation to hire women on an equal basis with men.

A student involved in such a situation will do herself and her fellow students a favor by first telling the counselor that interviews will have to be arranged for women as well as for men, and if this does not change the counselor's mind, then report the violation of the law to the nearest office of the U.S. Labor Department or to the State Equal Rights Commission, if her state has such an enforcement agency.

CASE 10. The technician has no legal case, since her admission to medical school was denied, not on the basis of sex, but on *age* and *marital* status. If the discriminatory decision had been made in a job situation, rather than in a graduate-school admissions case, she probably would have been able to use the law to force equal consideration for her application. The laws that apply the Amendments to the Elementary and Secondary Education Act (mentioned previously in this chapter) and Title VII of the Public Health Service Act are very specific about prohibiting discrimination based on color, religion, national origin, and sex, but they don't mention *age*. If the medical technician can prove, however, that *men* are not asked how old they are, or what their marital status is when they apply for admission to the same medical school, she might still win. In that case, even though *age* was used as an excuse, in actuality she would be faced with a case of sexual discrimination.

CASE 11. The young woman who wants to go to a vocational school to study automobile mechanics has that right under the new 1974 law. Although the law generally does not apply to secondary schools (only colleges and graduate schools), it does apply to *vocational* schools, even at the secondary level. What's more, if a young man decides that he would like to study beauty culture, he too would have the right to demand to be admitted into that course. If the school has no facilities for would-be female auto mechanics or would-be male beauticians, they will have to make arrangements to provide them.

Important New Rights for Students and Parents

On December 31, 1974, schools and colleges lost their right to keep secret records on students and to transmit them, without students' and parents' knowledge, to third parties. Under a law known as the Students' and Parents' Right and Privacy Amendment to Public Law 9–247, parents of children under eighteen now have access to *all* information schools keep on their youngsters, including psychological test scores, personal impressions of teachers on the student's home life, etc., as well as grades. No such information may be transmitted to a third party (an employer, the police department, the FBI) without the parents' written consent. The only exception to the transmittal provision is that material may be sent to other educational institutions to which the student has applied. But even in these cases, parents have the right to inspect the files and to challenge any information they may consider inaccurate or unfair.

After the students are eighteen years old, they have the right to inspect their own files, to challenge any aspects they consider questionable. For students, the only exceptions to this rule are letters of recommendation written before January 1, 1975, financial statements from parents, or medical data. However, even in the case of medical information (including psychological data) the student has the right to have a medical professional go over the record and issue a challenge in his or her behalf.

All institutions of learning, graduate and professional schools included, are covered by this federal law, as long as they receive *any* funding from the Office of Education of HEW. This means almost all public and private schools, since money for textbooks, transportation, etc., from the Office of Education is included in most school budgets.

Chapter IV

EMPLOYMENT RIGHTS

Case Histories

1. You have been working for three years as a reporter on the women's page of your local newspaper. Recently you discovered that young male reporters working on city-desk or sports-desk assignments earn twenty-five percent more than you do, even though some of your stories (especially those on food prices, abortion, and so on) have appeared frequently on the *front* page of the paper. You also learn that a job covering the courts has recently become available, and that the managing editor is interviewing several male reporters with less experience than you have for the position. Since you've always been interested in law (you majored in government in college) and you would like to stop working for the women's page in any case, you decide to apply for the court job, and to ask for a raise.

Your managing editor tells you that the paper *always* has paid women's-page reporters less than "regular" reporters, since their jobs are "slightly different." Also, under no circumstances will the paper consider you for the court-reporting job. "We just feel that this kind of situation is not suitable for a woman," he tells you. "You would have to cover sex perversion, murder, and other kinds of unpleasant cases. We think that the readers wouldn't accept that. Also, you would have to cover night court, and we don't want any of our girls out after dark." You point out that you've covered night meetings of various women's groups, and that nobody seemed to object to those assignments, but you are told that you will have to stay in your present job, at the lower salary, or quit.

If you take your case to court, could you win either (a) a salary comparable to the male reporter's with the same number of years' experience, (b) a chance to try out for that court job, or (c) both?

2. You have recently been divorced and the modest amount of child support money you have been awarded is not nearly enough to keep you and your two children (both under six) above the poverty level. Before you were married you worked as an executive secretary in a large company, and you would like to get your old job back.

When you go to the personnel department of your former employer you get a good deal of sympathy from the interviewer, but very little else. "It's the company's policy that we don't hire women with children below school age," she tells you regretfully. "We feel that a mother belongs at home with her youngsters—and besides, she would probably miss a lot of working days when the children are sick or something else is wrong at home." You point out that you *can't* stay home, unless you wish to starve, and that since your mother has agreed to care for the children, you foresee no baby-sitting problems. However, the interviewer remains firm. "Company policy is company policy," she says. "Actually, for some jobs—for instance as a receptionist in the executive office suite—we don't even hire *married* women, because our executives prefer young, pretty, single girls."

You know that you are not being discriminated against because you are female, but because you are a mother. Is the company's policy legal, or could you take the case to the Equal Employment Opportunity Commission and win?

3. You are a teacher in a suburban public-school system. You are married, and three months' pregnant. One of your supervisors notices your expanding waistline, and inquires about your state of health. You tell him that you are pregnant, feel great, and with your doctor's approval, intend to go on working until the end of the school year (about four more months). Your supervisor tells you that according to the board of education's regulations in your town, you will have to quit work by the end of the fourth month of pregnancy.

"We made that rule because we felt that some of the children might ask awkward and embarrassing questions if a teacher is obviously pregnant, and besides, some of the parents object," he tells you.

You are outraged by this seemingly unreasonable rule, and decide to take your board of education to court. Do you have a legal right to continue working as a teacher if you can continue to perform your job adequately, or can you be forced to quit because of the Victorian attitudes of the board and some of the parents?

4. You and your husband are both employed. He works as a management trainee in a local company, you as a nurse in your community hospital. Your husband earns $10,000 a year, you earn $8,500. Recently you found a house you both love and that is well within your budget. When you apply to your bank for a mortgage, you are told that only your *husband's* earnings will be counted toward your credit rating. "We never count a woman's income," the bank's credit officer informs you. "Women decide to quit, or get pregnant —and then the bank is stuck." You tell the official that you don't plan to get pregnant until your husband's income has increased substantially, and even then you plan to work part-time. "Company policy is company policy," he tells you. "We just don't make exceptions, unless we have a physician's proof that the woman has been sterilized, and even then we count only a percentage of her earnings toward a family credit rating."

Has the bank the right to deny you a mortgage because they refuse to count your earnings? Is there any government agency where you could file a complaint, or would taking the case to court help you to get that much needed loan?

5. You have been looking for a job as an interior designer. One Sunday in the "Help Wanted" section of your local newspaper, you find an advertisement for a position that seems to be exactly right for you. You have all the qualifications the potential employer is seeking, and from every point of view it looks as if you are ideal for the job and the job's ideal for you. However, the ad appeared under "Help Wanted, Male."

When you try to make an appointment with the firm that advertised, you are informed that they won't even see you. "We made it perfectly clear in the ad that we wanted a *man*," you are told. "That's why we placed our advertisement where we did. If we'd wanted a woman, we'd have placed it under "Female," or if we didn't care, we'd have specified: "Male *or* Female."

Does the firm have the right to refuse to interview you under these circumstances? As a matter of fact, is it even legal to specify sex in a "Help Wanted" advertisement?

6. Both you and your husband work, each making about $8,000 a year. When you calculate your federal income tax, you find that you pay twenty percent more when you file a joint return and split your taxable income than you would if you were both single. Are you making a mistake in calculating your tax return?

7. You have been employed in the personnel department of a large company for more than ten years. For most of the time, even though you did exactly the same work as the male employment counselor in the next office, you have earned twenty percent less than he did. Recently, in compliance with federal law, your salary has been adjusted to the same level as his. But what about all those years during which you were paid less than your male counterpart? If unequal pay for equal work is unconstitutional now, was it not *then?* And is there any way you can collect some kind of damages or back pay for the time during which you were apparently illegally underpaid?

All seven of these examples are based on actual cases. Identifying facts have been disguised to protect the women involved.

As far as jobs are concerned, women are still the most-discriminated-against minority in the American population. According to Representative Martha W. Griffiths, who was elected to the U.S. Congress from Michigan in 1955 and retired from Congress this year, and who has conducted a steady and frequently successful battle for the rights of working women, "Women are in a job ghetto, which in spite of legislation passed to improve their opportunities, is exceedingly hard to escape."

Representative Griffiths was the only female member of the Joint Economic Committee of the U.S. Congress, which in July 1973 held six days of hearings on the economics of sex discrimination in employment. In her opening statement she pointed out some startling facts. "Women have been unfairly treated as secondary workers and second-class citizens for too long," she said. "It is a little recognized fact that most women work because of economic need and not to satisfy their own whims. Two-thirds of all women in the labor force are either single, divorced, widowed, separated or have husbands who earn less than $7,000 per year. But how are such facts treated by the business and political worlds? Women experience unemployment ratios substantially above males, and over a period of time the ratio of female unemployment to male unemployment has worsened. In 1972, the unemployment rate for women was 6.6 percent, compared to 4.9 percent for men. This means that 2.2 million women were unable to find jobs. . . .

"Even those women who are able to find jobs work primarily in women's occupations. The median school years completed is the same for the female labor force as for the male labor force. Yet, with the same educational background as men, women have different jobs, usually with less responsibility and less pay. For example, among college graduates only 5 percent of all employed women are managers, compared with 20 percent of all employed males. . . . Among professional and technical workers the percentage of women has remained the same for the last twenty years, while in the category of clerical workers, the percentage of women workers has risen from 62 percent to 74 percent. . . . Furthermore, women who are employed in the same occupations as men receive only a fraction of men's salaries. Why is a woman worth only 57 percent of a man? Women earn less than 60 percent of their male counterparts. In some occupations, such as sales workers, women earn only 42 percent as much as men. . . ."

At the beginning of the Joint Economic Committee's hearings Representative Griffiths asked these questions: Why does the average full-time working woman, who is as well-educated as the average working man, earn only three-fifths as much as he earns? Why are women's unemployment rates so much higher than men's? How vigorously are federal antidiscrimination laws enforced? Why do women have so much more difficulty than men in obtaining credit and insurance? Testimony at the hearings brought some of the answers to these questions.

Actually, there are five separate federal laws and executive orders designed to protect working women against economic discrimination. Four of the seven case examples come under one or more of these laws, and definitely should be decided in favor of the plaintiffs. The laws and regulations are as follows:

a. Executive Order 11246, which covers all institutions with federal contracts and/or grants of over $10,000. The order prohibits discrimination in employment (including hiring, upgrading salaries, fringe benefits, training, and other conditions of employment) on the basis of sex, race, color, religion, and national origins. It is enforced by the Office of Federal Contract Compliance.

b. Title VII of the Civil Rights Act of 1964, as amended by the Equal Employment Opportunity Act of 1972, which covers all institutions with more than fifteen employees, and prohibits discrimination in employment, including all the benefits in Executive Order 11246 on the basis of sex, race, color, religion, or national origin. This act is enforced by the Equal Employment Opportunity Commission.

c. The Equal Pay Act of 1963, as amended by the Education Amendments of 1972, covers all employers in interstate commerce, and prohibits discrimination in salaries against employees on the basis of sex. Originally applying to only nonprofessional workers, the 1972 amendment broadened the law to include professional workers as well. It is enforced by the Wage and Hour Division of the Employment Standards Administration of the Department of Labor.

d. Title IX of the Educational Amendments of 1972 prohibits

discrimination against students or others for admission and employment in all institutions receiving money by way of grant, loan, or contract. This obviously means all schools and colleges. The law is enforced by the Civil Rights Division of the U.S. Department of Health, Education and Welfare.

e. Title VII and Title VIII of the Public Health Service Act, as amended in 1971, prohibits all institutions receiving federal funds from discriminating against students and employees for reason of sex, and is also enforced by HEW's Office of Civil Rights, Division of Higher Education.

In addition to these federal laws, many individual states and cities also have passed laws prohibiting discrimination based on sex.

With all these laws on the books designed to protect working women, why is women's economic plight apparently not much better than it was ten years ago? Representative Griffith has several answers, but the one reason she keeps emphasizing is that federal agencies are understaffed, underfinanced, and simply cannot keep up with the backlog of complaints. "If a woman has a good case, she will probably win eventually," she says. "But few women have the patience to go through seemingly endless red tape to get their problem heard and adjudicated."

Dr. Bernice Sandler, director of the Project on the Status and Education of Women for the Association of American Colleges, has yet another answer: "No one minds that women work, as long as they work in low paying jobs such as secretaries, nurses and waitresses. But when women start asking for better jobs, *then* cries are raised about the destruction of the family, juvenile delinquency, the joys of motherhood, and reverse discrimination. No one really wants their secretary to quit work and go back to the home. Our nation has only just begun to turn its attention to women and to deal with the new fact of life: working women." She adds that federal and state regulatory agencies are usually staffed by men in the upper echelons, and that few of these men have an overriding interest in protecting the rights of women.

Dr. Elga Wasserman, until recently an adviser on coeducation to the president of Yale, says that many women may be hesitant to press too hard for the rights the law grants them. "We have all been taught that being too aggressive is somehow unfeminine," she says. "Women are often kept from insisting on their rights by the psychological and social conditioning to which they have been subjected since childhood. We have been taught to look for approval and emotional support, especially from men, and therefore we sometimes give up a battle we might have won because we are afraid of the emotional consequences of winning."

Case Solutions

What about the seven case examples? The women in these examples did not give up. Six decided to take their problems to court and the seventh asked an accountant, a lawyer, and finally her representative in the U.S. Congress to help in providing a solution. The following is how the seven cases were received, using all available remedies under federal and state laws:

CASE 1. The newspaper was clearly in violation of several federal laws, most notably Title VII of the Civil Rights Act. Although the editor maintained that working on the women's page was not the same as working on the sports page, the law provides that equal pay must be given for "substantially equal work." An investigator found that writing about the rising cost of meat, the experiences in a consciousness-raising group, the theories of a psychiatrist on the care and raising of children, and so on were "substantially equal" to writing about the exploits of the local hockey and baseball teams. What's more, the reporter had a right to ask for an opportunity to try out for the court job. The editor's paternalistic concern for her health and safety were not considered legitimate reasons for denying her a chance to work in a field that interested her and for which she was exceedingly well qualified. The reporter claimed and was awarded back pay (usually awarded in most such cases) for some of the time she had worked on the women's page, and the paper was ordered to give her a chance to try out for the court beat. Since the case was so clear-cut, the paper decided not to appeal the decision. What's more, other reporters working on the women's page are now being given salaries equal to male reporters in other sections of the paper.

CASE 2. The company to which the young mother applied for a job in was also in violation of Title VII, as interpreted by the U.S. Supreme Court in a recent decision. As Title VII cases mounted against employers, many companies tried to use not sex, but marital status and motherhood, as reasons for not employing women. The Supreme Court case was filed by the National Association for the Advancement of Colored People on behalf of a mother of several young children who had applied to an aircraft company for an assembly-line job, paying three times as much as the waitress job with which she tried to support herself and her youngsters. She was told by the company that it was "policy" not to hire mothers of children under six. In a lower court, the company's decision was upheld. However, the U.S. Supreme Court overturned that decision and ruled in favor of the mother. Since she had obtained other employment in the several years it took to guide the case through the court system, she was awarded $20,000 in damages, to be paid to her by the aircraft company that refused to hire her. The case is now used routinely as a precedent for similar situations in which motherhood is set up as a bar against the employment of women.

Marital status also may not be considered, regardless of whether the executives in the front office would prefer "a pretty, young, single girl." A suit filed on behalf of married airlines stewardesses who were either grounded or fired as soon as their status became known settled that question once and for all in favor of the stewardesses. Representative Griffiths told me that she became involved in the stewardesses' case when one young woman wrote her and told her that she had been fired by an airline after she announced to her supervisor that she had recently been married. Representative Griffiths wrote to the airline, protesting for her constituent, and received what she calls "a very arrogant, brief reply" in which the personnel manager of the airline told her that "the primary conditions for the employment of stewardesses is that they be young, pretty, and unmarried." Representative Griffiths wrote an indignant answer. "What are you running, an airline or a whorehouse?" she asked. This exchange of letters took place just before her reelection, and the airline publicized her answer widely, hoping that her bluntness might defeat her. It had the opposite effect. "Even my husband thought that a lot of voters would resent that letter," she said. "But for the next few weeks, as I campaigned in my district, I got nothing but compliments for my stand. Surprisingly, as many men as women congratulated me." Representative Griffiths maintains that many men as well as women resent the kind of attitude that relegates the female to a sex object. The Labor Department has decided that the term "young girl" also constitutes age discrimination.

CASE 3. The teacher would win. Two recent cases were filed: one in Cleveland, Ohio, and one in Chesterfield County, Virginia, protesting school-board regulations that require teachers to quit their jobs four or five months before a baby is expected. In the Sixth Circuit Court handling the Cleveland case, the judge found *for the teachers* and against the school board. In the Virginia case, the appeals court held *for the school board* and against the teachers. Since then, the U.S. Supreme Court has upheld the Cleveland decision *for the teachers.*

The whole problem of maternity leaves is not clearly spelled out in federal law. The Equal Employment Opportunity Commission has issued a set of guidelines that direct employers to grant maternity leaves for reasonable periods of time and to regard pregnancy-related disabilities in the same light as other personal disabilities. However, a guideline is not a law, and many employers have chosen to ignore the commission's directives as long as a problem has not been solved either by law or by legal precedent through the courts.

California has a state fund that provides benefits to California employees when they are disabled. The fund is maintained by a small tax on the salaries of the employees. The only disabilities under the law for which benefits were *not* payable were those caused or contributed to by pregnancy. During the time this case was pending, California changed its administration of this fund and now pays for disabilities caused by abnormal pregnancies. Several women challenged this California law on the basis that it denied them the equal protection of the law guaranteed them by the U.S. Constitution by discriminating against them on the basis of sex. The U.S. Supreme Court decided that California's denial of disability benefits for disabilities resulting from a normal pregnancy (usually the day of childbirth and the period of recovery) did not violate the Constitution's requirement of equal protection. The Court noted that there was no condition for which one sex was paid benefits and the other was not. In a footnote, the Court implied that different treatment of pregnancy did not constitute sex discrimination. Since this decision, one federal district court has applied this footnote to a case involving a private employer's disability-income plan and held that Title VII does not forbid excluding pregnancy-related disabilities from such plans.

There are three states (Connecticut, Massachusetts, and Hawaii) that have laws regarding maternity leaves on their books, and a working woman who wants to inquire about her status under *state* law can find out by calling her state's department of labor, her local state employment service, or her legal-aid society.

CASE 4. This example, in which a woman's earnings were disregarded by a bank in establishing a couple's credit rating, is one of thousands of similar cases across the United States. In New York and several other states, individuals have gone to court to fight this particular form of discrimination. However, testimony before the National Commission on Consumer Finance a few years ago recorded graphically how widespread this kind of inequality is. Unmarried women complained that they could not get loans for cars or homes.

Divorced or widowed women complained that their credit was suddenly cut off. Married women complained that although they always had held charge accounts and credit cards in their own names, business organizations wanted to change over the cards to their husbands' names. According to the National Commission's report, "Banks, Savings and Loan Associations, credit card companies, finance companies, insurance companies, retail stores, and even the federal government discriminate against women in extending credit. And they discriminate against women in all stages of life . . . whether single, married, divorced or widowed; with or without children; rich or poor."

As of October 1974, discrimination against women in granting credit is no longer legal. An amendment to a federal deposit insurance bill has brought women one more equal opportunity—to borrow money. The provision bans discrimination in consumer credit based on sex or marital status. The bill, known as the Depository Institutions Amendments Act, 1974, passed both Houses of Congress.

Under the bill, the Federal Reserve Board must develop enforcement regulations for federal agencies within a year and it will be with federal agencies that complaints must be lodged.

The legislation follows women's complaints that they have been denied charge cards, bank loans, or personal credit for reasons other than personal income or credit history. So, the couple in Case 4 could complain that they were being denied credit because the wife's earnings were being disregarded.

Many women's groups feel that the law is not strong enough because there is no requirement that a person denied credit be told why this was done. The bank, if it wished, could still refuse the loan and simply give some other reason —such as, they didn't like the location of the property the couple intended to buy. Most lawyers expect that there will be a large number of court cases before the provisions of this new law are really clarified.

CASE 5. The interior designer had a clear-cut complaint not only against the employer who refused to interview her, but perhaps against the newspaper that carried "Help Wanted" advertisements in separate male and female categories. On June 21, 1973, the U.S. Supreme Court upheld the validity of a Pittsburgh ordinance that prohibits newspapers from carrying sex-designated employment advertising. The Court ruled that such a prohibition *did not* constitute interference with freedom of the press, as claimed by the publisher, but was a "commercial" activity. As one woman attorney put it, "Most newspapers are ignoring the decision, and still separate their want ads according to sex . . . but that doesn't mean that the job seeker has to take that distinction seriously. I, and most of my friends, don't even bother looking under 'Help Wanted . . . Female' any more. Most of the good jobs are advertised under 'Male' and the advertiser has no right to discriminate, period."

CASE 6. The couple found that unfortunately they had *not* made a mistake in calculating their federal tax return. Contrary to what many people believe, single people now enjoy a distinct tax advantage over married people. "There is a growing concern that tax laws create undesirable incentives, as well as inequities which are particularly unfair to women," Representative Griffiths said.

"If a woman who earns $2,000 per year marries a man who earns $3,000, together they will pay more in federal income tax than if they had remained single. And the 'marriage penalty' increases as income rises. If a woman who earns $14,000 marries a man with the same income they now owe an extra $984 income tax for the privilege of being husband and wife; if one of them has a child from a previous marriage, their 'marriage penalty' will rise to well over $1,000. And, of course, a disincentive to marriage is also an incentive to divorce." Representative Griffiths said that she personally knows of one couple, both professors at a university in her state, married and childless, who decided that they would be able to save $1,500 a year by getting a divorce. They did just that, and continued to live together as they had before the decree was issued. They used the tax money they saved to finance a sabbatical leave in Europe. "I think this is pretty

unfair," Representative Griffiths said. "It becomes even un-
fairer when you consider that, as a couple, both pay the
maximum amount of social security, and only one of them
will ever collect all that's due to him or her under current
laws." She is drafting legislation to correct this situation, and
hopes it will pass within the next few years. Meanwhile, the
couple in Case 6 has no alternative (except for getting a
divorce) but to pay the tax they owe.

CASE 7. The woman has an excellent precedent for demanding that she be reimbursed for two of those years in
which her pay was illegally lower than that of her male counterpart. In June 1974 the U.S. government brought suit
against the Corning Glass Works, which cost the company
more than one million dollars at one plant alone.

The case involved a differential between night-shift and
day-shift inspectors. Originally, state laws in New York and
Pennsylvania (where two of the plants were located) prohibited women from working nights, and the differentials were
established ostensibly, in order to induce men to take on the
"less desirable" night shifts. But even after women were
allowed to work nights, the custom of hiring only men per-
sisted. Night inspectors continued to get higher pay. The U.S.
Supreme Court concluded that the "situation reflected a job
market in which Corning could pay women less than men for
the same work . . . ," exactly what the Equal Pay Act of 1963
was trying to cure.

Across-the-board night-shift differentials were all right, the
court ruled, but women would have to be given equal access
to those higher-paying jobs. The court also decided that
women who had applied for night-shift work, or who might
have done so had they not known about the company policy,
were entitled to back pay. At one plant, a woman inspector
collected $780.

Other companies, looking at the U.S. Supreme Court's decision, decided to settle their employees pay-differential
complaints out of court. The American Telephone and Tele-
graph Company settled a suit similar to the one brought
against Corning Glass by agreeing to pay $30 million to

25,000 managerial employees who were victims of discrimination. In 1973, perceiving the wave of the future, the same company agreed to pay $45.7 million to nonmanagement employees.

Immediately following the Supreme Court decision, such diverse organizations as Rutgers University and Bethlehem Steel were accused of discrimination in pay by federal investigators. The federal government has informed many smaller companies, operating in interstate commerce, that they may have federal inspectors looking over their payrolls if there are any complaints from women and other minorities. Retail stores and publishers have been singled out as often operating on sex-biased pay scales.

Meanwhile, several suits have been filed charging age-biased pay discrimination. As of June 1974, Greyhound, Trailways, and McDonnell-Douglas were being sued for discriminating against older employees.

So, if you know that you have been paid less for doing the same work as a male colleague, you may well have an excellent case when you sue for back pay. If there are other women in your company who have a similar problem, the best way to proceed might be to file a complaint with the Equal Employment Opportunity Commission. In many instances where such complaints have been filed, the companies involved have made voluntary settlements for back pay to female employees against whom they discriminated for years.

What can you do, if you feel that your rights as a working woman have been violated? First, find out which, if any, of the federal laws mentioned in this article apply to you. Your best source of information would be your state department of labor or your state employment service. If there has been a possible violation, complain to the *correct* government agency. You might also want to find out if there are any *state* laws that cover your problem. If there are, you may get faster action on the local level than through Washington. Also, complain as quickly as possible, as there may be a time limit on complaints. If you have any doubts about the accuracy of the information you have obtained or about complaint procedures, contact your local chapter of the American Civil Liberties Union, the National Organization for Women, or the Legal Aid Society.

New Rights for Widowers

Since equal rights laws usually work two ways, widowers received an important new benefit in 1975 from the U.S. Supreme Court.

On March 19, the Court struck down as unconstitutional a thirty-six-year-old provision of the Social Security Law that authorizes survivors' benefits to the *widow* of the deceased worker but denies them to a *widower* in the same position.

The Court ruled unanimously that "the Constitution forbids gender-based differentiation that results in the efforts of women workers required to pay Social Security taxes, producing less protection for their families than is produced by the efforts of men."

Chapter V

RIGHTS IN MARRIAGE AND FAMILY

Case Histories

1. You are nineteen years old and your fiancé is twenty. You have decided that you want to get married next month. You are both in school but hold part-time jobs, so you can support yourselves without any help from either his parents or yours. However, both sets of parents are firmly opposed to the marriage; they feel that you are too young. They have indicated that they would stop you legally from going through with the wedding.

You ask a lawyer friend whether they could really stop you, and you find out, to your infinite surprise, that there's nothing *your* parents can do, but *his* parents can. In your state, women can get married without their parents' consent at age eighteen; men have to wait until they are twenty-one. So, if you insist on getting married now, his parents might be able to have the marriage annulled. Is the lawyer right? If he is, are you living in a state with a very peculiar set of legal standards that don't apply anywhere else?

2. You are twenty years old, unmarried, and pregnant. You're still in school and so is the father of your unborn child. But both of you feel that eventually you might want to get married. In any case, you don't want an abortion—you want to have the baby. Your parents are appalled at the thought. They insist that you have an abortion immediately. They point out that you have no way of supporting yourself and your child. And besides that, in your state, you are legally a minor, so they have every right to supervise your medical care, which in their opinion includes termination of the pregnancy. They plan to make arrangements with a doctor to do

this as soon as possible. Can a parent or a legal guardian force you to have an abortion against your will?

3. You have been married for two years, and in your opinion, your marriage has been on very shaky ground. You have been considering a divorce, although your husband is reluctant to agree. Meanwhile, you have made plans to go to graduate school to prepare yourself for a profession. You have been very careful about birth control, but you become pregnant anyhow. The thought of having a baby when your marriage is breaking up is unacceptable to you. You make arrangements for an abortion and discover to your great surprise that your husband violently objects to the idea. He insists that he will stop you from having the operation. You feel that he wants to punish you for planning to leave him by forcing you to have a child you don't want and neither of you can afford, but he says, "After all, it's my baby too, so I should have certain rights." He threatens to make trouble for you and your doctor if you insist on going through with the abortion. Can he?

4. You are twenty-five years old and have become fairly well known in your home town as a television reporter. You have recently been married, but you would like to keep your maiden name (which you use professionally) legally, for purposes of a driver's license, a bank account, credit cards, voting registration, and so on. Your husband has no objections to this, but apparently your state does. When you try to renew your driver's license, the clerk refuses to issue one, except in your married name. The city clerk won't let you vote unless you agree to change your name on the voter's list. Your local department store refuses to continue to let you use your old credit card—the credit manager wants you to take out a new one in your husband's name. Even your landlord objects to the sign you have put up on your mailbox with both your husband's name and your maiden name. He says it looks bad—as if he were renting to an unmarried couple. At first you considered the whole situation rather silly, but you are beginning to get angry. Can your community (as represented by the registrar of voters, the auto-licensing bureau, the

credit bureau, the landlord, etc.) refuse to allow you to use your maiden name legally?

5. You are planning to get married within the next six months, and you and your fiancé certainly don't believe that your marriage will end in the divorce courts. But all around you marriages are breaking up and you see couples bitterly fighting each other in court over alimony, child support, property rights, and so on. You don't ever want to get into this kind of legal hassle yourselves. You've heard of divorce insurance, as proposed by the National Organization for Women, and you know that, at present, no insurance company (not even Lloyds of London, which according to popular legend, will insure *anything* for the appropriate premium) is issuing divorce insurance policies. Is there any premarital agreement you can make that will avoid a court fight later, should you decide to end your marriage? For instance, if you, as a wife, agree to interrupt your education now to help put your husband through graduate school, would a signed statement from him, that under all foreseeable circumstances he would pay for *your* further education, stand up in court?

6. You have been married for five years and have never signed a check. You don't have any charge accounts either. You get a weekly household allowance from your husband which has not gone up as much as the cost-of-living index. Every time you need a pair of stockings for yourself or a new sweater for one of your children you have to ask for the money. What's more, you don't have any accurate idea of what your husband's income is. You have suggested a joint income-tax return, but your husband has indicated that, even for tax purposes, he'd rather have you as a dependent than a partner. From a lawyer friend you learn that in your state, as in most states, there is a law that your husband has to "support" you and your family. You want to know whether the law spells out exactly what it means by "support." Do you, for instance, have a legal right to know what your husband's salary is? Do you have a right to demand the kind of "support" that might normally be expected at his income

level (e.g., a winter coat that is not eight years old, and a car you can use to go shopping for groceries instead of walking two miles every time you run out of milk)?

7. You live in one of the several states that have recently passed "no fault" divorce laws. These laws provide that marriages can be dissolved for "irreconcilable differences," with neither of the spouses being declared legally guilty or innocent. You are considering divorce, and actually have very good grounds to bring action (your husband has been involved in a year-long affair) but you'd rather keep your dirty marital linen out of court. If you get a "no fault" divorce, will the fact that your husband is not found guilty of any wrongdoing affect your chances of being awarded adequate alimony and/or child support?

8. You have been divorced and been awarded some alimony and child support, which isn't nearly enough to keep you and your two children above the poverty level. You hold a full-time job, but you still have a very difficult time, especially when you deduct child-care expenses from your income. Meanwhile, you have heard that your ex-husband has received a substantial increase in salary. (He probably understated his income during the divorce proceedings, but you had no real proof that he wasn't telling the truth.) If you go into court to ask for more money than you are now receiving, what are your chances of winning? Also, your husband has threatened to leave the state (he says that his company will simply transfer him to another plant at his request), and then "you can whistle for the money." How difficult is it to enforce support payments across state lines?

9. You have been living with a man for eight years. You never went through a marriage ceremony, but you have always considered yourself his wife, and so has almost everyone who knows you. You have two children. One day he announces that he is leaving you. He has decided to marry someone else. You feel that you have been living in a form of common-law marriage and therefore are entitled to at least some alimony and child support. Are you?

Through new legislation and court decisions, the legal lot of women has been vastly improved during the past ten years. This is particularly true in the areas of employment and education. However, as attorney Kathryn Emmett put it, and in the opinion of most lawyers interviewed, marriage and family law is still "a bastion of real and latent male supremacist views."

Most laws regarding marital and other family relationships are based on British common-law principles. And in common law, one man and one woman married to each other do not equal two people. They equal one marital unit, and that unit is definitely male-dominated. Basic to common law is the idea that the man supports his wife and that, in return for this support, she owes him certain services and must bow to many of his decisions. The services include sexual intercourse and homemaking. The decisions to be obeyed include where the family shall reside, how it shall live, and how the family's income and property will be used. Not only do husbands have certain legal powers over their wives, but parents have them over their children as well.

According to many lawyers (both male and female), American marriage-and-family law is ripe for reform. Several states are beginning to rewrite their statutes to eliminate some of the more glaring inequities between men and women, and to give children more legal rights. Hawaii, for instance, has rewritten its entire legal code to eliminate all sex differences in its statutes, including those governing marriage and the family. Court decisions also are beginning to point in the direction of more equality. However, as the nine specific case examples above will show, we've still got a long way to go. All examples are based on actual court cases with facts sufficiently disguised to protect the identity of the individuals concerned.

Case Solutions

CASE 1. The young man's parents could indeed have stopped the marriage. In some states, women are allowed to marry without parental consent two to three years *earlier* than men.

According to Leo Kanowitz, in *Women and the Law,* "the historical basis for sex-based differences can be found in early legal presumption of differences in physical capacity to produce children." Although the "legal presumption" turned out to be psychologically and legally incorrect, the laws remained on the books because, according to Kanowitz, there also were several underlying sociological presumptions. "One is that the married state is the only proper goal of womanhood," he says. "The other, that the male, and only the male, while not to be denied the benefits of marriage, should be encouraged to engage in bigger, better and more useful pursuits."

So a law that on the surface seems to favor women (after all, it gives them the right to decide earlier than men whether or not they wish to marry) is probably kept actually to "protect hard-working, ambitious males from designing, materialistic females," as one lawyer put it.

What actually happened to the couple in Case 1 is that the young man's parents went to an attorney to try to stop the marriage. He told them that he could go to court to do so, and that they probably could win a decision against their son, but he strongly suggested that they reconcile themselves to the situation. "If you refuse him permission to marry, or insist that a marriage he contracts without your consent be annulled, you'll have gained a very temporary victory, and you'll probably lose your son," he told them. "Next year, when he is twenty-one, he can marry anybody, anywhere, at any time he wishes." The parents accepted his advice and the couple is now married.

The state in which the parent-son conflict occurred has several bills before its legislature to allow both men and women to marry at eighteen without parental consent. It is expected that one of the bills will pass—unless the Equal Rights Amendment to the U.S. Constitution passes first. That, of course, would make the unequal age laws unconstitutional.

CASE 2. The young woman lived in a state in which the

legal age of majority for both men and women is twenty-one.
However, her parents could not force her to have an abortion
she didn't want. They probably could not have done so even
if she had been much younger than eighteen. If a minor
refuses to have a life-saving operation or medical treatment
to preserve her health, a physician probably could treat her
with her parents' consent and over her protests. However,
lawyers interviewed were sure that no court would order an
abortion against the wishes of the mother, regardless of her
age, unless her life were in imminent danger. The attorney
consulted in the case again urged the parents to be reasonable and to accept the fact that their daughter wanted to
keep the child. She had the baby and since has married a
young man who is not the baby's father, but who has adopted
the child.

CASE 3. On the other hand, the woman in this case had the
abortion, even without her husband's consent. The U.S. Supreme Court's decision on abortion states specifically that for
the first three months of pregnancy, the decision on whether
or not she wishes to have a baby is up to the woman and her
physician. There is no mention of the father of the unborn
child. However, a great many hospitals and doctors insist on
a husband's signature, giving permission to perform an abortion. They fear that the father might sue.

In a precedent-setting ruling, an Illinois Circuit Court
judge ruled that a husband has no legal right to prevent his
wife from having an abortion. The husband had gone to court
in an attempt to prevent his wife from aborting her pregnancy. Lawyers interviewed agreed that the ruling was entirely consistent with the U.S. Supreme Court's decision on
abortion. States are permitted to make laws and regulations
to protect the health of the woman only during the second
trimester (second three months). Other kinds of state laws
can be made to cover interruption of pregnancy during the
last trimester. Lawyers thought that a similar case would be
won if the abortion were performed before the end of the
second trimester of pregnancy. Lawyers, as well as physicians, advise that if a woman is considering an abortion, it
makes good legal, as well as medical, sense to get it as early

as possible. Pregnancy time is counted from the first day of the last menstrual period.

The young wife in Case 3 first went to a doctor who insisted on her husband's permission. She pointed out that she did not need his agreement, nor did she think she could get it. When the doctor refused to perform the operation, she went to a local hospital clinic which did an out-patient suction abortion without any unnecessary questions. She since has been divorced and has started law school.

CASE 4. The television reporter lived in Connecticut, a state that does not require a woman to take her husband's surname, although she is free to do so, if she likes, as he is to take hers. Few states now set up specific requirements in this area, but official and business organizations can still make a good deal of trouble for married women who choose the unorthodox way. (Only Hawaii requires that a married woman take her husband's surname.)

For instance, the Motor Vehicles Department insisted that the reporter *must* register her car and renew her driver's license under her new name. She took a copy of the state statutes with her to prove to the clerk that this was not necessary, and the clerk finally, with much shaking of head and clicking of tongue, agreed to do as the reporter asked.

Her name on the town voting list had been changed automatically. (The town clerk was an avid reader of society pages, and changed names as wedding announcements appeared.) She found that in order to be allowed to vote under her old name, she would have to take the case to court. In a similar case, which had been filed recently, the court had decided a married woman could register to vote or maintain her registration under her "maiden" name.

A letter from her lawyer to the department store with a threat to close out her account because a woman cannot be denied credit for reasons of sex persuaded the store to allow her to pay her bills under any name she chose, just as long as she did so promptly. "We won't cut off your credit just because you seem a little peculiar," one female credit manager told her.

She was informed that her mailbox belonged not to her

landlord, but to her and the U.S. Postal Service, and that she could label it with any name she chose.

Her lawyer warned her that she should be consistent in any documents filed with the U. S. government. Social Security and income-tax returns should be filed under the *same* name every year. "If you switch around from your maiden to your married name and back again, you might get tangled up in all kinds of red tape," she was warned. Since she wished to file a joint income-tax return with her husband, she was advised to do so in her maiden name, but to add after it: "also known as Mrs. John Smith" (her husband's name) so that the Internal Revenue Service would know why there were two names on the return of a legally married couple.

The reporter had an easier time keeping her own name, because she decided to do so *before* she was married. It's very difficult to get one's maiden name back again once one has used one's married name, unless one also gets a divorce, one lawyer warned. "Several states will make a woman go through a whole legal-name change, just to get her maiden name back," he said.

Some states have more liberal laws allowing women to keep their maiden names for all official purposes. Others are more restrictive (i.e., Hawaii). However, most states tend to follow the Connecticut pattern. If a woman has a question on what the law is in her state, she can call her local bar association, the American Civil Liberties Union, or the Legal Aid Society, which probably will be able to clear up the matter. In most jurisdictions, one is allowed to assume any name one wishes as long as it is not used to defraud others.

CASE 5. Premarital property agreements are generally valid in court. This is part of common law, under which "settlements" were frequently made giving the wife the right to a certain amount of the husband's property and her own dowry in case of the husband's death, or in rare cases in which the marriage was dissolved. If the fiancé owns property at the time of the marriage, it certainly could be put in a special trust account or in escrow for the wife's education, for instance.

If he owns no property and is pledging future earnings, the situation is less clear. Most lawyers felt that a written pledge to support his wife in school or to turn over part of the family savings in case of a marital breakup probably would stand as a legal contract.

On the other hand, any agreements made before marriage as to custody of as yet nonexistent children probably would not hold up in court. Children are the responsibility of the state as well as of the parents. Any agreement about custody and/or child support would have to be made at the time of the legal separation or divorce. Of course, there's nothing to keep a couple from promising each other that they won't get into a court fight should the marriage end badly. But a promise under those circumstances is not a contract and is not legally enforceable.

Insurance experts interviewed took a very dim view of the concept of divorce insurance, incidentally. "Those couples who don't feel sure of themselves and each other would probably take out a policy. Those who are sure that their marriage is made in heaven wouldn't," one underwriter said. "The very presence of the policy might constitute a self-fulfilling prophecy. We would be underwriting a lot of potentially bad marriages. The whole idea sounds a bit like writing life insurance on those people who have reason to suspect that they are afflicted with a mortal illness, or automobile insurance on those who drive ten year-old cars with faulty steering mechanisms."

CASE 6. Here the wife lived in one of the forty-two *common-law states,* an unlucky circumstance for her. Had she been able to persuade her husband to move to one of the eight so-called "community property" states (Arizona, California, Idaho, Louisiana, Nevada, New Mexico, Texas, or Washington) her husband's earnings would have been classified as the spouse's joint property (community property), and she probably could have insisted in court that he disclose the amount of his wages and other benefits. However, in a common-law state the husband's earnings are his separate property (the wife's, of course, are hers too, if she has any) and he cannot be forced to share either information or actual cash with his family as long as the wife remains married to him. He is obligated to "support" her. Support is very narrowly defined in most states: it means he has to keep her reasonably well-nourished, provide adequate shelter, give her enough clothes to keep her from freezing in winter and sweltering during the summer, and pay for medical care. If he does not make even this minimal contribution, she may purchase what the court defines as "necessities" on credit and he will be obligated to pay the bills. "Necessities" is as narrowly defined as "support": e.g., a winter coat that keeps her warm although it has been out of style for five years probably would be considered adequate.

Any property that she owned before she married or any wages that she earns on her own are hers to control. However, the average young wife with small children usually has no money of her own, and in a common-law state must depend on her husband's generosity. Even in most community-property states, the husband is regarded as the "manager" of the joint estate.

The wife in Case 6 had three alternatives. (a) She could settle for the situation as it was, accepting whatever crumbs her husband chose to give her. (b) She could leave him and sue for separation or divorce. In that case he would have to disclose his income and she would be awarded by a court decision a percentage of his earnings and of the property he owned. Or (c), she could get a job, being careful to put all her earnings in a bank account solely in her name. A husband in a common-law state exerts considerable control over a joint account. She chose the third of the three alternatives, but fights over money have continued and she has filed for a legal separation.

CASE 7. The wife's instincts are probably right. Even though she can sue her husband for adultery and get a divorce that legally puts him in the wrong, she probably will be emotionally (and possibly even financially) better off getting a "no fault" divorce. Only seven states (Illinois, Massachusetts, Mississippi, Montana, Ohio, Pennsylvania, and

South Dakota) still insist that one party be blamed as the culprit when a marriage breaks up. All other states now legally accept what many marriage counselors have known for a long time: rarely is there one totally "guilty" and one completely "innocent" party in a divorce. Most frequently, two people who are not suited to each other and who bring out the worst in each other's personalities simply need to get out of a bad situation.

Technically, neither partner in a "no-fault" divorce (more correctly called a "dissolution of a marriage") will suffer financially because the couple chose to end the marriage as amicably as possible. Before a no-fault divorce can be granted, a property settlement and agreement on alimony, child custody, visitation rights, and so on will have to be filed with the court. Some states now require that not only the husband and the wife, but any minor children, have *separate* legal representation, since experience has shown that couples are sometimes so eager to leave each other that the rights of youngsters to support, inheritance, and other things are neglected. This may mean an additional lawyer's fee. Even so, no-fault divorces are generally less expensive than "guilty" versus "innocent" cases. The usual cost for attorneys' fees for no-fault ranges from about $350 to $500. If there is any kind of contest, lawyers' bills probably will exceed $1,000.

Even in no-fault states, couples often complain about high lawyers' costs. Women are in an especially painful bind, since they often have no money of their own and have to count on their husbands to pay for their lawyers. (Both parties should be represented, each by his or her *own attorney*, even in a no-fault situation, lawyers warn, since otherwise the divorce might later be invalidated if the nonrepresented partner charges collusion.) Many lawyers don't want to take the case of a penniless woman and depend on the court to get a legal fee from her husband. Other lawyers indicated that they *do* take such cases. It may take interviews with several attorneys before a willing and able one is found.

California seems to be the one state where the lawyerless

divorce is not only possible, but popular. Several organizations sell "divorce kits," costing from $20 to $75, that include all the necessary forms with instructions on filling them out and filing them. Last year almost twelve thousand couples got "do-it-yourself" divorces in that state. California attorneys are naturally very unenthusiastic about this practice and have filed suit in California State Supreme Court contending that the "do-it-yourself" divorces are "dangerous" and that the kit sellers are "little better than unethical opportunists."

Many "no-fault" states have a provision that if one party leaves the other party for a given period (usually about two years) "irreconcilable differences" have automatically been established, and divorce can be granted. One of the true disadvantages of the no-fault system, especially for women with children, is that it becomes exceedingly difficult to hold up a divorce indefinitely in order to obtain an equitable settlement. In "fault" states, a wife can just refuse to give her husband a divorce indefinitely (and vice versa). In a no-fault state, that becomes almost impossible when one partner just moves out.

The young woman in Case 7 decided to go the no-fault route, after financial and custody details had been worked out to her satisfaction. She found that she had to change lawyers twice. Her first attorney told her the divorce would cost $500, and then indicated that she should just go along with what her husband's lawyer offered. "You're so attractive, you'll be married again in a year," he told her. The second lawyer insisted that since she had a potential adultery case against her husband, "We should throw the book at him and get everything we can." A third attorney handled the property settlement, all other legal matters, and the divorce up to the final decree for $350.

CASE 8. The divorcee had every right to go to court to ask for more money. Although the financial statement filed by the husband regarding property, salary, and other income is a sworn document and he can go to jail for perjury if he is caught in an obvious lie, a great many men understate their income and potential income in court, according to several divorce lawyers. "When a man is on straight salary and doesn't earn any more than appears on his Internal Revenue Service W-2 form, he really can't fudge," one lawyer said. "When there are expense accounts, income from free-lance work, investments, or from other sources, it's often very difficult to establish what his true earnings are. Also, divorce court is one place where men tend to underestimate their future earning potential. The same man who may have told his three best friends that he'll be vice-president of his company next year may tell the court that he is about to lose his job due to the energy crisis."

The woman in the case was advised to keep an exact account of what it cost her to support herself and the children (including the cost of working herself—that is, extra clothes, transportation, lunch money, as well as child care fees) for three months. Then her lawyer took the case to court, found out that the husband had indeed almost doubled his income since the divorce, and got her a sizable increase. Most of the increase was awarded for child support. The ex-wife had not been aware at the time of the divorce that she had to pay federal income tax on the alimony she received, and that her husband could deduct the payments from *his* taxes. Child-support payments are not deductible by the person paying, nor taxable to the person receiving them, and are therefore usually much more advantageous for the woman. Many husbands who might agree to an increase in alimony will balk at a raise in child support for just that reason. Also, when a woman remarries, alimony almost always stops, while child-support payments don't.

In the near future, alimony may become a two-way street in all states even if the Equal Rights Amendment does not pass. The fact that a woman may be required to pay alimony to her husband has been advanced by opponents of ERA as one of the reasons why the amendment should be defeated. Recently, in Georgia, a judge ruled against alimony to a woman because the state's law had no provision for alimony for men. He ruled that the state law went against the equal-

protection provisions of the U.S. Constitution. The case is
now under appeal. Other courts have disagreed and many
states have already changed alimony laws to make wives
responsible for husbands who are unable to support themselves. In community-property states, husbands always have
been entitled to half of everything that the couple acquired
during their married years, even if the entire property con-
sisted of the *wife's* earnings. Many motion-picture actresses
with annual incomes of six figures have paid dearly for their
divorces from underemployed and unemployed husbands.

Husbands do sometimes leave the state if alimony and
child-support payments become too burdensome. This is
why one judge told me that he "never awarded the wife so
much of the husband's income that the man would stop
working or just take off." "In the long run, that course is
self-defeating for the wife," he said. "She'd spend all her time
and much of her money in court trying to catch up with
him."

Actually, a man is responsible for money awarded to his
wife and children by a court, and can be held in contempt
and jailed if he doesn't pay. Many states have contracted with
each other to try to catch up with defaulting ex-husbands and
fathers under the Uniform Reciprocal Enforcement of Support Act, which allows a wife to take a defaulting husband
and father to court in his new home state to insist on payments. Lawyers point out that the man can claim hardship
and ask the new court to lower his obligations, however. This
happens quite frequently. So, in his own way, the judge I
interviewed may not seem very judicial, but he certainly is
practical.

CASE 9. If you live in a state that recognizes common-law
marriage, the court would regard you as the man's lawful
wife with the same rights and responsibilities as if you had
gone through a formal marriage ceremony. He would have
to get a divorce from you in order to be able to remarry and
you would be entitled to all of the other benefits a wife he
formally married would receive—that is, alimony, a share of
the property, and so on. You might also be entitled to Social

Security widow's benefits if he dies while you are married and he was eligible for such coverage. For inheritance purposes, you would be considered his surviving spouse. Of course, if the man has acknowledged paternity of the children in this case, he would be under an obligation to support them. If he has not, you might have to go to court to prove that the children are his before being awarded child support.

There are, however, very few states that recognize the validity of common-law marriages. Among those that do are Alabama, Iowa, Kansas, Montana, Ohio, Oklahoma, Rhode Island, Pennsylvania, South Carolina, and Texas, as well as the District of Columbia. Even in those jurisdictions, the relationship must meet the common-law requirements of marriage, including a present agreement to be husband and wife, followed by consummation of the marriage. Some states also require that the parties hold themselves out to the general public as husband and wife.

The whole problem of who is entitled to what when two people who live together without a marriage ceremony split up (a situation not confined to the young, since many older, widowed people simply live together to prevent the loss of widow's benefits by remarriage) is often unclear. In those states that do not recognize common-law marriage, if the relationship is ended by death, the survivor may not be able to claim any inheritance rights or survivor's benefits. If the parting is less than harmonious, there may be problems in proving what belongs to whom and who paid for what. Those who choose to live together without benefit of wedlock should realize that they are taking some expensive chances. It may prove worthwhile to consult an attorney on the possibility of drawing up a legally enforceable contract and wills to set forth your wishes in the event the relationship should break up, either because it no longer suits one or both of the parties or because of death.

There are some other true inequalities in family law. For instance, in most states a husband now can sue a wife for desertion if she refuses to leave her job and follow him to another town or state if he is transferred. She cannot sue him under similar circumstances. In some states a wife cannot borrow money, establish a business, or sign a contract without her husband's permission. In others, he can decide to move her and the family into his parents' house, and if she refuses to follow him, he can charge her with leaving him. All of these inequalities automatically will be eliminated if the Equal Rights Amendment passes the required number of state legislatures in 1975. Actually the Equal Rights Amendment has by 1979 to pass state legislatures but its supporters feel that its chances will be greatly diminished if it does not pass in 1975. None of the lawyers interviewed could think of one significant right, in the area of marriage and family law, that a woman would lose if ERA were passed.

Chapter VI

REENTERING THE JOB MARKET

Case Histories

1. You are forty-two years old, and previously worked as head of the bookkeeping department in a large wholesale clothing distribution center. Fifteen years ago, when your first child was born, you left and spent the intervening years caring for your husband and two children. The children are now in school; one is planning to go to college eventually, and the family could use a second income. You hear that your former employer is looking for a bookkeeper. You get out your old textbooks and find that, with a little brushing up (which you do at night school), your skills return rapidly.

When you go to see your former employer to apply for the job, he tells you regretfully that they don't employ anybody over forty full time. "It raises our insurance rates," he explains. "You can have a job on a part-time basis without the fringe benefits, such as medical coverage, vacations, pension rights, et cetera. You'll find that most large companies don't want to hire people over forty for the same reasons I gave you. I'd advise you to take the part-time job. It's probably the best deal you can get. Of course, we also pay our part-time people less than we do our full-time help. That's been company policy ever since we started this business," he says. Can this employer legally refuse to employ you because of your age, and put you into a lower job category than a young woman just graduating from business school?

2. Your husband's business has recently felt the effects of the current recession. You both decide that it's time you went back to work. Before your children were born you held a job in the public-relations department of your local hospi-

tal. You have learned that a similar job is now open—as a matter of fact, it has been advertised in the newspaper, under "Help Wanted, Male." You know that the hospital cannot discriminate against you because you are a woman, so you apply for the position. The personnel manager quickly assures you that, of course, he knows that "a qualified woman" should have the same opportunities as a man. "We placed that job opening under the 'male' column because we were afraid that we'd get female applicants with small children who would miss a lot of work days because the sitter didn't show up, or the kids got sick," he points out. You realize, of course, that by that description of the kind of job applicant he does not wish to consider, he means someone exactly like you, a mother with children under school age. You tell the personnel manager that your sister has agreed to look after the children, and that there really should not be a child-care problem, but he is still unwilling to take a chance. "Now, if you showed me some evidence that the youngsters were enrolled in a good day-care center, I might take a second look at your application," he says. Do you have to make child-care plans that suit your employer's ideas and not your own? May he legally refuse to employ you because he is afraid that your status as a *mother* (not necessarily as a woman) might interfere with your performance on the job?

3. You had been working for a large industry in your home town as a secretary, and because of your exceptional talents, had been in line for their management-training program. Just before the program started, you found that you were pregnant. You always had intended to go on working (your mother, a widow, lives with you and would be more than pleased to take care of the baby). You ask for a maternity leave, which is granted, and you return at the specified time (three months after the baby is born) ready and eager to start the training program. The personnel director tells you that you certainly can have your secretarial job back, but that management training is strictly for childless women. "We actually only started accepting women in the training program because the federal government insisted that we

couldn't discriminate," he said. "We would prefer to provide this kind of opportunity to men only, but that's apparently illegal. Then we decided that we would include only unmarried women (the kind who don't get pregnant before the course is over). We were told that that's illegal too. But you are not only married, you already have a child. That clearly makes you ineligible. No politician would be so unreasonable as to expect us to train *mothers* for management. Why, you might even get pregnant again next year." You suspect that the personnel manager is wrong, and that your baby does not disqualify you from rising in your chosen career. Who is right?

4. You are considered a gourmet cook by your family and friends. Whenever someone is giving a large party, you are asked to help with recipes, meal planning, and so on. Sometimes, you even have been paid to prepare part of the meal, to bake a special cake, or to make your superb quiche Lorraine. The pay always has been minimal (usually barely enough to reimburse you for the ingredients). One day it occurs to you that, with your special talent, you might be able to start a successful catering business. There is no similar business in town—families who want to have large parties catered have always hired a firm from a nearby city, which charges extra for serving customers twenty-five miles away. Besides, you know perfectly well, from having tasted their products, that you're a much better cook than they are.

In thinking over your project you realize that you will need a much larger stove, additional equipment, a small advertising budget—in other words, about $2,000 worth of capital. You have no money of your own. The family's checking account is in your husband's name. You go to your bank for a loan. The loan officer (who admired your salmon mousse at a recent wedding reception) feels that your business venture has every chance of success, and is perfectly willing to lend you the money you need. There is only one snag: he requires your husband's signature on the note.

You know that your husband, who in most ways is a perfectly sane and normal man, has one peculiarity: he has a

phobia against debts. You try to persuade the bank manager
that your business venture is really very sound, offer to put
up your engagement ring (which is worth about $2,000) as
collateral, and as a last resort, even offer to have your mother,
who owns her house free and clear, cosign the note. The bank
officer is adamant. "It's bank policy that we don't grant loans
to married women unless we have their husband's signature
on the note," he tells you. "What do you do about *unmarried*
women?" you ask. "In that case we usually require a signature from the father or some responsible *male* relative," the
loan officer explains. If you didn't find the bank's procedure
so insulting, you probably would consider it funny. Why
would an institution that advertises loans on television for
cars, engagement rings, and even electric guitars to any male
who is over eighteen and "reasonably responsible" refuse a
loan to a super-responsible woman who has been their customer for several years and who wishes to start a business
that even the loan officer considers almost bankrupt-proof?
Does the bank have the right to do this to you?

5. You have just resumed your career as an architect after
several years of homemaking and child-caring. The small
office in which you work carries income-protection policies
on all its professional staff members. "We have found that the
usual two-week sick-leave rules we have here don't work out
too well for us," the senior partner explains. "For instance,
Harry, our chief draftsman, had a heart attack last year; he
was out for six months. We had to hire someone to replace
him, and architecture is not the kind of business that can
afford to carry two people's salary when only one is working.
So we would have had to cut poor Harry off after two weeks
—which would have been disastrous for him and his family.
That's why we carry income-protection policies. If someone
gets sick for more than two weeks, the insurance company
pays his salary, and we can afford to hire a temporary re-
placement."

When the senior partner calls in his insurance agent, he
finds to his shock and surprise that income-replacement policies for women cost a good deal more than those for men. He

is now in a quandary. He simply could not buy the same protection for you that he does for the rest of his professional staff, but he is a fair man and considers this alternative unacceptable. (Later, he finds out it's also illegal, since he does a lot of work under federal contracts and therefore has to provide the same benefits for women as he does for men.) He can hire you as a part-time employee, and thus put you on a slightly different status than the rest of his professional staff (a dodge that also may be of dubious legality). Actually, he feels that the insurance company may be discriminating illegally against women, so he calls his lawyer. What will the lawyer tell him?

6. Your family recently has had some high medical bills, and although you have two small children, it becomes necessary for you to go back to work in order to pay off the debts. You are a nurse, working for a hospital that has no day-care facilities. Your husband is the foreman in a large metal-processing plant that has established a day-care center for the children of its female employees. Paying for a baby sitter while you go to work would be too expensive—it would take so much of your pay that you might as well remain at home. One evening, as you are trying to juggle your debts for the month, a thought occurs to you. Why can't your children attend the day-care center in your *husband's* place of work? Your husband agrees that this might be exactly the solution you have been seeking. The next morning he has a talk with the personnel manager of his company and is informed that the center is only for the children of *female* employees. Your husband asks why the company wishes to discriminate against *him*. The personnel manager points out that the day-care center (which costs the company a few thousand dollars a year) was established to make it possible for the children of *mothers* who were heads of households or who had to work to provide a second income to do their jobs without worrying about what to do with their youngsters during working hours. Your husband points out that this is exactly the case in your particular situation. It's necessary to have both parents work, and you *both* need a safe and attractive place for your

youngsters. What if he were a widower? Would the center refuse to accept his children in that situation? The personnel manager indicates that such a problem has not, as yet, arisen. "Under those circumstances, we might rethink our policies," he says. "But meanwhile, the children of *male* employees are not eligible for day care." Your husband feels that this policy may constitute discrimination against *men*, and decides to discuss the problem with his union's lawyer. What would he tell him?

Case Solutions

In Cases 1, 2, 3, 4, 5, and 6, the employers are violating federal laws that prohibit discrimination based on sex.

In Case 1, the employer is also violating a law that prohibits discrimination based on age.

The laws that apply are essentially the same as the ones discussed in Chapter IV, which deals with the employment rights of working women. If you are reentering the job market, you may wish to read that chapter as well.

CASE 1. The employer has no right to refuse you a job that is open, and for which you are qualified, solely on the grounds that your age bracket might raise his insurance rates. He cannot place you in a lower-paid, lower-status job because you happen to be forty-two years old. As a matter of fact, since you are probably more skilled than a young woman who has just graduated from business school, he may be required to pay you *more* than he would her.

He also cannot deny you any of the fringe benefits that employees (both male and female) enjoy. You are entitled to the same sick leave, vacation pay, pension rights, and so on as everyone else in your job category. Since the plant is a large one, operating in interstate commerce, Title VII of the Civil Rights Act of 1964, as amended by the Employment Opportunity Act of 1972, covers all institutions with more than fifteen employees, and prohibits discrimination in employment (including fringe benefits). The Equal Pay Act of 1963 also applies to your case.

If the plant in which you worked did not operate in interstate commerce, federal law might not be applicable. In this case you would have to find out (from your State Employment Service) whether your state has legislation similar to the federal statutes. By 1974 a majority of the states did. However, the definition of working in interstate commerce is a very broad one. For instance, if a clothing store sells only in the state in which it is located, but receives its merchandise from other states, it is considered to be operating in interstate commerce. If a builder constructs houses only in State A but receives his lumber and other supplies from States B and C, he is considered to be working in interstate commerce. There are very few retail or wholesale businesses that confine their activities to one state alone. In such cases, of course, only state law would apply.

CASE 2. The personnel director of the hospital legally could not ask you what your child-care plans were *unless he asked exactly the same question of every prospective male employee.* Few employers know this, and even fewer women know that they have the right to refuse to answer. Most prospective employees probably would disclose their plans in any case (they don't want to make a poor impression on the person they hope will give them a job). However, if the employer turns you down on the sole ground that he doesn't approve of your child-care plans, and fears that you will be absent too often from your job because you have to stay at home with the children, you can claim discrimination. The laws that apply are similar to those in Case 1. A hospital may, of course, claim that it does not operate in interstate commerce, since most of its patients come from the local community. However, supplies, medicines, and other necessary implements of medical care do go across state lines, so the hospital's claim would probably be negated by a court. What's more, you are probably protected also by Title VII and Title VIII of the Public Health Service Act, as amended in 1971, which prohibit all institutions receiving federal funds from discriminating against students and employees for reasons of sex. There are few hospitals in this country that have not received federal training or research funds, or that have not recently expanded or improved their facilities with federal Hill-Burton funds.

CASE 3. The employer is in violation of the same laws as the one in Case 1. Equality of opportunity means that he has to allow you into the training program if you are qualified in every other way except that you are a woman and have a child. The only way he could justify his refusal to grant you that training opportunity is if he also excludes men who are fathers. There is, of course, one condition that applies to all three cases. If you cannot do your job adequately because of your age or your obligation to your children, the employer is entirely free to fire you. National statistics have shown, however, that older women returning to the work force generally have a better attendance record than employees (male and female) as a whole. What's more, women who are the mothers of young children seem to manage their home lives and their work lives very well. There is no evidence in statistics supplied by the U.S. Department of Labor that such women miss more work days, or have to be dismissed from their jobs more often than the average worker (again, male or female) in the work force as a whole.

CASE 4. The would-be caterer would have been out of luck if she had applied for a loan before October 1974. A great many banks required the signature of "a responsible male relative" on a bank loan. Some states that have equal credit laws prohibited this practice, but there was no federal legislation covering the situation. In October 1974 both houses of Congress passed an amendment to the Federal Deposit Insurance Bill that bans discrimination in consumer credit based on sex and marital status. In other words, the bank no longer is allowed to require a woman to have a man's signature on a loan application unless it also requires a man's application to be countersigned by a woman.

Credit practices of banks have annoyed and insulted a great many women. As a matter of fact, they have led some of the most gentle homebody types into the feminist movement. At a conference on Business Opportunities for Minority Women in Washington, D.C., last year, one enterprising black and Puerto Rican woman after another complained of this particular practice. There were women who had run successful businesses for years and who wished to expand. Their husbands were occasionally unemployed and often disabled by illness. Still the disabled husband would have to sign the credit application of a woman who already had proven her worth in the market place. Many of these minority women felt that the credit rules were aimed directly at *them,* because they were black, Puerto Rican, Indian, or Chicano. They were surprised to learn that their white sisters had exactly the same problem. They will not have these difficulties any longer if the law is properly enforced.

CASE 5. The architect must be able to get her income-protection policy, if her employer does work for any federal agency, including the Department of Housing and Urban Affairs, although he will have to pay the higher premium for her. Executive Order 11246, which covers all institutions with federal contracts or grants of over $10,000 (and no architect could design a good tool shed for less than $10,000 these days), prohibits discrimination in hiring on the basis of sex, including discrimination in fringe benefits. The employer, unfortunately for him, will have to pay the higher premium requested by the insurance company or buy lower coverage for the same price he spends for the men. Insurance companies operate on actuarial statistics, and there are no federal laws that prohibit them from interpreting their statistics in a way that makes sense to them financially. If an insurance company is really out of line, the State Insurance Commission probably will protest. However, higher fees for women's income protection are charged by almost every company that writes such policies. The employer may be happy to find out, on the other hand, that if he also carries life insurance on his professional staff, the cost of his female members' policies may be less than that of males in the same age bracket. Insurance companies realize that, according to the best available current statistics, women live longer than men—therefore, the lower policy cost.

CASE 6. The husband can take advantage of laws that probably were passed to protect women employees. He has every right to claim that his children need day care because both parents work. The fact that no day-care facilities are available at his wife's place of employment means that because he is a man he would be unjustly deprived of a privilege that is granted to one sex (women). The day-care center is a fringe benefit, and several laws cited in this book indicate that no employee can be deprived of fringe benefits because of *sex*. That means *male* as well as female sex. Many equal-opportunity laws that protect women protect men as well, a fact that a great many males who oppose such laws do not realize. If they did, they might change their attitudes.

Chapter VII

WILLS, ESTATES, AND TRUSTS

Case Histories

1. You have been discussing making a will. You have a small life-insurance policy, a savings account in your own name with less than $1,000 in it, a few pieces of jewelry (worth about $800) that you inherited from your mother, and a checking account that, at the end of the month, usually contains about $100. Otherwise, you own all property (including the house you live in, the car you drive, some stocks and bonds, and a larger savings account) jointly with your husband. Your husband thinks that the idea of making a will is ridiculous. "Nobody is going to fight over that small savings account or the jewelry anyhow," he tells you. Most of what you own, you own *jointly* with me. I would get that anyhow, if you were killed in an automobile accident. Why do you have such morbid thoughts about death and wills? I think instead of spending money on a lawyer to draw up a will, you should see a psychiatrist to find out why you dwell on such unpleasant subjects." You are not at all sure that your husband will get your half of the property automatically if you die without leaving a will. Are you right?

2. Your husband is making a new will. In his old one, he left everything to you, for your use and that of your children. Now he wants to put everything in trust. "We have made a good deal of money during the past twenty years," he says. "I'm not sure that you would know how to cope with the estate. You might make some foolish investments. I think it would be safer to let the bank handle the capital and to leave you the interest on the estate. That, plus what you'll get out of my pension and social security should see you through

very comfortably." You point out that, with present inflation, what seems like enough money to live on today may be a pittance tomorrow. Besides, emergencies might come up when you would have to use some of the capital. "The bank will take care of all that," your husband says. Are your worries justified? Are there advantages in putting the whole estate in trust with a bank acting as trustee? Does the bank charge for such services?

3. Your husband died and never made a will. But regularly, at every wedding anniversary, he announced to the assembled guests that, of course, he was leaving everything he owned to you, his beloved and loyal wife. Now a flock of relatives, including his brothers and sisters, are claiming part of the estate. They tell you that his repeated public announcements didn't constitute a legal will. Besides, they claim he was a little tipsy when he made them, what with all that anniversary champagne. You are not at all sure what the true situation is. Obviously, you will have to engage a lawyer, but before you do you'd like to know whether all these assorted relatives have any right to a part of your husband's estate. Do they?

4. Your husband died unexpectedly at a very young age. His estate was left in trust with specific instructions that the interest be used to support you and the children, but that the trustees' permission would be required to release any of the capital. Now it turns out that one of your youngsters needs orthodonture, you have to have surgery, and the town sewer commission has just assessed you $2,000 to help build a town sewage system. Obviously, your interest payments won't cover all these unexpected costs. The trustees of your husband's estate are his brothers, who are both notorious misers. They feel you could get along somehow, if you just put your mind to it, and refuse to release any of the capital. Do you have any legal recourse to reverse their decision?

5. During his last few years you and your husband just didn't get along very well. You never got a divorce, but you spent most of the year in your sister's house in Florida, while your husband lived in your home in New York. When he died

you found out that he had changed his will, leaving his entire estate to your children and not a penny to you. Can a man totally disinherit his wife? If he does, can she go to court with a reasonable chance of having the will changed?

6. Your husband has died and left an airtight will, leaving everything to you and the children. Among his possessions were the house you live in, a car, and some fairly valuable works of art, which were bought years ago when their value was much lower. The probate judge (who in your state isn't even a lawyer—he's a political appointee who, by profession, is an electrician) insists that the house, the car, and the paintings will have to be appraised for tax purposes. The appraiser will get a percentage of whatever the estimated value of your property is. The probate judge appoints his brother-in-law (a licensed plumber) as the appraiser. You suspect that the appraisal will be high, since the fee charged for it depends on the value of the property. Is that whole transaction illegal, and if so, what can you do about it?

7. You have been hearing advertisements on the radio from a bank that urges the public to establish "trust savings accounts," which the ads imply will work just like every other savings account (i.e., the depositor can remove the money any time he or she chooses) but which will go to the person named as the beneficiary of the trust, *tax free*, on the depositor's death. The whole idea seems peculiar to you. But if the transaction is indeed legal, it also seems like a sensible thing to do. Are such trust accounts legal and do they really save inheritance taxes?

8. You have been living with a man for more than five years. You would have been married a long time ago, but his wife refused to give him a divorce. Everyone among your acquaintances regards you as a couple, although most also know that you are not legally married. You also know that in his will this man has divided his estate equally between you and his children. You accidentally meet his wife at a party and she tells you that, if he should die, she certainly would get your share of his estate, because "you can't disinherit a legal wife, and besides, I'd claim that you exerted undue

influence on my husband." Has she got a point?

9. Your father died and left you a large sum of money under the condition that you use it to go to his alma mater to get a degree in chemistry. You don't like the college and your interest is in English literature. If you decide that you want to go to the college of your choice and study the subject that interests you, do you automatically forfeit the inheritance?

Case Solutions

Death is an unpleasant subject. Most of us prefer not to think about our own death, let alone plan for it. However, the distribution of one's property after death is one of the few aspects of that process that is within the individual's power to control. As a general rule, one can dispose of property following one's death only by making a will that complies with the statutes of the state in which one lives. If a person dies, leaving property, with no will, the statutes of the state will determine who will receive the property and these statutes may or may not fulfill the wishes of the former owner.

CASE 1. One of the exceptions to the rule that a will is needed to control postmortem disposition of property is the situation in which property is owned jointly with rights of survivorship by two persons (in some states, this kind of ownership by two married persons is called tenancy by the entirety). In Case 1, if you own property jointly with *rights of survivorship*, with your spouse, on the death of one, title to the property passes to the survivor. However, if you both own the property but there is no mention of rights of survivorship (called tenancy in common in many states), your interest in the property may not pass to the surviving owner on your death but will become an asset of your estate. It will then be disposed of by the law of intestacy of your state if you do not leave a will that states how you wish to dispose of your interest. Without a will, the other property mentioned in Case 1, such as the savings account, jewelry, and checking account, will also pass according to statute.

Since the laws of intestacy vary from state to state, you should check with an attorney to see who will inherit your property if you die without leaving a will. For example, under Case 1, in Connecticut, without a will, the husband would get one-third of his wife's property (over and above what they owned jointly with rights of survivorship) and her children would share equally the remaining two-thirds. If she did not have children, he would get up to $5,000 and half of everything over $5,000. The other half would go to her parents. If her spouse does not survive her (or if she had no spouse at her death), her surviving children would share equally in her property. If a single person leaves no children, his or her parents would inherit, or, if no parent is surviving, then the deceased's brothers and sisters would inherit. Under Pennsylvania law, on the other hand, a surviving spouse, when the deceased leaves no children, inherits up to $20,000 and half of the remainder of the estate. The deceased's parents (or brothers and sisters, if no parent survives) inherit the other half. If, however, the deceased leaves one child, the spouse gets one-half of the estate and the child gets one-half. If there is more than one child, the spouse takes only one-third and the children share the other two-thirds equally.

If your state's laws of intestacy do not accomplish the distribution you wish, then the best way to ensure your desires are accomplished is to make a will. In a will you can spell out exactly who will get what in the event of your death. You can make sure that the family heirlooms or mementos go to a person to whom they will have meaning. You can, if you wish, disinherit a relative who otherwise might be entitled to inherit but whom you dislike. You can make a gift to your pet charity. And, if you have children, most importantly, you can nominate a person whom you trust to be the guardian of those children. If you die without a will, the courts will not have any guidance as to your wishes regarding who you think would do the best job of raising your children.

CASE 2. In most jurisdictions, one can leave property to a trustee to administer for the benefit of a third person. In Case 2, this is what the husband is doing. It can be a very worthwhile mechanism for ensuring that someone's needs will be met, if one is unsure that the person would handle the property wisely if it were given outright. It relieves the beneficiary of the need to make decisions of how the property should be invested and allows the person setting up the trust (often called the trustor or settlor) to decide who will get income following the beneficiary's death and who ultimately will get the property forming the basis of the trust. If the husband in Case 2 leaves the property outright to his wife, she can decide to use it all up during her lifetime or decide whom to leave it to on her death. Using the trust allows the husband to decide how much she will get during her life and how often, and who will get the property after she dies. One can choose a trustee who has expertise in money management and give the trustee directions as to how much the beneficiaries should get and under what conditions. The trustor can direct that the trustee pay over principal in certain circumstances or merely allow the trustee to do so if the trustee thinks it necessary. Professional money managers usually do charge a fee for serving as trustee. Of course, one of the primary reasons for deciding to use the trust mechanisms may be that it makes possible a reduction in taxes. In such a situation, it is always best if you and your spouse consult a tax adviser and/or an attorney *together*.

Even if you own nothing now in your own name, it is a good idea for you to know what the size of your spouse's estate is, what tax implications there are, what options are open to you, where his will may be, who his lawyer and accountant are, and what you can expect if something should happen to him. While it may be unpleasant to contemplate, you may become a widow unexpectedly. You and your spouse can ease the trauma of that eventuality by planning intelligently together for that time. Too many women have found themselves having to cope, not only with the emotional shock of losing a husband, but also with managing on their own for the first time, paying bills and taxes, having had no conception of how much money it cost, totally, to maintain the household or how much money would be available in the future for such purposes.

CASE 3. Here the answer will depend on state law. You should, of course, consult a lawyer. As a general rule, most states require that a will be in writing. If your state follows the general rule, chances are that a court would not deem these anniversary protestations to comply with the statutory requirements and therefore would find that your husband died intestate (without a will). The distribution of his estate, as in Case 1, would be determined by the state law of intestacy. In Missouri, you might be entitled only to one-half of his estate, with his brothers and sisters sharing equally in the other half. In Connecticut, on the other hand, if your husband left no surviving children or parent, you would get all of the estate. A verbal statement of a person's wishes with respect to the distribution of his property after death, even if soberly made, is no substitute in most cases for a written will. Even a promise to make a will may offer little protection to the intended beneficiary.

CASE 4. It may be possible that the trust agreement contains directions to the trustees as to when they should invade the capital (corpus) of the trust and that the trustees are refusing to comply with the provisions. In such a case, it may be possible to seek an order of the court directing them to comply. If, however, the trust agreement leaves such decisions to the sole discretion of the trustees, a court would be very reluctant to interfere.

CASES 5 AND 8. Both of these cases involve a husband's attempt to disinherit his wife. Most states make it impossible to disinherit a spouse totally. These states provide to the surviving spouse an option "to take against a will." What this means is that the survivor can claim what she (in these cases) would have received had her husband died intestate. The rest of the will would stand as it affects the other beneficiaries, but the surviving spouse gets her share first. However, in Case 5, you may be faced with an exception to this option in cases where a wife has wrongfully deserted her husband. In states that recognize this exception, a woman who has left her husband (and husbands who have deserted their wives or refused to support them) is not given this option and can be disinherited. The option, in other cases, exists, too, even if the deceased did make provision in the will for the spouse. A surviving spouse can decide whether she (or he) is better off taking what is left to her under the will or whether she should exercise her option to take against the will. This option is often exercised when the spouse is left nothing outright, but the estate (or a portion of it) is left in the hands of a trustee for her benefit. She may decide she would rather have her intestate share outright than receive income from the trust during her lifetime. If you are faced with making such a decision, an attorney familiar with the laws of your state can advise you on the nature of your options and the relative merits of each choice.

CASE 6. Probate courts (called surrogate's court in New York) are those courts that supervise, among other things, the administration of estates. It is this court that will appoint someone to manage the estate (an administrator or administratrix, executor or executrix if there is a will), pass on questions of who should inherit the estate, decide questions raised by ambiguous language in a will, and supervise the administration of the estate. The powers of the judge or surrogate are generally defined by statute. If state statutes allow, the judge, in Case 6, can appoint anyone to appraise an estate. Usually, however, the statutes will provide a mechanism for challenging the opinion of an estate's worth, especially as it influences the amount of tax that may be due. Your lawyer can advise you on the procedures available under the laws of your state.

CASE 7. One of the reasons that persons try to plan their estates is to minimize the taxes that may be imposed on them during their lifetimes (such as income taxes) and on their estates at the time of their deaths (estate and inheritance taxes). Federal estate taxes are generally imposed on estates of over $60,000. One's taxable estate is composed of property over which one had control at the time of death. It would appear that, in Case 7, the depositor does have control of the savings account and it is unlikely that it would be excludable from your taxable estate. The advantages such accounts have is that they cannot become part of the depositor's probate estate. In other words, the account becomes the property of the beneficiary automatically on the depositor's death without the need for first going through the probate court.

CASE 9. Wills and trusts are documents worthy of respect. Courts place great stock in them because they reflect the wishes of the person who drew them. Since you cannot ask a dead person if she or he would mind if a change were made, courts allow changes in very, very few circumstances. One of the few instances in which courts have refused to accept a will is if it can be shown that it does not reflect the true wishes of the person making it because that person was unduly and insidiously influenced by someone. Courts will not accept a will if it can be shown that the person did not have the capacity to understand what she or he was doing. They will not enforce provisions of a will that are illegal and will allow changes in provisions that prove impossible to fulfill. However, if an inheritance is made conditionally, such as in Case 9, and the condition does not contravene state policy, the conditions generally will be enforced.

By now it should be evident this is one area of the law in which curbstone legal advice can be very expensive. The money you spend seeking the counsel of an attorney experienced in estate matters is a good investment. The peace of mind you can have after putting your wishes in the form of a will or after being told you do not need one by someone who knows this area of the law does not have a price tag on it. An experienced lawyer can help you evaluate your own estate and help you to minimize your tax liabilities. Wills are as useful to single persons as they are to married ones. If you are married, you and your spouse should plan together for the day when either of you will have to manage alone. Legal counsel can be invaluable in raising issues neither of you may have thought about. Many people understandably are reluctant to discuss their property and such personal matters as net worth with other people. Attorneys are bound by their code of ethics to treat your discussions confidentially. An attorney cannot be effective unless you are completely candid about what you have, what you want to do with it, and why. While a lawyer may not like what you want, it is the attorney's job to help you accomplish it, if at all possible.

Chapter VIII

MEDICAL RIGHTS

Case Histories

1. You are twenty-four years old and have three children under five. You and your husband have decided that you don't want to have another baby in the near future, and that you need the most reliable form of contraception available. You are delighted to learn from your family physician about a foundation that provides birth-control services free of charge.

When you see the doctor at the foundation he informs you that you will be part of a research project monitoring the side effects of birth-control pills. If you volunteer for the project, you will be given free medical services and supplies. You are provided with pills and a tube of vaginal cream, which you are urged to use along with your medication. You follow the physician's prescription and, as far as you are concerned, the pill has only one side effect: you are pregnant within two months.

Later you discover that you were given a placebo (a sugar pill) because you were part of a double-blind study designed to discover whether many, if not most, of the side effects women report when they are taking birth-control pills are actually imaginary. The experiment is financed in part by a drug company that manufactures the principal ingredient in birth-control pills. Only some of the "volunteers" were actually supplied with the medication. Others, like you, were given a sugar pill that looked exactly like the real thing. Do you have a legal right to claim damages from the foundation, the physician who treated you there, and/or the drug company that financed the experiment in which you took part?

2. You have suffered repeated gallbladder attacks and are referred by your family doctor to a surgeon to discuss an operation to remedy the situation. The surgeon also advises the operation, makes arrangements for a bed at a local hospital, tells you how long you will be out of commission, what the effects of the operation will be, and so on. The only matter you do not discuss is his fee, since you know you have a medical-insurance policy that covers you for all "usual and customary" medical expenses, including surgical fees.

About a month after the operation you receive a bill for $250 from your surgeon. You immediately get in touch with your insurance company and are told that the doctor charges $250 more for a gallbladder operation than most other surgeons in your community. When you ask the doctor about his charges he tells you that he is considered a specialist in surgery on gallbladders and related organs and that indeed, he *always* charges more than "a regular surgeon." He assumed that you knew this when you asked him to operate. Who is responsible for paying that $250? You or the insurance company?

3. Your five-year-old marriage has been unhappy for some time. You are left alone on weekends a good deal and you suspect that your husband's frequent business trips with his secretary may indicate that they are having an affair. One lonely weekend you receive a dinner invitation from an old college friend. You have a great time with him, and you spend the night together.

Within a few weeks you learn that you are pregnant and your physician arranges for an abortion. Six months later your husband tells you that he wants a divorce because he wishes to marry his secretary. If you make any trouble for him, such as contesting the action, or asking for alimony, his lawyer will subpoena your doctor and his records into court to prove that you have been unfaithful and have had an abortion. Under the law, is such a subpoena allowed?

4. You are twenty-seven years old, have been married for six years, and have just given birth to your third child. Your medical history makes the use of birth-control pills inadvisa-

ble. An IUD (intrauterine device) proved to be painful and caused a good deal of bleeding. You don't consider other methods of birth control reliable. Therefore, you decide that you wish to have a tubal ligation, or a voluntary sterilization. Your physician indicates that your community hospital has what is called an age-parity rule. In your case they will permit sterilization only if you have at least five children. There is no other hospital nearby in which you could have the operation without causing serious inconvenience to yourself and your family. Does the hospital administration have the right to refuse to perform a sterilization operation you have requested, and which your physician considers to be in your best interest?

5. Your first child was born by the Lamaze method of natural childbirth. There were no complications and your gynecologist agrees that you can use the same system for your second child. However, the baby arrives slightly ahead of schedule when your own doctor is away on his vacation. His substitute, whom you meet in the hospital labor room, tells you that you need general anesthesia, and over your protests, administers it.

After you get home you think about your experience and you begin to wonder whether you *really* needed that anesthetic and, if so, why? Your own doctor had by now returned, but his explanations seem evasive and confusing. You ask to see your hospital records. You are informed by the hospital administrator that hospital records are never made available to patients, only to physicians. Can the hospital withhold your own records from you?

6. Your parents disapprove of your life style, your friends, and your politics, and besides, they suspect (incorrectly) that you are taking hard drugs. They insist that you sign yourself into a psychiatric hospital for observation and treatment. If you refuse to go voluntarily, your father indicates that he will retain an attorney to have you committed. You have no money to hire your own lawyer. A friend tells you that in your situation, you are entitled to free legal services from the local Legal Aid Society. Your father says that this is patently

ridiculous. He makes $50,000 a year, so why should *you* be
given free legal help. Who is right?

Case Solutions

Medical-legal rights differ from other kinds of rights in one
important way: they usually are covered by *case law* rather
than by statutory law. Case law means that situations similar
to the one currently in the court have been brought before,
and that decisions will be based on precedent. As one attorney interviewed put it, "Case law is usually based on British
Common Law, which goes way back in history and protects
such important rights as a person's control over what is done
to his or her own body, privacy, and other factors affecting
medical-legal decisions. You might say that case law usually
represents the best *common-sense* solution that can be applied to a given situation."

Another important aspect of the medical-legal process is
that cases tend to come into court as "torts" rather than as
criminal proceedings. A tort is a case in which one person
sues another person or institution for damages. The state
becomes involved only by providing the courtroom, judges,
and so on, and by enforcing any judgment that is rendered.
Nobody goes to jail as the result of a tort—that would require
a criminal proceeding brought by local, state, or federal law-
enforcement agencies. Medical cases only very rarely become criminal proceedings. The lawyers interviewed could
recall only a few examples, usually dealing with practicing
medicine without a license, violations of federal or state drug
laws by a physician, or the performance of an illegal abortion
(before the United States Supreme Court eliminated most
state laws restricting abortions).

The difference between case and statutory law, and between a criminal procedure and a tort, may seem very technical, but they are important to anyone who has a medical
grievance and who wants her day in court. She probably will
have to engage an attorney and sue in order to get her problem resolved.

There are attorneys who specialize in medical malpractice suits. You probably can find one by calling your local bar association or asking your family attorney. Usually, if an attorney accepts such a suit, he or she will do so on a contingency basis. If you win, the lawyer gets a percentage (usually about one-third) of whatever the judgment is. If you lose, the lawyer gets only his out-of-pocket expenses. Working on contingency is considered a perfectly ethical practice, because many clients in damage suits don't have the money to pay regular legal fees. However, most lawyers will take only those cases about which they feel fairly confident (since they don't want to waste valuable time on a losing cause) and that involve more than $1,000.

How would case or statutory law apply to the six examples at the beginning of this chapter?

CASE 1. This case, which concerns the experiments with placebo birth-control pills, has received extensive publicity in law journals. It also has been discussed in detail in a recently published law textbook, *Experimentation with Human Beings* by Dr. Jay Katz, professor of law and psychiatry at the Yale Law School, and by Barbara Seaman in her book *Free and Female*.

The case first surfaced when the physician in charge of the experiment gave a paper at a scientific meeting on a "double-blind" study to determine whether the incidence of headache, nausea, nervousness, vomiting, depression, and breast tenderness would be substantially higher in women taking actual birth-control pills containing estrogen than in those who were given a harmless, but ineffective, inert substance. The women in the experiment were mostly poor Mexican-Americans who already had several children (and who, incidentally, might not even have *heard* about any of the possible side effects of birth-control pills, a fact that would tend to distort the experiment's findings). Of the seventy-six women who received the placebo, ten were pregnant at the end of four months. The experiment was cosponsored by a drug firm manufacturing the ingredients in birth-control pills, and which might well have been interested in proving that the much discussed side effects were largely imaginary.

Several reporters and representatives of women's-rights groups who heard about the experiment closely questioned the physician directing the project on what information had been given the "volunteers." He indicated that the word "placebo" was never mentioned, nor were the women told that some would be given dummy pills. He insisted that the patients would not have been able to understand such information. He said that everybody was instructed to use the contraceptive cream, but admitted that the pregnancy ratio turned up in the study was "entirely consistent with other test results using vaginal creams or foam alone." He added that, had the state's courts permitted, the pregnant women would have been offered a free abortion. Unfortunately, all this occurred before the U.S. Supreme Court decision and the state abortion law did not cover this particular situation. So the test subjects presumably had babies they did not want and could not afford to support.

At last report, a woman's-rights group, the Third World Woman's Caucus, was attempting to bring a suit on behalf of these women against the experimenters. The case, of course, goes to the heart of one of the most important of all medical precepts: *informed consent.*

Informed consent is a basic principle of common law and has been upheld as a legal requirement in countless court cases throughout the United States. Informed consent on the part of the patient or his legal guardian is required before any medical procedure may be undertaken, routine or experimental. The problem is that different physicians define this doctrine in various ways. The women in the pill experiment were told that they were part of a study to test the side effects of birth-control medication. They were not told that, by the very nature of the experiment, a much higher risk of pregnancy might be expected. Without this important bit of information, was the consent really *informed?* Eventually the court will have to resolve that question.

Recently, another case involving informed consent made

headlines. In June 1973, a one-million-dollar damage suit was filed against a federally funded family-planning agency in Montgomery, Alabama, by the Southern Poverty Law Center, a nonprofit agency. Nationally known lawyer Melvin Belli agreed to assist in the case. The action was taken on behalf of Minnie Relf, fourteen, and her sister, Mary Alice Relf, twelve. According to the girls' attorney, the two youngsters had been surgically sterilized after their mother, who can neither read nor write, had signed a document with an "X," authorizing the operation. Immediately after the permission slip was signed the girls were taken to the hospital and the surgery was performed, on the sole ground that it would "prevent pregnancy."

The lawyer for the youngsters maintains that the mother understood only that her signature permitted a physician to "vaccinate" the girls. The director of the clinic maintains that sterilization was explained to the woman in terms she might be expected to understand. Was informed consent given in this case? Were alternatives offered to a procedure that will make it impossible for either of the two youngsters ever to have children of their own? Was the fact that the Relfs were on welfare more important to the authorities in this case than the legal rights of the children and their mother? The courts will have to decide these questions too. Meanwhile, the federal government has suspended the flow of money to the agency responsible for the sterilization. The U.S. Justice Department and a congressional committee are also investigating the problem.

Right now many other cases dealing with a patient's "informed consent" on the side effects of various drugs (especially various birth-control pills) are also in the courts. Lack of "informed consent" is one of the most common reasons for medical suits.

CASE 2. This deals with an even more frequent legal problem: medical bills and who is responsible for paying them. According to Ann Cote, ombudsman for New York Hospital (a position in which she interprets the patient's position to the hospital, the hospital's to the patient, and frequently mediates between the two), more patients complain about their bills and threaten to sue the hospital because they think they are being overcharged than for any other single reason. Physicians also have found that few patients bother to sue until they get a bill they consider outrageous.

According to the best available case law, the patient who had the gallbladder surgery is indeed responsible for that additional $250, above and beyond "usual and customary" fees prevalent in her community. Her insurance contract made that fact abundantly clear. However, many people unfortunately don't read their insurance contracts. Also, patients tend to be noticeably shy about bringing up the question of fees with their physicians. Miss Cote feels that the doctor *should* raise the point, especially if his charges are higher than those of other physicians in the community. But if he doesn't, and the patient is reluctant to do so on her own, the bill may come as an unpleasant surprise. Also, unless there are extraordinary mitigating circumstances, she probably is legally liable for the full amount.

According to Miss Cote, the patient also has a right to ask for a complete and itemized account of her hospital bill, even if the bill is paid in full by her insurance company. "Most hospital billing systems are computerized, and contrary to what some billing clerks may tell you, computer operations *do* make mistakes," she said. "If you have any questions, don't just meekly pay while fuming on the inside. Speak up."

CASE 3. This deals with the legal problem of the inviolability of communications between physicians and their patients. Most people believe that everything they tell their physician is totally private, and that no doctor ever can be forced to violate this confidence. Unfortunately, this is not true. Certainly, communications between a person and his or her personal physician are *confidential*. That means that the patient's doctor in Case 3 certainly would not call up her husband, her mother, or even his own wife to discuss the pregnancy and subsequent abortion without the patient's knowledge and consent. However, few laymen realize that there is a difference between "confidential" and "privileged." Confidential means that your doctor cannot give out information about you without your consent to anyone, *except a court*. In most states the *only* truly privileged communications are those between a lawyer and his or her clients, and a clergyman and his or her parishioners. A few states also make communications between a patient and a psychiatrist privileged. However, other types of physicians are rarely covered. Under the law of the state in which this young woman lived, her physician and his records could indeed have been subpoenaed into court in a divorce case. To protect their patients, many doctors might refuse flatly to answer questions, and as a matter of custom, few judges would send such doctors to jail for contempt of court. But it could happen.

Also, it is very important for a person talking to a physician to know in *whose employ* the physician is. For instance, if an employer sends you to a doctor for a physical examination before you are hired for a given job, the doctor works for the *employer*, and is empowered automatically to give information to him. If you take a physical exam for an insurance policy, the doctor is working for the insurance company, and anything you tell him will go into your insurance record.

CASE 4. A great many hospitals (especially those affiliated with religious organizations) still have age-parity rules for sterilization procedures. If the hospital receives any kind of federal funding (and almost all do), the hospital administration is on very dubious ground legally if they refuse to perform a procedure which the patient requests and to which her doctor agrees. A precedent was established in 1970, in the case of *Linda McCabe* v. *Nassau County Medical Center*. Mrs. McCabe asked to be sterilized, and the medical center (a public hospital) refused. She went to court and asked for an injunction against the hospital's refusal, as well as for damages. She insisted that the refusal to allow her the operation had caused her great mental anguish. As soon as the case was filed, the hospital administration reversed itself and allowed the operation to be performed. Mrs. McCabe, however, insisted on proceeding with the damage suit. The court decided that Mrs. McCabe did indeed have the right to demand the operation, but that her suit for damages was no longer valid, since she indeed had been sterilized. Several of the justices disagreed with the dismissal of the damage suit. All agreed that the hospital had been in the wrong in refusing to allow the operation, since it had denied her her constitutional rights of privacy and equal protection.

Most hospital administrators and boards know about the *McCabe* case. If they don't, a reminder might be in order. Usually a hospital that has age-parity regulations on female sterilization will back down if the patient threatens to take the case to court. Of course, the patient's physician has to agree to perform the operation (no doctor can be *forced* to perform a sterilization procedure, any more than he or she can be forced to perform any other form of surgery).

In some states, the husband's consent is necessary before a sterilization can be performed. Interestingly enough, there seem to be no similar rules about vasectomies on males. One of the reasons for this apparent inequality is that a vasectomy is an out-patient procedure that may be done in any qualified physician's office. But a state law that maintains that a wife must obtain her husband's agreement (perhaps even in writing) before she can be sterilized, but does not require that a husband must have permission from his wife before undergoing a vasectomy, has the kind of unequal legal standard that would be remedied by the passage of the Equal Rights Amendment.

CASE 5. This centers on the question of who owns your medical records. Many physicians and most hospitals hedge on this question. However, in actual practice, you will be given general information about your condition, but your access to your physician's or the hospital's written records probably will be limited unless you take the case into court. The young mother who wanted to know exactly what was done to her and why, preceding the birth of her baby, probably will have to be satisfied with what the doctor and the hospital are willing to tell her, unless she wants to go to court and sue, in which case her *lawyer* can demand her complete transcribed records.

Attorney Kathryn Emmett, who specializes in medical-legal cases (she was one of the lawyers on *Women* v. *Connecticut*, which was brought by four hundred women to eliminate the state's restrictive abortion laws), says that most hospitals will release a complete set of records only to a physician, another hospital, or an attorney, if a suit has been filed. Her own experience with the hospital in which she had her last baby was very interesting. She had a client who was suing another hospital because a procedure to induce labor had, according to the client, been misused. Attorney Emmett, whose labor also was induced, wanted to know what had been done in her case. She wrote to the hospital on her own personal stationery, asking for this information, and was told that records could be sent only to her physician or an attorney. She then repeated the request on her legal stationery, and promptly received the records.

Hospital administrators generally refuse to give the patient his or her complete records because they feel that they contain much speculation and other "raw" material, which might be frightening or upsetting. Attorney Emmett also thinks that some hospitals and physicians would find it embarrassing to have patients read what had been written about them. According to her, such notations as "this is a troublemaker," "complains a lot," "hypochondria," "has a very low pain threshold" or "may sue!" abound.

CASE 6. This case is the one example that is totally covered by a statute (in this instance, the Sixth Amendment to the Constitution). Anyone threatened with a deprivation of liberty (such as an involuntary confinement in a mental hospital) is entitled to "assistance of counsel for his defense." The courts repeatedly have found that this means *free* assistance if the person who is threatened cannot afford to pay. In this particular instance, the young woman's father was her legal adversary. Therefore, *his* ability to pay for a lawyer had absolutely nothing to do with *her* right to obtain legal services free of charge.

This question often has arisen when a person is confined to a mental hospital, an alcohol or a drug-withdrawal clinic, or some other mental-health facility against his or her will. In the past, many mental-health professionals have maintained that such confinement is not covered by the Bill of Rights, since the person is being hospitalized (presumably for his or her own good) for treatment, not for punishment. The courts increasingly have found that a person, unless he or she is a danger to others, has the same right to refuse psychiatric treatment as any kind of physical treatment.

Courts also increasingly have questioned the length of time a person is confined to a mental-health facility, and under what conditions. Recently the National Association for Mental Health filed an action in federal court in Washington, D.C., demanding that patients who work as gardeners, kitchen helpers, or perform other chores normally done by paid workers receive some kind of comparable salary.

As questions regarding the rights of patients arise more frequently, several studies have been undertaken to clarify some of the issues raised. Senator Edward Kennedy heads a congressional committee that is delving into the protection that should be offered to human research subjects. The American Hospital Association has issued a "Patients' Bill of Rights," which that group feels should be adopted by every hospital it accredits in the United States. A Commission on Medical Malpractice, sponsored by the U.S. Department of Health, Education and Welfare, issued a report last year dealing with the basic causes of the rising number of malpractice suits, and focusing on such issues as a patient's right to decent medical care, informed consent, and access to medical records.

Malpractice suits have become a major problem to physicians and hospitals, and indirectly to their patients. According to the report of the Commission on Malpractice, the yearly cost of the average physician's malpractice insurance has risen from $7,061 in 1960 to $37,610 in 1972. Of course, the cost of this insurance is passed along to the patient as part of his medical bill. Hospitals often pay staggering insurance fees, and they too are part of the rising cost of hospital care.

Too often, malpractice suits are the result of misunder-

standing and lack of communication, Anne Cote said. Many
of the lawyers interviewed agreed with her. Here are some
of the suggestions they made to patients or potential patients
on how to protect themselves from situations that might
require a court case to straighten out:

a. Ask a physician all the questions you feel you need in
order to make an informed decision about treatment. Don't
let a physician, a hospital administrator, a nurse, or anyone
else in the medical establishment make you feel that you are
taking too much of their valuable time by requiring clear and
precise answers. Don't sign any paper you have not read and
understood completely.

b. You are entitled to know exactly what medication you
are taking, what it is supposed to do for you, and what the
side effects might be. When in doubt, ask. Also request your
physician and your pharmacist to label, by name, all prescription drugs.

c. If you are in a hospital, and you feel that your rights as
a patient and human being have been violated or ignored,
complain. Learn something about the hospital's procedures
and grievance channels before you are too sick to cope. For
instance, if the hospital has an ombudsman or a patient advocate on its staff, that person usually can deal with your problem most efficiently. Going to the hospital director over the
heads of nursing supervisors, senior residents, or the billing
department probably will be just a waste of time. Your complaint will bounce right back to the person charged with
dealing with your particular type of grievance.

Also, if you have a complaint, express it *as soon as possible.*
Grievances that are received six months after a hospital bill
has become overdue are suspect, because they generally are
regarded as a dodge to avoid paying a legitimate debt.

d. Hospital computers are not always right. If your bill
looks doubtful, ask for an itemized statement. Keep asking
questions until the answers satisfy you.

e. If you feel that your legal rights have been seriously
violated, and that you must bring suit to recover damages,

find an attorney who specializes in medical malpractice suits.
Don't assume that he is an ambulance chaser because he asks
for one-third of the damages you recover. He probably is
taking the case on contingency, and will get nothing if you
lose.

Remember that to recover relatively small sums of money
(in most states up to $200) you are entitled to use a small-
claims court, where you won't need an attorney.

f. Never allow a physician, a hospital administrator, a
nurse, or anyone else entrusted with your health care make
you feel unimportant, ignorant, or powerless. Obviously,
these specialists have a great deal more technical knowledge
than you do, but it's *your* body they are treating and it's
therefore *your* right to understand what's happening to you,
to suffer as little physical and psychological discomfort as is
medically and humanly possible, and to be respected as a
patient and as a human being.

Chapter IX
RAPE

Case Histories

1. You have been following the latest FBI statistics on rape and realize that this particular crime against women is increasing at a frightening rate. Although you actually have never been raped, occasionally you have been followed, propositioned, and generally annoyed by unwanted attentions from strange men. You also have read that a rape case is often hard to prove, that prosecution can involve investigations that may be as embarrassing and painful to the victim as they are to the perpetrator. So you wonder, if you were raped, should you even bother to report that fact to the police? Would your previous sexual history become part of the court record, for instance, if the rapist's lawyer tried to prove that you are a promiscuous person? Since you are twenty-six, young, and attractive, and have lived a fairly unconventional life, would you be believed? If your story were not believed, and the rapist were released, would that fact constitute a legal assumption that you *invited* his attentions?

2. A friend has called you in a panic. A young man whom she had dated twice had forced his way into her apartment that evening and had raped her. She doesn't know what to do. After all, the man was not a stranger. Still, he had attacked her and forced her to have intercourse against her will. He had not used a weapon—he was simply bigger and stronger than she. And she somehow had never got around to taking the judo or karate lessons she had planned on. She is furious at the man and would like to see him punished. She also is worried that he might do similar harm to other girls. However, since the man *was* her date and since he did not

use a weapon, can she claim that she was raped?

3. You live in a neighborhood that is noted for its high crime rate. Because there have been several rapes in your block, you recently purchased a spring-blade knife, which you carry in your coat pocket where it cannot be seen. Recently someone told you that your state has a law against the carrying of "concealed weapons" and that your knife certainly would fall into that category. You might be prosecuted just for keeping your weapon handy. Don't you have the right to protect yourself?

4. Your young cousin was raped by a young man she since has seen around her neighborhood. She knows who he is and where he can be found. She also has three large, strong brothers, who are naturally furious at what has happened to their sister (who, incidentally, didn't report the rape to the police because she was too ashamed). They have cooked up a scheme that involves having their little sister invite the young man over to the house the next time she sees him (pretending that she was impressed with his forceful, masculine approach). Her brothers will be there, waiting, with chains, baseball bats, and other instruments of destruction "to beat the living daylights out of that bastard." Your cousin is wary of that approach. She feels that her brothers might get into serious trouble if they take the law into their own hands. They maintain that there is "an unwritten law" that allows them to avenge their sister. Who is right?

5. A neighbor's apartment was broken into while she was asleep. The criminal raped her, and stole her color television set and some jewelry. She is afraid to report the rape to the police, because her fiancé is an exceedingly jealous man, and she feels that he might wish to break the engagement, even though the incident clearly was not her fault. On the other hand, she would like to see the perpetrator punished, and possibly get her property back. She asks you whether she should report the theft but not the rape. Is she committing some kind of crime (for instance, obstruction of justice) if she withholds pertinent facts from the police?

6. Your husband, from whom you are separated (you are

filing for divorce, but the divorce is not yet final) uses his old door key, since you forgot to have the lock changed, and forces his way into your apartment, beats you up, and rapes you. He gloatingly invites you to call the police. "You can't accuse me of rape, because I'm still legally married to you," he announces. "You can't even complain that I gave you those black eyes, because a wife cannot testify in court against her husband." You feel that there has to be something wrong with his reasoning. Is there?

Case Solutions

CASE 1. The answer in this case is not easy or unequivocal. The number of reported rape cases has indeed been rising steadily. Statisticians are not quite sure whether this increase means that more women are raped or that more women are *reporting* rapes, partly owing to better and more humane police techniques, and partly because of the encouragement they have received from the women's movement not to play the role of the defenseless victim. However, officials still estimate that there are four to ten times more rapes committed than reported.

Many women apparently ask themselves, "Is it worth going through the misery and embarrassment of having to tell about your experience in great detail, first to the police, then to a prosecutor, and finally in open court?" There is no avoiding this necessity: they will have to relive, in their own minds, everything that has happened to them over and over again if they wish to see the rapist prosecuted.

What's more, they will have to fight their own instincts in making sure that evidence necessary for indictment and prosecution is preserved. The immediate impulse of the average woman, after being raped, is to take a bath or shower. She almost inevitably feels soiled. This is exactly what she *should not* do. She should not even change her clothes. The most important evidence of rape is the presence of semen in her vagina, on her clothing, or both.

So, if she wishes to prosecute her attacker, she will have to call the police immediately. A squad car probably will take her to the nearest hospital, where a gynecological examination will be performed, and a vaginal smear (to determine the presence of semen) will be taken. During the examination a police officer will be in the examining room. In some jurisdictions, the police department now tactfully assigns a female officer to this detail, but the woman must be prepared to have a *male* police officer watch the whole procedure.

Even if she does not wish to report the rape incident, a woman should see a doctor as soon as possible after she has been attacked sexually. She needs a physical examination, and certain precautionary medical steps probably will be taken. Most physicians will give a rape victim a shot of preventive penicillin against possible venereal disease. Others may suggest that she take a large dose of estrogen (the so-called "morning after" pill) to make sure that the rape does not result in pregnancy. If there are any lacerations or bruises, these also will be treated. Of course, if she does not wish to report the incident to the police, the physician will protect her privacy, and any treatment that is given will be kept in strict confidence. Obviously, no police officer will be present during the examination under those circumstances.

However, if she does wish to go ahead and charge her attacker, the physical exam is just the beginning. She will be questioned extensively about the attack itself, whether or not she knew her attacker, what her life style and previous sexual experience have been, and any number of other topics that may seem to her quite unrelated to the outrage that has been perpetrated against her.

Prosecutors don't like to take rape cases into court unless they have a reasonable chance of conviction, and it's still more difficult to convict a rapist than almost any other kind of criminal.

If the victim is young and attractive, and if she has not been badly beaten, stabbed, or otherwise seriously injured, jurors still may wonder whether she did not, consciously or unconsciously, invite the attack. She may even be asked if she enjoyed it. As one prosecutor put it recently, "The only way to be sure of getting a rape conviction is when the victim is under 12, over 70, half dead or a nun."

In spite of such cynicism, more rape convictions are being obtained these days. Rape laws are changing. Only a few years ago, rape was one of the few crimes in which "corroboration" was essential before an accused criminal even could be indicted. "Corroboration" was often defined so narrowly that a woman almost needed a witness to the act in order to be assured of a trial. The corroboration clause is being eliminated in many states now, and rape is being treated as a *crime of violence* rather than a sex crime. Other states are making it illegal to question a woman about her past sexual history in or out of court. Such questions were formerly permitted, supposedly to establish the witness' credibility. Prosecutors and judges are realizing that, since it's illegal to ask an accused burglar whether he has ever before been arrested or convicted of burglary, it's manifestly unfair to women to ask them if they have engaged in sex acts that did not violate any laws, before the alleged attack. If you want more information about rape laws in your state, your bar association or legal-assistance organization can help.

Some police departments now have rape squads, usually including several female officers, who may be expected to be more sympathetic to the victim. Several communities have women's centers or rape centers, which a victim can call before she calls the police. Often such organizations will send a volunteer (sometimes a woman who has been raped and who has gone through the whole reporting procedure herself) to assist the victim at the hospital and at the police station.

Knowing that you may be embarrassed, harassed, and that your case may turn out not to be strong enough to convict the rapist may make it difficult for you to force yourself to report the attack. But the same man who attacked you probably will attack other women. Some mental-health experts believe that rapists who are allowed to get away with their crimes tend to become more violent. The man who simply threatens a woman with a beating actually may beat, stab, or even kill the next woman he attacks.

Certainly you will be doing society a favor if you report the

rape. Actually, even with all the difficulties and embarrass-
ments that your action may cause you, you still may be doing
yourself a favor as well. For most of us it's better to get a
traumatic situation into the open and to do something constructive about it than to keep it hidden inside ourselves,
feeling helpless, depressed, and furious, perhaps for years to
come.

CASE 2. The young woman here certainly has been raped
in the legal sense of the term. Rape is defined as forcing a
woman (or a female child) to perform sexual intercourse
without her consent. Even though the victim knew the man
and had dated him, he still raped her.

All the difficulties that face a woman who reports a rape
will be tripled in Case 2, however. The man almost certainly
will say that she consented. However, with a sympathetic
prosecutor she still may be able to persuade a jury that her
attacker is lying. Again, one of the principal reasons for reporting the incident is that he probably will try to commit
the same crime with another woman, and that even if he is
not convicted the anxiety of going through a police-question-
ing session, the embarrassment of seeing his name in the
paper as an accused rapist, and the lawyer's fee he will have
to pay if the case gets into court may convince him never to
attempt such an attack again.

CASE 3. The spring-blade knife may get its owner into
serious trouble. It definitely would be classified as a concealed weapon. Even if she used it on a potential rapist, she
still might be arrested for possession of the knife, although
she probably would not be accused of assault, since she employed it in self-defense.

What's more, any kind of weapon can be used against the
owner. The chances are that a rapist, or any other experienced criminal, is stronger than the victim and may use
her own knife or gun on her.

So what can a woman do to protect herself? Carrying a
loud whistle is sometimes helpful. Although we all have been
told that no one will respond to a cry for help, even if a rape
takes place in broad daylight at the corner of Main and

Church streets, this is not always true. Police officers may be nearby and certainly will respond to the whistle. Often civilians will help the potential victim. The cases in which nobody does anything are the ones that get into the newspapers. There are countless others in which women have been saved from rapists and muggers by the police, a neighborhood storekeeper, or just a helpful stranger.

Learning self-defense techniques can be very useful. Some YWCA's now run self-defense classes, and there are commercial judo and karate schools with special programs for women. In many cities police departments have been conducting courses in self-defense for women. A well-placed kick can be as effective in fighting off an attacker as any weapon. Even a small woman, with judo methods, can learn to throw a large man over her shoulder, using his superior weight and size to her advantage.

The book *Our Bodies, Ourselves,* published by the Boston Women's Health Collective, includes a very constructive suggestion. If a potential rapist corners you in a hallway or an elevator, don't yell "Help"—yell "Fire." That usually brings a prompt response from everyone within hearing distance of your voice.

CASE 4. The young woman in this case had better warn her brothers that if they take revenge on her attacker they may land in prison. They probably will be accused of assault and battery. The whole idea of the "unwritten" law is more myth than law. Juries may be swayed to recommend mercy when brothers injure their sister's attacker, or the judge may be persuaded to give the men a lighter sentence, but still they have committed a crime, and if caught, will be prosecuted and probably convicted.

Recently, two cases received wide publicity. In California, a woman shot a man who allegedly raped her. She tracked him down and shot him within about a week of his attack on her. She was accused of premeditated murder, convicted of murder in the second degree, and received a sentence of five years in jail.

In Philadelphia, another young woman urged the rapist to

visit her apartment (pretending that she had enjoyed the experience). When he arrived, she blasted him with a shotgun. She too was arrested and charged with murder. It was pointed out to her that she had not shot her alleged attacker in self-defense (as would have been the case had she had that shotgun handy when he actually attacked her). She had *invited* him to her home. The fact that he previously had raped her was irrelevant.

So, no matter how embarrassing a report to the police might have been, the young woman would have been infinitely smarter had she called the police department right after the rape took place. At least, she might have had a police officer present as a witness when she invited the rapist to her apartment—and she most assuredly should have left that shotgun in the closet.

CASE 5. The woman certainly can report the loss of her television set and other property to the police without mentioning the rape, if this is what she chooses to do. If the perpetrator is found, and she picks him out of a lineup, she will have an easier time getting a conviction for theft than for rape. Unfortunately, juries are still more apt to believe a woman when she complains that her property has been stolen than that her body has been violated.

However, it would seem advisable (although not legally required) that she tell the police about the attack as well. Again, she may be preventing similar crimes against other women. If the man is convicted of burglary, it may be a very good idea to have at least a police complaint of the rape on hand when he comes up for parole. What's more, he may be able to get psychiatric treatment while he is in jail, which might prevent him from raping women when he gets out. If the authorities don't know that they have a rapist on their hands, they can't do anything about his violent nature. If they do, they at least can try. If she chooses not to tell the whole story, she would not be obstructing justice, however. She has the right to press charges or not.

CASE 6. The husband is wrong on all counts. According to the legal definition of rape, a man can indeed be accused of raping his own wife. What's more, since he beat her, he also can be accused of assault and battery. His idea that a wife cannot testify against her husband is a myth that a great many people share. She cannot be forced, under common law, to testify against him (just as he cannot be forced to testify against her). But she has every right to press charges voluntarily against him, and under the circumstances certainly should do so.

Chapter X

WHAT YOUR CHILD SHOULD KNOW ABOUT THE LAW

Case Histories

1. In a small Connecticut town fifteen-year-old William Brown was giving a party, complete with loud rock music, cokes, and potato chips. His parents (unwisely, as it turned out) had decided to leave the youngsters to their own devices and go to a neighborhood movie. Sometime around midnight Bill responded to a loud knock at the door, and was confronted with two policemen who told him that several neighbors were complaining about the noise. Bill apologized, and told the officers that he would certainly lower the volume on the hi-fi and tell his friends to quiet down. At that point one of the officers said that he also had been informed that someone was smoking pot at the party, and although he didn't believe the story, he would like to come in and check it out. Bill allowed the officers to enter the house. No one on the first floor was doing anything illegal, but the officers found two of Bill's guests with marijuana cigarettes in a second-floor bedroom. Everybody at the party was arrested and charged with juvenile delinquency and possession of illegal drugs.

2. In a suburban department store in Texas, thirteen-year-old Mary Williams browsed through the record department, picked out three records, and slipped them absentmindedly into her shopping bag. Ignoring the signs that directed her to pay for her purchases at the nearest cashier's counter, she moved toward the exit door. Before she had left the store she was stopped by a man who identified himself as a store detective and insisted that she accompany him to the manager's office. There she was accused of stealing and the police were called. After a police officer arrived, Mary (who had been told

that she had the right to remain silent and the right to ask for an attorney to be present during questioning), sobbing and frightened, said that she had only meant to pick up a birthday card in the greeting-card department, which she thought was near the exit door. She was going to mail the card, along with the records, to her best friend, and certainly had meant to pay for all the merchandise. The detective pointed out that the greeting-card department was on the second floor of the store, nowhere near the exit toward which Mary was apparently heading. She was taken to the station house, her parents were called, and by the time they arrived their daughter had been formally charged with juvenile delinquency: shoplifting.

3. In a Midwestern college town a group of youngsters was picketing the local welfare department to protest a cut in welfare benefits. A contingent of police officers arrived and informed them that they were breaking a local law that prohibited "parading without a permit." Since they obviously didn't have a permit, they would have to leave or face arrest. The indignant youngsters pointed out that they were picketing peacefully, which, they maintained, was their constitutional right. They certainly didn't consider their protest a parade. They refused to leave and were arrested, taken to the nearest police station, and booked on a charge of juvenile delinquency: creating a public nuisance, parading without a permit, and resisting arrest. (Several members of the group had decided to go limp and had to be dragged to the police van.)

4. On a rural road in Vermont two thirteen-year-old boys with one flight bag full of dirty laundry and five dollars between them were picked up by a local police officer. He asked their names, their ages, where they were going, and from where they came. It turned out that they had run away from home (a New York suburb) and were looking for a nearby commune. The officer, who had picked up dozens of runaway youngsters in the past year, took them in the police car to the station house and called their worried parents, who promised to drive to Vermont immediately to pick up their

children. Until the parents' arrival, the youngsters would be held at the police station. Legally, they could have been charged with juvenile delinquency: running away from home. However, the officer decided to postpone any formal action until he had had a chance to discuss the situation with their families.

Case Solutions

All youngsters involved in the four situations given above were having their first brush with the law. How they and their parents handled the problem could have affected the rest of their lives.

As it turned out, all of these cases ended relatively happily for the youngsters involved. However, they could have saved themselves and their families a great deal of pain and anxiety if they had been taught a few basic facts about the law.

CASE 1. Bill should not have invited the officers to enter his home without a warrant. At least, he should have asked them to come back when his parents got home, even though he didn't know anything about the pot-smoking upstairs.

CASE 2. Mary should not have answered *any* questions without legal advice from an attorney.

CASE 3. The protesters should have followed police orders and taken their complaint to the city attorney.

(Cases 1 to 3 will be discussed in more detail later.)

CASE 4. The two runaways should have realized that taking off from home without their parents' knowledge was not just a lark—under the circumstances their action could be defined as juvenile delinquency. They were lucky that an understanding police officer didn't book and charge them. He just sent them home to their relieved families after giving them a stern warning not to take to the road again.

Children, like adults, hear a great deal about "law and order" these days. However, few children understand what laws really are and how they apply to them, and what legal rights and responsibilities they have. Parents rarely discuss law with their children and few schools provide more than a minimum amount of information. However, youngsters discuss law and law-breaking among themselves almost as frequently as they discuss sex, according to William Mecca, supervisor of professional services at Family Service of New Haven, Connecticut. Mecca, whose specialty is working with young people, says, "Of the two topics they discuss most, they know least about law, and they spread all kinds of misinformation in their group." These are some of the most common misconceptions:

a. "Nothing serious can really happen to me because I am a juvenile."

This is, of course, a totally false assumption. Actually, in many states, laws are more stringently applied to children than to adults. Many different offenses, such as minor shoplifting, loitering, hitchhiking, and so on, are lumped under one category: juvenile delinquency. In the case of an adult, most of these charges either would be dismissed or the culprit would be given a warning or a fine. Shoplifting charges are generally more serious when a child is involved, many police officers maintain. "When a well-dressed adult takes a tie or a scarf off the counter and walks out the door, most store managers will just follow him or her and ask that the merchandise be returned or paid for," a police officer said. "If it's a charge customer, they may just quietly include the item on his next bill. The same store manager will insist on pressing charges against a child 'to teach him a lesson.'" Had Mary Williams been an adult, she almost certainly would not have been stopped before she actually had walked out of the store. Even if she had left the store with the records, she might not have been arrested—just warned not to come back.

Police and judges also tend to take a dimmer view of drug-possession cases involving young teenagers than those involving adults. "We don't bother raiding adult parties, even if we are reasonably sure that pot is being smoked," one police officer in a small Connecticut town said. "We figure these people must know what they are doing. We know that marijuana is illegal, but it's used so widely around here that we'd not have time to do anything else if we raided every suspicious adult party. However, if we know of a teenage pot-smoking party, we do something about it. We feel that kids often don't know what they are doing and should be stopped."

What's more, certain actions that are perfectly legal for adults are illegal for children and can get a youngster into serious trouble: for instance, running away from home (no matter how unloving and uncaring the home), truancy, or marrying without a parent's permission. Some charges on which children may be arrested and sentenced are so vague that they never would hold up in an adult court: "being in need of supervision," "incorrigibility," "creating a nuisance," or "loitering." Until the spring of 1972, Connecticut had a special law that applied only to girls under twenty-one: "being in manifest danger of falling into habits of vice." It was used to pick up adolescents who were out on the street at night, or who were otherwise troublesome to the community.

Whatever the cause for an arrest, a juvenile-delinquency proceeding before a court that is empowered to take a child away from his family, friends, and community is a terrifying experience for almost all youngsters and a painful one for their parents.

In some ways, of course, juvenile court differs from adult court. Hearings are closed to the public and the press to prevent publicity. There is no jury; only a judge. The point of the proceedings is supposed to be to "rehabilitate" the child, rather than to punish.

However, juvenile-court judges have great latitude in the disposition of cases. Any charge of "juvenile delinquency" potentially can send a youngster to reform school or to some other institution for children. Some inexperienced judges even may feel that a short time in a reformatory (which may have such a harmless-sounding name as "Green Valley School for Girls" or "Running Brook School for Boys") will teach the child respect for the law.

However, all the psychiatrists and social workers, most of the judges and police officers, and many of the police department officials interviewed agreed that even a brief stay in a "training school" or a "juvenile detention center" might be psychologically disastrous for a sensitive youngster. As for teaching respect for the law, many considered these institutions crime incubators, since most are understaffed (particularly with mental-health professionals and teachers); some are overcrowded, dilapidated, and filthy; and in them, young, relatively inexperienced, and naive juveniles tend to become pawns of older, more experienced offenders.

If a child is left in the home and sentenced to a period of probation, his or her juvenile record seriously may cloud future prospects for education and employment.

At best, even if the child is cleared of all charges, a juvenile court experience is no joy ride.

b. "Children don't have any legal rights anyhow."

Contradictory as it may seem, this false idea is often held by the same youngsters who believe that nothing serious can happen to them because they are juveniles. In fact, in the history-making *Gault* decision, the United States Supreme Court decided that in court, children have many of the same constitutional rights as adults. For instance, a child or his belongings cannot be searched without a warrant unless the child is caught red-handed in the commission of a crime.

CASE 1: The police search of William Brown's home in Connecticut turned out to be an illegal one. Bill had not been warned that he could refuse entrance to the warrantless police officers. In order to find the pot-smoking guests, the officers had to go upstairs (nothing was evident on the first floor). Because the youngster's rights had been violated, charges against everybody (including the two culprits who were actually using drugs) were dismissed.

A child also has the right to refuse to answer questions, the right to be represented by an attorney, and the right to confront witnesses against him.

Children also have rights under various civil rights statutes. The Civil Rights Act of 1968 made it illegal to discriminate in employment because of race, religion, or sex. Many states have passed statutes to conform with this law. For instance, during the summer of 1972, a sixteen-year-old East Providence High School student, Eileen McMahon, applied for a job as golf caddie, traditionally reserved for boys. The caddie master rejected her because he didn't believe that a girl could carry two golf bags for eighteen holes. Eileen asked for the right to prove she could do so. Her application could not be rejected solely on the grounds of her sex, even though she was only sixteen years old.

Youngsters also cannot be refused employment because they belong to minority groups, if the job for which they are applying is in any way connected with commerce between states (federal laws apply here), or if their state has a fair-employment statute of its own.

As of January 1975, students in a public school cannot be suspended for more than ten days without notice of the charges against them, an examination of any adverse evidence, and a chance to present their side of the story. The United States Supreme Court, in its majority opinion, decided to extend the protection of "minimum due process" and thus became a participant in a long-standing debate on the extent to which minors are entitled to the same constitutional guarantees as adults. This decision grew out of the case of nine students in Columbus, Ohio, who were suspended without a hearing or without even an opportunity to hear the charges against them.

The Court has still left open the question of students' rights in cases of long suspensions or expulsions. The opinion stated, however, that "more formal procedures" may be required in such cases. A case involving a disciplinary expulsion is now pending, and many lawyers expect that the decision on the ten-day-or-less suspensions may set a precedent for the more serious problem.

Any parent whose child has been suspended (or expelled) is urged to insist on knowing the causes that led up to the punishment and, if this seems indicated, to ask for a hearing.

All suspensions go on a youngster's school record and certainly might hurt his or her future job or college admission plans.

"A legal right is not what someone gives you—it's what no one can take away," former Attorney General Ramsey Clark once told a group of young people. Most lawyers feel that this statement sums up the situation for children, as well as for adults.

c. "If I'm innocent, I don't need a lawyer."

Most children and many adults believe that only guilty people need legal representation. Innocence is supposed to be its own best protection. Unfortunately, this is not always the way legal proceedings work out.

CASE 2: Let's take the case of Mary Williams again. By the time her parents arrived at the police station, she was almost hysterical, had contradicted herself several times during questioning (she agreed to be questioned without a lawyer present because she *knew* she was innocent), and was under arrest. The general impression that both Mary and her parents received from the desk officer was that she really didn't need a lawyer. After all, the charge was relatively minor. What's more, the verdict was almost a foregone conclusion. The records were found in Mary's shopping bag, she couldn't answer questions without being caught in contradictions, and what's more, attorneys could be pretty expensive.

Mary's parents, after discussing the situation with their daughter, were really convinced of her innocence. She always had been a rather absentminded, forgetful girl, and to them her story could be not only plausible, but likely.

The first witness at the juvenile court hearing was the store dectective who said that he saw Mary take the records, put them in her tote-bag, and walk toward the exit. However, Mary's lawyer in cross-examination extracted the information that Mary actually had not *left* the store when she was stopped. More importantly, he also found out that the greeting-card department to which Mary had said she was going had indeed been located near that exit until two weeks before the alleged theft, when it was moved to the second floor.

The police officer, when questioned, testified that he found the records in Mary's shopping bag. On cross-examination, he amplified his statement and said that Mary hadn't tried to stop him from searching her bag. Although she did contradict herself at the police station, she certainly seemed emotionally upset enough to be confused.

The facts brought out by the attorney plus Mary's own story convinced the judge that she was innocent of stealing. The case was dismissed and Mary went home, vastly relieved and determined not to be absentminded again when she went shopping. She also decided to find a baby-sitting job during her summer vacation to help pay the lawyer, whose bill came to about $100.

That $100 may have been the best investment Mary's parents ever made in her future. Justine Wise Polier, who for thirty-six years has been a judge in the New York Family Court, probably has heard more juvenile cases than any other American jurist. She firmly and emphatically insists that anyone (especially a child) who is accused of a crime that may involve deprivation of freedom on conviction, should have a lawyer at his or her side. A recent United States Supreme Court ruling backs up her point of view. The Court unanimously decided that a person accused of even a minor misdemeanor that can result in a jail term of *just one day* is entitled to *free* legal counsel, if he cannot afford a lawyer. The decision applies to children as well as to adults, Judge Polier points out.

"Far from resenting a lawyer's presence in court, most juvenile court judges welcome it," she adds. She also feels strongly that a child who is *guilty* of the action for which he or she was arrested needs an attorney. "Court calendars are crowded, probation officers busy, and real treatment facilities for children overcrowded or nonexistent," she says. "A lawyer can help a judge to make a disposition that is fair and best for the child involved."

She also feels that parents should be made aware of free

legal-assistance programs in the community to serve children. "Those who need free legal help most often are the ones who don't know it's available," she says.

Parents who can afford to retain a lawyer for their children should make sure that the youngster knows who the family lawyer *is* and where and when he can be reached. "Last year our sixteen-year-old, Johnny, was arrested for loitering while on a cross-country hiking trip," one father said. "He was looking for a youth hostel at the time. It happened about six o'clock in the evening. He couldn't reach us because we were out to dinner, and he didn't know who our lawyer was. So he spent the night in a county jail in the same cell with a drunk, a homosexual, and a man accused of armed robbery. He is going on another hiking trip this summer, and I'm making sure that he carries the family lawyer's office and home telephone numbers in his wallet, right along with the family doctor's."

Charles Pulaski, associate professor of law at the University of Iowa, who has defended many youngsters in court, tells all his friends' teenage sons and daughters to call home at once if they are arrested. "It's better to face the music at home than in jail," is his advice. "I have seen children who were more afraid of their parents' anger than of a juvenile-delinquency record," he says. "They will refuse to notify their parents and just plead guilty on the court's promise of a light sentence or probation." He tells of two boys who were arrested for hitchhiking and obstructing traffic on a highway while on a weekend camping trip. They were arrested, taken into court, and asked whether they wished their parents called. Since the boys had promised to take a bus, they were afraid to make the call. The judge appointed a temporary guardian for the court case (that's quite legal) and allowed the youngsters to plead guilty. They paid a fine with their bus money and went on with the trip. Only later, when one of them applied for a summer job in a defense plant, did he learn that he had a "juvenile delinquency" record.

d. "All juvenile court records are completely closed, and no one will ever find out that I have been in trouble with the law."

Children and their parents often find out to their sorrow that "closed" records have a way of leaking to potential employers, college admissions officers, and others. A record can make the crucial difference of whether or not a youngster is admitted to the college of his or her choice or whether he or she gets a certain job. It may bar him or her from being admitted to officers' training school in any of the armed services. In some cases, it even has created difficulty for young people applying for a passport.

According to Judge Polier, the idea of a completely confidential file in a juvenile case is a myth. "We don't allow the press to print the names of juvenile offenders, but it's almost impossible to keep arrest records totally secret," she says.

A story in *The New York Times* of June 25, 1972, bears her out. "The New York Police Department will curtail its controversial practice of keeping dossiers on juvenile offenders and passing along unsubstantiated information to other authorities," the story began. "In a compromise with lawyers who challenged the practice as unconstitutional, the department will continue to keep records on children between the ages of 7 and 16, but will deny access to them to all public and private agencies."

The records didn't contain just information on misdeeds for which the youngsters had been *convicted*, but also facts on alleged violations of the law of which the children had been cleared, or for which they had not even been prosecuted for lack of evidence. "One of the reasons the practice of handing around these records is so bad is that there seems to be a 'Gresham's Law of Information' . . . the bad information about a child drives out the good, simply because it's more accessible," a lawyer acting for the children told a reporter.

Judge Polier knows of many cases in which youngsters were asked by potential employers, college admissions officers, and others, "Have you ever been arrested?" (The question was not "Were you convicted?"). The youngster may suspect that even a simple arrest record may damage his future. He doesn't want to lie, so he finds himself in an impossible trap. Judge Polier thinks that asking such a question should be illegal, and that arrest records of juveniles (especially if they were not convicted) should be erased.

Attorney Pulaski points out that in Connecticut and several other states an attorney can petition to have the record erased. "In that case, the youngster should be informed that an erased record means there was no arrest," he said. "And he or she can answer 'no' with a clear conscience when confronted with a question about a past arrest."

To petition to have records erased is another reason why a child should be represented by an attorney in a juvenile-court proceeding.

Besides clearing up these common misconceptions, parents should also explain a few other important legal facts to their children.

Few children know the difference between a law and a rule. School rules (such as dress codes, smoking regulations, etc.) are made and enforced by the school board and/or the principal. Employment rules (length of coffee breaks, rest periods, punching in and out on time clocks) are made and enforced by the employer. A youngster can get into trouble with the institution that made the rule if he ignores or breaks it. The teacher can keep him after class and a principal can suspend him. An employer can fire him. However, he cannot be taken into court and charged with a crime for breaking a rule—only a law.

Judge Polier points out one important exception to this principle: Children who break rules consistently in school or in the community can be charged with such *legal* offenses as "being in need of supervision" or "being chronically disruptive." This kind of complaint can and often does result in a juvenile-court hearing.

Youngsters also should be aware of the fact that a person (including a child) shares responsibility with a lawbreaker if he or she *in any way* participates in the crime or profits from illegal gains. If Jim allows Joe to hide his marijuana cigarettes in the glove compartment of the car, Jim also will be arrested if the drug is found, and probably will be convicted of possession of illegal drugs. If the search of the Brown house in Connecticut had been legal, Bill would have had an exceedingly difficult time proving that he was uninvolved in the use of marijuana on the premises, even though he didn't know what was going on upstairs.

A child who accepts a present from another child, knowing the object is stolen, is considered an accessory to and a participant in the theft. A child who takes a joy ride in a car a friend has "borrowed" from a parking lot without the owner's permission can be held criminally responsible for being an accessory to auto theft.

CASE 3: Participation in demonstrations that result in violence usually will mean arrest for everyone involved, even those who had absolutely no intention of engaging in a confrontation with the police. Incidentally, "going limp" and forcing an officer to drag one to a waiting police van has been interpreted as "resisting arrest" by the courts. Youngsters should be told that if they are arrested, they should go along quietly, and insist on calling their parents and/or a lawyer as soon as they get to the police station. The only charge that was upheld against the protesters in the Midwestern college town was one "resisting arrest." Requiring the youngsters to produce a parade permit was indeed an infringment of their First Amendment right "peaceably to assemble, and to petition the government for a redress of grievances."

Children should be encouraged to discuss knowledge of unlawful activities with their parents. They certainly should be warned to stay away from scenes of such activities (e.g., if the corner store sells pot and LSD along with the comic books, find another comic-book store), and from persons known to be committing illegal acts (teenagers who raid their friends' parents' liquor cabinets and bring the loot to a beach party). Parents also might want to remind children that almost as many youngsters are arrested for *illegal drink-*

ing as for smoking pot. If Joan knows that alcohol will be flowing freely at Susie's sixteenth birthday party as soon as Susie's parents have left for the movies, Joan should find a good reason not to go to the party. In a police raid, nondrinkers probably also will be arrested.

Parents, of course, should react with common sense and discretion to their children's confidences. In the case of Susie's party, a talk with Susie the next time she comes by might be indicated. A call to the police most certainly is not. If parents get their children's friends into trouble needlessly, they will lose the youngsters' trust, and the next time they may not hear about potentially alcoholic parties or other more serious problems.

Obviously, children should be taught enough about the property rights of others to keep them from destroying, defacing, or borrowing such property. However, they also should be made aware that they have property rights too. A mother who makes her young son pay for the window his baseball broke at a neighbor's house but refuses to make her own best friend pay for repairs to her son's bicycle, which she accidentally hit with her car, is teaching her youngster not only selective law, but selective morality. If the cleaner loses or ruins Barbara's best leather coat and refuses to pay for it or replace it, it may seem like a great deal of trouble for the parents to go to the small-claims court to force him to restore Barbara's property. However, Barbara should learn from her parents that they really believe in "equal law, equally enforced"—even if it means that time and effort will be needed to protect her rights. Incidentally, children cannot take cases into the small-claims court on their own, but parents can do so on their behalf. In most states, the small-claims court handles cases that involve sums of $200 or less, and an attorney is not needed.

Parents should indicate to their children that First Amendment rights concerning freedom of speech, opinion, and assembly are respected in the household. Adolescents especially often say or write things that outrage their parents, neighbors, or even teachers. Under the law, they have the right to do this. On the other hand, a youngster also should know that the laws that protect him also protect others. Shouting down a speaker whose point of view varies from that of a young audience is not only rude, it's also an infringement on the speaker's First Amendment rights. Parents should firmly discourage their children picketing auditoriums to keep out unpopular speakers, not only because such activity can lead to an arrest for disturbing the peace, but because it also infringes on the right of free speech and free assembly.

Young children often need to be reminded that American law is based on an assumption of innocence. When Peter comes home and says, "I think Johnny stole my bike—do something about it," a parent should not rush to the phone to call either Johnny's mother or the police. This is an excellent time to give Peter a simple lesson in American law: "How do you know that Johnny stole your bike? Did you see him do it? If not, what makes you think it was *Johnny?*" are entirely appropriate questions. It will be helpful to a youngster's sense of law and fair play to hear his mother or father report the stolen bike to the police without mentioning Johnny's name, unless Peter has really produced some solid evidence that Johnny may be the guilty party. Just not liking Johnny or having been told by a friend that "Johnny is the kind of kid who steals things" simply isn't enough to point the finger of suspicion at Johnny.

Parents of older children often are confronted with youngsters who announce that they knowingly will break a law as a protest measure. Both parents and potential protesters may be perfectly aware that sitting in at the board of education or the mayor's office, or distributing leaflets in a shopping center without getting the owner's permission, can get them arrested for disturbing the peace, creating a public nuisance, or blocking traffic.

Parents should discuss with their children that protesters have gone to jail for engaging in activities that seem quite moral to them, but that are nonetheless illegal. If a youngster is willing to break a law to defend a principle, he or she must be made aware of the possible legal consequences (including possibly arrest and jail) and be prepared to take his punishment, if necessary. One mother told her seventeen-year-old son, who was planning to participate in a peace march which had the potential to turn into a violent confrontation with the police, "If you feel what you are doing is right, and therefore, you *must* do it, I guess you'll have to go ahead. You may feel that it's your *duty* to march on the recruiting station to protest the war in Vietnam. But it's the policeman's *job* to keep you out, so don't complain to me if you get caught in a situation where the police retaliate with tear gas or night sticks." The boy joined the peace march, but left when the marchers got into a battle and rock-throwing fight with the police.

James F. Ahern, former New Haven police chief—who achieved national prominence for the leading role he played in keeping that city "cool" on May Day in 1970, when thousands of protesters arrived to vent their anger over a Black Panther trial and the Vietnam War—emphasizes the importance of honesty between parents and children on the whole subject of law. Ahern, who joined the police force in 1954 after studying for the priesthood, has worked with thousands of angry, discouraged, sick, and just plain mischievous young people who get into trouble with the law. Because of his experience, particularly with young people, he was appointed to the Presidential Commission on Campus Unrest and serves as an associate fellow at Yale University in law enforcement.

"Too many parents find it necessary to defend *all* law, no matter how stupid, and all law enforcement, no matter how unfair," Ahern says. In discussing law with his own children he always has emphasized that all laws are certainly not perfect, and that many need drastic changes. He admits freely that enforcement is often capricious, that not all policemen are honest and fair, and that corruption exists in the court system.

"To try to tell an angry, troubled seventeen-year-old kid that the legal system is perfect is like telling a seventeen-year-old: 'Yes, Virginia, Santa Claus brought your Christmas presents by sliding down the chimney,' " he says. Youngsters should be told unpleasant, as well as pleasant, truths about law and law enforcement, and should be encouraged to participate in the political system to change those aspects they find reprehensible.

Ahern is delighted that eighteen-year-olds now can vote and make a direct contribution to the political process. "One of the reasons many young people get into trouble is because they feel alienated and helpless," he says. "They may still be alienated . . . but with 17.5 million young people between the ages of eighteen and twenty-one eligible to vote, at least they don't need to feel helpless any more. Instead of breaking laws they consider unreasonable, unfair, and discriminatory, they can work to change them. I am convinced that there is a great deal about law and law enforcement that needs the kind of change many young people want."

Chapter XI

HOW THE EQUAL RIGHTS AMENDMENT FOR WOMEN WOULD AFFECT YOU

Case Histories

1. Susan and William James have been married for five years. At the time of the wedding, Susan had just received her master's degree in chemistry and William was a third-year medical student. Since then, Susan has worked with a research team on new approaches to chemotherapy for cancer and her salary has supported herself and William, who is just finishing his residency in internal medicine at the same hospital where Susan is employed.

She had always assumed that when her husband completed his training, they would either stay in the town where they now live (she thought both liked it there) or move to another university town where she would have an opportunity to continue her career and perhaps study for her doctorate in chemistry. William, however, has just informed her that he is tired of "the big-city rat race" and is planning to join his brother's practice in their old home town in another state. Susan knows that there is no university with a good graduate program in chemistry within two hundred miles of that town, nor is there a university-affiliated hospital where she might continue her research. She also knows that her husband has turned down a teaching job at the medical school and an offer to join a local group practice. He refuses to consider offers from other universities, or to move anywhere but to his old home town (Susan suspects his mother's influence), and has indicated that she, as his wife, is obligated morally to follow him wherever he chooses to live.

What she didn't realize until William pointed it out to her a few days before is that she also is obligated *legally* to live in whatever place her husband chooses as their home. In the state in which they now live and in the state where William proposes to move, desertion is considered grounds for divorce. The courts have interpreted a wife's refusal to accompany her husband to his chosen "place of residence" as "desertion." Susan's lawyer tells her that a husband's refusal to live in his wife's choice of residence is *not* interpreted as desertion. In other words, if Susan refuses to live in William's home town (which, incidentally, she detests), where she will not be able to practice her profession, he can divorce her. She cannot divorce him for forcing this choice on her.

2. Doris Johnson is a secretary in the office of a large construction company. When she was in college she majored in physical education and was the state's discus-throwing champion, and still participates regularly in regional track meets. She dropped out of college when her father died suddenly, because her salary was needed to help support her mother and four younger brothers and sisters. Although she is an excellent secretary, her job bores and annoys her. She knows that she would prefer to work outdoors, in an occupation in which she could use her physical strength and coordination.

Recently, she talked to one of the men who operates a huge construction crane, lifting steel and concrete girders into place at one of her company's building sites. As a joke, the man allowed her to climb into the cab of the crane, to sit in the operator's seat, and to lift one of the girders, under his careful supervision, of course.

Doris discovered that with some training she would be able to do this job easily. It requires good physical coordination (which she certainly has) and considerably less strength than an average afternoon of practicing the 100-yard dash. She also discovered that the men operating these cranes make more money in a day than she does in a week. So she took what seemed to her the next logical step. She asked her boss to consider her for a crane-operator's job. "Of course, everybody in the office split their sides laughing," she reports. "The union to which all crane operators belong excludes women as a matter of policy. The union steward told me that women were 'constitutionally' not suited for doing hard, physically demanding labor. I pointed out to him that I was in much better condition than the man who had showed me how to operate the crane. He was overweight and got out of breath just climbing into the cab. He'd probably have a heart attack at the very idea of participating in a track meet. But the union steward was adamant. 'We passed those rules to protect women from being *forced* into this kind of job,' he told me." Doris told him with some asperity that no one was forcing her to do anything, except possibly to remain a secretary, because all the outdoor jobs she liked routinely excluded women. The union steward and her boss remained firm: "Rules are rules," they said.

3. Jean Rogers has been married for seven years and has three children. Never, during all those years, has her husband, John, told her how much money he makes, how much he keeps in the checking account, or what savings or other property he owns. It is obvious that the family is not poor. They live on a ranch in a western state. There seems to be plenty of money to bid on prize cattle, buy farm machinery, and pay for John's various expensive hobbies. However, Jean has no checking account of her own and no access to the savings account. Her husband gives her a household allowance for food and cleaning supplies. They have no charge accounts. Every time she wants to buy a pair of shoes for one of the children or a dress for herself, she has to ask him for the money. He usually gives it to her, sometimes after extended questioning to find out if the purchase is "really necessary."

Since Jean works twelve hours a day, seven days a week, on the ranch, she recently consulted an attorney to find out if she did not have some rights to the income she and her husband apparently were earning jointly. It turned out she did—but only if she chose to file for divorce or a legal separation. The law in her state maintains that a husband must support his wife "in an adequate manner." The word "adequate" is not defined, and the courts usually have found that if the family is properly fed, housed, and clothed, support is "adequate." If she wishes to end the marriage, she probably can force her husband to disclose his income and give an accounting of what property he owns. However, if she wants to keep the marriage intact, the law can do nothing for her.

4. In a small town in New York, a twenty-one-year-old woman, whom we shall call Joan Smith, is trying to join the local police force. She is five feet four inches tall. New York State requires that a patrolman must stand at least five feet seven inches, which is considered "average" size for a man. The applicant's attorney contends that his client only should be required to meet female standards of height and that such standards have not been set.

In addition to complaining about her height, the police chief also objects to the fact that, as a new police recruit, she would be "riding around on night patrols, unescorted," which the job requires.

Her attorney has produced in court a petition bearing over thirteen hundred signatures of citizens who disagree with the police chief. The total population of the town is about nine thousand. Among those supporting her career ambitions is her father, a police lieutenant. Incidentally, she holds a college degree in political science.

Case Solutions

The way the problems faced by all four women are solved may be drastically altered when the Twenty-seventh Amendment to the United States Constitution passes the thirty-eighth state legislature.

This is how the amendment (which passed the U.S. House of Representatives on October 12, 1971, by a vote of 354 to 23, and the U.S. Senate on March 22, 1972, by a vote of 84 to 8) reads:

> Section 1. Equality of rights under the law shall not be denied or abridged by the United States or by any state on account of sex.
> Section 2. The Congress shall have the power to enforce, by appropriate legislation, the provisions of this article.

Section 3. This amendment shall take effect two years after the date of ratification.

Section 3 means that a two-year period is allowed after ratification so that necessary changes in federal and state laws can be made to bring all laws into compliance with the Constitutional amendment. A Constitutional amendment is officially ratified when two-thirds of both Houses of Congress and two-thirds of all state legislatures have passed it. The U.S. Congress has done so. At the time this book went to press, nineteen of the required thirty-eight states had also done so. (The majority of legislators and constitutional lawyers expect this amendment to be part of the basic law of this country within the next year.)

What does the Equal Rights Amendment (generally referred to as ERA) really mean to women? Is it a legal technicality, as some claim? Will it automatically and drastically change all our lives, as some of its proponents and almost all of its opponents assert or warn (depending on which side of the issue they stand)?

According to U.S. Representative Patsy Mink of Hawaii, who has supported the amendment, "It will legally establish that women are people." However, Representative Mink sees few *immediate* drastic changes in our lives, because she feels that a great deal of litigation will be needed to establish that the law really means what it says. "ERA will give us a basis to fight for equal rights in employment, pay, choice of residence, credit, custody of children, division of property in marriage, and all the other areas of life that concern women," she said. "The Amendment gives us a solid legal foundation on which to win our case. It's not only desirable . . . it's necessary."

Representative Mink is a graduate of the University of Chicago Law School and was a professor of business law at the University of Hawaii before she was elected to Congress. She is a tiny, attractive woman devoted to the cause of equal rights for women, which she lists as one of her major interests in her official biography. From personal experience she knows that discrimination against women in employment can be damaging to even the most gifted young lawyer. "After I graduated from law school, I couldn't get a job, anywhere," she said. "Potential employers told me that they didn't want to take a chance on hiring me. I was married, and they apparently expected me to have little interest in a career."

Would this kind of discrimination become impossible, if ERA becomes the law of the land? "Probably not immediately," Representative Mink says. "You see, law firms told me that they wouldn't hire me, not because I was a woman, but because I was *married*, and might be expected to follow my husband if he chose to move, or I might get pregnant, or something. . . . Of course, nobody would refuse to hire my husband because *he* was married, and might consider moving because of *my* career choice." (Representative Mink's husband, John, is vice-president of Earth Sciences, Inc., in Washington, D.C.) "Even after ERA passes its last hurdle, we shall still have to fight discrimination. It may mean taking cases to court, or passing additional federal and state legislation."

In her own state of Hawaii, which she served as attorney for the Territorial House of Representatives in 1955, legislators are already looking at all state laws to eliminate conscious or unconscious bias against women. "Whenever the law says 'men' or 'women,' we are substituting such nouns as 'individuals' or 'people,'" she says. "For 'husbands' or 'wives,' we are substituting 'spouses,' for 'mothers' or 'fathers,' 'parents.' This is one way we expect to remove all sex distinction in our state laws. I hope that other states are making a similar effort."

Even with ERA, Representative Mink feels additional federal legislation to guarantee equal rights and opportunities for women will be needed. "On the federal level, we shall have to pass additional laws to make sure that women really receive equal opportunities with men, particularly in education," she adds. "Education is really where it all starts. . . ." In order to accomplish this, she introduced H.R. 14451, the Women's Education Act of 1972.

"The Congress hereby finds and declares that present educational programs in the United States are in need of modernization of curriculum, text, vocational and physical education programs, techniques of teaching and counseling, and the administration and planning of educational programs, as they relate to women, in order that they shall fully participate in American society," the bill states, and then it carefully adds, "Nothing in This Act shall be construed as prohibiting men from participating in any of the activities funded."

Senator Samuel J. Ervin, Jr., of North Carolina, one of the Senate's outstanding constitutional lawyers, opposes ERA as energetically as Representative Mink supports it. He disagrees that the law's effects will be gradual and beneficial; he thinks that they will be immediate and disastrous. For one thing, Senator Ervin points out quite correctly, under ERA women will be subject to the draft under exactly the same conditions as men. The idea of women as combat soldiers or military pilots clearly horrifies him, both from the point of view of the women involved, and from the perspective of the United States Army, whose combat efficiency, he feels, might be impaired if the law were truly enforced.

Senator Ervin further feels that American family life would be seriously disrupted if women's and men's roles were made legally interchangeable, and if many of the special protections and privileges that women now enjoy under the law were removed.

"While I believe that any law making unfair or unreasonable distinctions against women should be repealed . . . I have the abiding conviction that the law should make such distinctions between men and women as are fairly and reasonably necessary for the protection of women and the existence and development of the race," he said in a speech in the Senate opposing ERA.

"When he created them, God made physiological and functional differences between men and women. These differences confer upon men a greater capacity to perform arduous and hazardous physical tasks. Some wise people even profess that there may be psychological differences between men and women. To justify their belief, they assert that women possess intuitive powers to distinguish between wisdom and folly, good and evil. To say these things is not to imply that either sex is superior to the other. It is simply to state the all-important truth that men and women complement each other in the relationship and undertaking on which the existence and development of the race depend," the Senator continued.

Based on this statement alone, it would be only too easy to label Senator Ervin either a male chauvinist or a fine Southern gentleman, depending on one's own bias on ERA and the status of women. However, the Senator defies labels. He is recognized by those who agree with him and by those who oppose him as one of this country's outstanding experts on the United States Constitution. Included among his admirers on most legal issues is Representative Patsy Mink. He repeatedly has taken stands that might be considered unpopular with his constituents, including well-publicized battles with the FBI and opposition to such administration-backed measures as preventive detention and the increased use of wiretapping. He is the one voice in the U.S. Senate that can be counted upon to oppose any kind of media censorship.

Senator Ervin maintains that the role in which women are cast is dictated by social custom, as well as by biology, and that no law will erase this. He feels that "women are equal to but different from men," and that the differences cannot and should not be erased by a constitutional amendment.

A booklet circulated by his office, *The Equal Rights Amendment . . . An Attractive Slogan, But Is It Good Law?* which unequivocally opposes ERA, bears some surprising signatures. Included among the listed opponents are Cesar Chavez, director of the United Farm Workers Organizing Committee; Dorothy Height, president of the National Council of Negro Women; Sarah Newman, general secretary of the National Consumers League; Dolores Huerto, vice-president of the United Farm Workers Organizing Committee; plus such long-time feminists as Mary Keyserling, the retired director of the Women's Bureau, U.S. Department of Labor, and the late Mary E. Switzer, former director of the

Social and Rehabilitation Service of the U.S. Department of Health, Education and Welfare.

Many of those who have publicly and privately opposed ERA feel that the law would eliminate certain special privileges that unions have gained for women, such as rest periods on the job, maternity leaves (unless paternity leaves are also instituted), and even chairs on assembly lines. Others, like Representative Mink, feel that some of these protections probably will be extended to men (although she considers the "paternity leave" issue a red herring), because unions simply will not give up benefits that they have won for some of their members.

Others who do not oppose ERA on principle share some of Senator Ervin's fears about family life. As one woman judge who is a strong advocate of equal rights for women put it, "We'll just have to make sure that the principle that *both* parents are responsible for the care of minor children does not also mean that *neither* is responsible."

Regardless of the arguments for and against ERA, the constitutional amendment almost certainly will be part of our basic law soon. What immediate and long-range effects can we all expect?

In looking at the four case histories previously mentioned, how will the lives of Susan James, Doris Johnson, Jean Rogers, and Joan Smith be affected?

CASE 1. Susan James probably has an untenable marriage in any case. No law will turn her unreasonable, selfish husband into a fair person. Laws were not made to correct personality flaws in either husbands or wives. However, with ERA he probably no longer will be able to divorce her because of his unilateral decision of where the couple should live. Such divorce laws are expected to be declared unconstitutional.

CASE 2. The union that bars Doris Johnson because she is a woman will have to prove that she is "physically unable" to operate that crane. Automatic exclusion of women from certain occupations will become impossible. But Doris probably will have to take her case to court, as will many other women who wish to insist on their rights to jobs formerly reserved for men. Blacks already have found that the Equal Opportunity Law didn't necessarily open the doors of craft unions and other tightly closed organizations.

CASE 3. Jean Rogers' situation also will have to be taken to court. Laws that put the husband in automatic control over all family-owned property certainly will be tested. However, who owned what at the time of the marriage may still be the deciding factor in the outcome of such cases.

CASE 4. Joan Smith's attorney apparently feels that she has a viable case against the police department *now*, or he would not have taken the matter to court. Her exclusion from the police force may be in violation of the Equal Employment Opportunity Law, but her case would be strengthened immeasurably by the passage of ERA.

The best projection of what can be expected from ERA appears in the *Yale Law Review* of April 1971. The article was written by three women lawyers, Barbara Brown, Gail Falk, and Ann E. Freedman, plus Professor Thomas I. Emerson, Yale University Law School's top expert on constitutional law. Both proponents and opponents of ERA quote this article as the best authority on the subject. Here are some of its conclusions on the U.S. military, criminal law, domestic relations, protective labor legislation, jury duty, and so on:

a. Women will be drafted for military service on the same basis as men. (Proponents of the law indicate that this certainly will speed the development of an all-volunteer army.)

b. Height and weight standards (in the military and in other occupations) will have to be revised. (This affects Joan Smith's case.)

c. If the armed forces draft women, all facilities, including athletic ones, will have to be made available to them.

d. Women will not necessarily be excluded from combat duty because of their sex. (However, in countries where women are already drafted, e.g., Israel, few actually go into combat, although some have been trained as fighter pilots.)

e. ERA would not permit a legal requirement, or even a legal presumption, that a woman take her husband's name at the time of marriage.

f. A court would do away with the rule that refusal to accompany or follow a husband to his chosen place of residence amounts to desertion or abandonment (thus solving Susan James' legal problem).

g. Under ERA, courts are not likely to find *any* justification for the continuance of laws that exclude women from certain occupations. (That should please Doris Johnson.)

h. Laws that restrict or regulate working conditions for women probably would be invalidated. (This worries the unions.)

i. Courts may be expected to hold that laws that confine liability for prostitution to women only would be invalid under ERA. (It no longer would be legal to arrest a prostitute without also arresting her client.)

j. Seduction laws, statutory-rape laws, laws prohibiting obscene language in the presence of women, and laws allowing the arrest of women considered to be "in manifest danger of falling into habits of vice" would be held unconstitutional.

k. States probably would be required to eliminate differences based on sex in public-school and public-university systems.

l. States that now grant jury-service exemption to women with children either will extend the exemption to men (if the men are charged with the responsibility for the children's care) or eliminate such exemptions altogether.

Women who worry about ERA usually are most concerned with the effect the constitutional amendment will have on custody, child-support, and alimony laws. There is no doubt that some changes will occur.

According to the *Yale Law Review* article, women are given custody of minor children in ninety percent of all divorce cases now, either by statute or because of common-law principles. ERA may require family-court judges to award custody to the parent best qualified to care for the children, possibly the father.

The law now presumes that a husband and father is responsible for support of his wife and minor children in case of divorce or separation. Under ERA such a presumption no longer would hold. In actual practice, it doesn't hold now.

Most support payments awarded to women are not nearly adequate to provide even common necessities for themselves and their youngsters. As one lawyer interviewed put it, "Judges rarely award wives and children the money they will really need. They award what they consider to be an amount that *will not make the husband too uncomfortable.*" The reason for this is an entirely practical one: uncomfortable husbands quit their jobs and leave the state. Attempting to collect alimony and child-support payments across state lines is exceedingly complicated and difficult. Most ex-wives usually just give up and either go to work or on welfare.

State laws that *automatically* award alimony rights to a wife if she is the "innocent" party in a divorce case also no longer would hold up under ERA. However, few wives who can support themselves receive much alimony now. The rare case of a wife who receives a huge settlement or alimony award gets a great deal of newspaper publicity. This usually occurs only if the husband desperately wants the divorce (in order to marry someone else) and if the wife is willing and able to hold out for a large settlement. Young, childless, working wives often don't even ask for alimony. Even under ERA, older wives who never have worked and are unlikely to find jobs to support themselves almost certainly will continue to be awarded alimony or settlements. However, women who are in the financial catbird seat at the time of the divorce may be asked to pay alimony or settlements to husbands who are unable to support themselves.

On paper, ERA drastically would alter domestic-relations laws. But most lawyers and judges believe that in actual practice very little would change. Most mothers want custody of minor children—few fathers do. Alimony payments to childless, working women are rare now. Both parents now are responsible for the support of minor children, regardless of what the law states. Only infrequently are court-ordered child-support awards large enough to provide adequately for a mother and children without additional earnings from the mother, help from her parents, or welfare.

Attorney Catherine Roraback, a long-time advocate of

women's rights, puts the question of ERA in perspective. She was barely out of law school when, as one of the lawyers for Planned Parenthood, she helped to prepare the case *Griswold* v. *Connecticut,* which resulted in a U.S. Supreme Court verdict finding Connecticut's anti-birth-control laws unconstitutional. She now is the principal attorney for a group of more than five hundred Connecticut women to overthrow that state's antiabortion law, and already has won a U.S. district court decision on this question. "I worry about ERA quite a bit," she said. "The idea of erasing protective labor laws for women, for which many feminists had fought hard, bothers me. Changes in domestic relations laws worry me too. But, on balance, I have to support ERA strongly. It's important to both women and men that women finally be regarded as *human* individuals entitled to equal protection and equal responsibility under the law."

Chapter XII

RIGHT TO KNOW LAWS

Case Histories

1. If you are a taxpayer in Oak Brook, Illinois, do you have the right to know under what circumstances your village board voted to authorize a 3.3-million-dollar bond issue (to be paid off with the help of *your* taxes) in order to buy a privately owned water company?

2. If you are a PTA member in Bristol, Connecticut, do you have the right to know the reasons for some drastic changes in maternity-leave policies for public-school teachers, enacted in closed session by your board of education?

3. If you are a farmer in Wisconsin, do you have the right to know whether the United States government is planning to buy land (including possibly yours) in your area of the state for a national park?

4. If you are a close family member of a deceased serviceman, do you have the right to see the Army or Navy report telling how and under what conditions your relative died?

5. For that matter, if you are just a United States citizen, do you have the right to know the contents of government-research reports (paid for with your taxes) on the effect of new drugs, conditions in government-inspected meatpacking plants, or Medicare-supported nursing homes?

Case Solutions

According to the letter of the law you probably have the right to know all these facts, but in actual practice you may have to go to court to find them out.

The federal government is bound by the Freedom of Information Act to give you access to any unclassified document, file, or record held by a federal agency, except the United States Congress. Forty-eight states have some form of "Right to Know" law (the exceptions are Rhode Island and West Virginia) requiring open state and/or local meetings of governmental bodies, or the right of access to public documents or both.

However, in spite of all this apparent openness most governmental business at the local, state, and federal level is done in secrecy.

In Connecticut, for instance, the "Right to Know" law seems crystal clear. Under the statutes "all administrative boards, commissions, agencies, bureaus, committees, or other bodies of the state or any of its political subdivisions" (i.e., cities or towns) must open their meetings to the public. Unfortunately, the law has a loophole so large that it is almost totally ineffective. If the majority of the committee members vote to hold an executive session, the meeting may be closed to the public and to the press. Connecticut abounds in executive sessions. That's what happened in Bristol, when the maternity-leave policy was being discussed. No record of the executive session or the vote even was filed with the town clerk's office (under state law these documents *must* be filed within forty-eight hours). "The minutes should have been filed," the board chairman admitted to a reporter from the *Hartford Courant.* "We had no reason to hold it back . . . nothing to hide." Teachers and the Connecticut chapter of the American Civil Liberties Union may not be satisfied with that explanation, and go to court.

In New York State a legislative committee called to deal with public dissatisfaction on the calling of too many executive sessions voted to hold all of its discussion *in executive session.* New York has an "open meeting" law, which unfortunately, for the curious or suspicious citizen, does not apply to the *legislative* branch of state government.

California's law is more specific. All sessions of committees, at the state and local level, including legislatives ones, must be open to the public. Executive sessions are allowed only when an agency is considering dismissals, appointments, or complaints regarding public employees that might reveal data personally embarrassing or damaging to the man or woman under discussion. Even this very specific, apparently loophole-free law didn't stop the Merced City Council. They simply met in a restaurant before the "public" meeting to discuss their business, and then adjourned to City Hall to announce what they had decided in private to the citizens and the press. When a superior court ruled that these dinners were illegal and that the council could convene only in city hall, a veteran reporter from the local newspaper remarked that this probably wouldn't phase the council members at all. "They'll just have their dinners catered," he predicted. According to a publication by the University of Missouri's Freedom of Information Center, "the judge's signature was barely dry when the prediction came true: the Council privately supped in City Hall. The city attorney ruled that holding catered dinner sessions in council chambers did not violate the judge's injunction."

Some states actually make the withholding of information a misdemeanor, usually punishable with fines of several hundred dollars and/or imprisonment of 180 days and up. A governor of Nevada who privately discussed certain affairs of state that should have been public was actually arrested once on the complaint of an editor, and remained under arrest for three hours. In Indiana four members of a county parks and recreation board were charged with holding an illegal meeting to negotiate a contract and were indicted. The case is still in court.

A few years ago, a Texas mayor was fined $150 for closing a meeting. "That case is lost in a fog of appeals procedure," the Freedom of Information Center* reports.

So where does all this leave the citizen who feels that he or she has a right to know how and why government is

*The Freedom of Information Center is located in the University of Missouri School of Journalism and is concerned with all matters pertaining to freedom of the press.

operating the way it is, in order to participate adequately in the decision-making process? Is there really no way to find out on what basis a state government or town council arrives at its annual budget and why, and how tax rates are set at new levels? Why the board of police commissioners voted to build a new police station instead of hiring more patrolmen? Why the new high school is going to be constructed (with a swimming pool) at the east end of town when it would seem so much more logical to build it (without the swimming pool, but with a new library) at the west end of town? And what about those federal-research reports on drugs, meatpacking houses, or nursing homes? Is there no way to get the United States Government Printing Office to send them?

The citizen who wants to exercise his or her right to know is finally getting some help. The American Civil Liberties Union, operating at the federal level, has brought suits against the government on behalf of the Wisconsin farmer (Case 3) who wished to know what was going to happen to his land, and the relatives of soldiers and sailors who died in the service of their country but whose death records are not available (Case 4). State chapters of the same organization are also filing suits with state and local governments where existing "Right to Know" laws seem to have been violated.

Common Cause, a citizens' lobby group, has listed more open government discussion and action among its top priorities. In 1972 the organization published an excellent paperback book, *Money and Secrecy: A Citizen's Guide to Reforming State and Federal Practices*, which clearly and simply explains federal access to information laws and procedures, and carefully outlines every state's "Right to Know" law. It also offers a model statute, which an individual or organization may wish to have introduced into a state legislature, and which closes almost every conceivable loophole. The book is available for $2.95 from Common Cause, 2100 M Street N.W., Washington, D.C.

Common Cause also is organizing now on a state level to lobby for its model statute and help citizens to make the widest possible use of "Right to Know" laws that already exist. In Connecticut, for instance, Common Cause volunteers are assigned to monitor all legislative hearings. If a hearing is closed, they are instructed to ask why. "Ask a lot of embarrassing questions, especially when there's a reporter in the vicinity, and you can often get a meeting opened up again," one Common Cause organizer said.

The Freedom of Information Center at the University of Missouri is working with the news media to help inform citizens what their rights to information are. "Florida has the best and most comprehensive 'Right to Know' law in the United States," one Florida newspaper editor said. "Unfortunately, it's called 'the Sunshine law' and so a lot of people think it's some obscure statute regulating the weather bureau. We've been telling our readers that they should insist on attending legislative meetings and hearings that interest them, and that they have a right, under the law, to demand public minutes, records and other documents."

Ralph Nader's organization also has a "Freedom of Information" section, which is attempting to make accessible to the public documents that have been classified by the federal government for no apparent reason. The U.S. government has more than twenty million documents marked "Secret" locked up in special files. The Nader group feels that very little of this information really needs to be kept from the public, especially not such documents as research reports, paid for with tax dollars, and concerning matters of interest to the consumer.

As an individual citizen, you may wish to join with one of those organizations to fight for your "Right to Know." Or you may wish to work on your own by attending meetings of your state and local legislative and executive bodies (e.g., the state legislature's education committee or your own board of education, board of finance, or board of police commissioners).

If someone wants to keep you out, you may want to ask, "Why? What's the big secret?" And if you are being denied information illegally, you may wish to complain to the attorney general of your state or to one of the organizations mentioned in this chapter. If your "Right to Know" is really being violated, you'll probably get help, including sometimes a lawyer free of charge.

Usually, there won't be a court case. The threat of legal action is frequently enough to make secretive public officials mend their ways. Even if you go to court and win, the chances are that nobody will be fined or jailed. But you will have helped to open up the process of government, to remove dangerous and unnecessary curtains of secrecy, to let the sun shine in. That's probably what a poetic Florida legislator had in mind when he gave his state's law that confusing name.

Chapter XIII

WOMEN AS LAWYERS

Case Histories

1. You are a sophomore in college and plan to go to law school. You are now faced with picking a college major and your friends are telling you that you'd better plan on a pre-law course, including mainly such subjects as government, economics, and sociology. Personally, you would prefer to major in English. You are also in line to become the next feature editor of your college newspaper, and the same friends are telling you that you'd better forget all that journalism and join the college debating team if you hope to compete successfully for a place in a good law school. Are they right?

2. You are getting ready to take your LSAT (Law School Admissions Test), which is required by most American law schools. You have seen advertisements in your local newspapers that cram courses for this test are given in your community. You also have found several guide books in your college book store on how to pass the test successfully. Is it worthwhile to take one of these courses (which usually cost more than $100) or helpful to buy one or more of the books?

3. You have received your LSAT scores and you know what your overall grade average in college has been. You know that you are probably won't be accepted at one of the Ivy League law schools, since the competition for a place there is fierce and usually only top students will be accepted. You are in the upper quarter of your class and your LSAT score is in the upper 500's. Is there any way to learn which, if any, law school would consider your application seriously?

4. You have passed your LSAT with a very high score (670)

and are in the top five percent of your graduating class at college. You have decided that you want to go to law school, but that you definitely will need some financial assistance. Are there many scholarships or fellowships in law schools? How could you go about obtaining one?

5. You have a job as a reporter on your local newspaper covering the courts. You have become increasingly fascinated with law, and think that you might want to switch careers and become a lawyer. But until you are sure, you don't want to give up your present satisfying and rather lucrative occupation. What's more, you would not have any money to support yourself, or for tuition and books, if you quit your job. Are there any part-time law schools? For instance, could you go to school at night?

6. You have been accepted at a law school in Connecticut, but you know that eventually you will want to live in San Francisco. Does that mean that you should be studying law in California, since most certainly you will have to pass a California bar examination? Wouldn't a California university teach you more of that state's law?

7. You have taken a bar examination in Iowa, and because of family obligations, find that you have to move to Ohio. Will you have to take another bar examination in Ohio, in order to be able to practice your profession there?

8. You are in law school now and are thinking of going out on job interviews. There is one law firm in your town in which you are particularly interested, but you know that they have no women among their professional staff. Do large law firms still discriminate against women? You know that legally they cannot. Your state has a Fair Employment Practices Act, which includes sex, but what if the senior partners find some other excuses not to hire you? Is it worthwhile to try to crack an all-male stronghold?

9. You plan to go to law school, but you also are engaged to be married and eventually would like to have a family. Several male lawyers you know have told you that "law is simply not a part-time occupation." They are advising you to study social work, or teaching, or nursing, or "some profes-

sion where everybody is accustomed to married women with kids." Are a career in law and a marriage with children mutually exclusive?

10. You are forty years old, your children are grown, and you have decided that now is the time to fulfill your life-long ambition. You want to go to law school. You took your LSAT more than ten years ago and received a very high score. You were a summa cum laude graduate of a top women's college. What are your chances of getting into a good law school? Would your age be held against you?

Case Solutions

CASE 1. The sophomore who wants to go to law school is not alone. One hundred years after Myra Bradwell was denied admission to the bar by the U.S. Supreme Court because she was a woman, women are entering law schools and passing bar examinations in unprecedented numbers. In 1973, sixteen percent of the accredited law-school enrollment was female. Although national figures for 1974 were not yet released by the time this book went to press, early estimates indicate that women may now make up more than twenty percent of the total law-school enrollment. The 1973 enrollment figures were several percentage points above those of 1972, twice the percentage for 1970, and four times that of 1967.

Roger W. Williams, in the *Saturday Review World* of September 1974, observes that no other system of professional education in the United States has experienced such a rapid change.

The number of women undergraduates majoring in social science has not risen correspondingly. Law schools have indicated that they like applicants with well-rounded educational backgrounds. An English major, with an interest in journalism, would be given the same consideration as a government major with an interest in debating. Actually, writing skills are very important in law. Most lawyers spend more time researching and writing briefs and other documents than they do arguing in court. Admissions officers of major law schools are advising prospective applicants to choose the courses they like and that interest them during their undergraduate years. All kinds of extracurricular activities can be helpful to the budding lawyer. She may learn more about the world in which her future clients live by working as a reporter on her college paper or by tutoring in a ghetto school than by traveling around to other colleges with the debating team.

CASE 2. This student no doubt has received material from the Educational Testing Service of Princeton, New Jersey, which administers the LSAT, stating that cram courses, books, and so on won't help her. The test, according to the *Prelaw Handbook*, prepared by the Association of American Law Schools and the Law School Admission Council, is designed to "measure certain mental capabilities important in the study of law." It also includes a separate test to score writing ability.

According to the *Handbook*, "commercial publications and cram courses purport to help you prepare for the LSAT. These are, of course, unofficial and not approved by the law schools, the Law School Admission Council, the Association of American Law Schools and the Educational Testing Service. Such courses probably provide a familiarity with the types of questions in the LSAT, but at least that much is provided by the sample LSAT in this Handbook and by the sample questions in the free Law School Admissions Bulletin." (The *Handbook* can be bought at any college book store and the Admissions Bulletin will be sent to you on request by the Educational Testing Service.)

Personal experience of a great many would-be law students has shown that it *is* possible to improve test scores by practice, however. The test includes one section that requires a rather extensive comprehension of graphs and statistics, which many liberal-arts majors do not have. A student who does not understand the questions obviously won't be able to give the answers. So some tutoring for the test may be very helpful. You probably won't need an expensive cram

course, if you have a friend who has taken the exam successfully in a previous year and who is willing to spend time
helping you understand exactly how the test works.

Sample test books are helpful. The sample questions in the
Law School Admissions Bulletin tend to be easier than the
ones that actually are on the test. The books tend to pick
some of the harder ones, and explain why the most obvious
answer among the multiple choices may not be the correct
one. Also, the books' various test sections are timed exactly
the same way that the LSAT sections are timed. It helps to
get one or more of these books, plus a kitchen timer, which
rings when the allotted ten or twenty minutes are over. The
LSAT is what's known as a "time-pressure test." You can
teach yourself to answer as many questions as possible in the
short time you are given by skipping ones that puzzle you
and going on to the next one. If you have a few extra minutes,
you can go back to the unanswered questions. Incidentally,
wrong answers don't count against you, so it pays to guess. If
you have only a few minutes left at the end of a test section,
mark any answer. You have a one-in-five random chance of
being correct (there are five possible answers to each question).

CASE 3. The student here has a problem. Most law schools
consider your LSAT score plus your overall grade average in
deciding on whether or not to admit you. Other factors, such
as extracurricular activities, recommendations from professors, and so on may also be given some consideration, but if
you fall below their standard, many colleges almost automatically will discard your admission application.

The *Pre-Law Handbook** gives some indication of what
every accredited law school in this country considers an acceptable LSAT score and grade-point average. You can look

---

**The Pre-Law Handbook* is published every other year. There is a 1975
edition. The publisher is the Association of American Law Schools and the
Law School Admission Council. It can probably be obtained at any college
book store or from the Educational Testing Service, Princeton, N.J. The
price is $3.25.

up the law school of your choice to see if you fall within its guidelines. If not, look up some other, perhaps less prestigious, school to see if you might qualify there. The young woman in Case 3 may find a school that would suit her needs just as well as one of the Ivy League colleges.

CASE 4. The would-be lawyer also has a problem. There are very few scholarships or fellowships for law schools. An organization called the Graduate and Professional School Financial Aid Service (GAPSFAS) is designed to collect information about financial resources and obligations of students, their parents, and other responsible relatives, to analyze such financial data and to transmit this information to participating schools in allocating grants and loans. Decisions on awards are made not by the GAPSFAS, but by participating law schools themselves. (Not all schools are members.) You can get an application blank at your undergraduate school career-counseling or financial-aid office.

The chances are, however, that even if you are awarded a scholarship or a noninterest loan, it won't be nearly enough to cover your expenses. That means you will have to apply for a regular student loan at your local bank (which can no longer discriminate against you because you are a woman), or you may have to work for a few years and save money before you start a full-time law course.

CASE 5. The young journalist actually may have the answer to the financial problems of would-be law students. In many areas of the United States there are now law schools that give evening courses meant for people who are already working and who wish to study law part-time, either because they can't afford a full-time education or because they are not really sure that they want to switch careers.

Many state universities provide part-time evening law programs in major cities. Usually, these programs require four years of study rather than the three years that are needed to obtain a law degree on a full-time basis.

They offer distinct advantages to students who would find full-time study difficult, either for financial or for family reasons. The course offerings are usually similar to those in the regular daytime program. The quality of the education is just as good (and entrance standards just as demanding). If the student is a resident of the state whose university conducts an evening law course, she will find that tuition is quite low, considerably less than in a private law school. Also, tuition payments are spread out over four years, rather than three.

There are some private universities that conduct part-time programs leading to a degree. Tuition there generally is much higher than at state universities.

Many of the law schools offer a student an opportunity to switch to a full-time course and to get her degree in three years, rather than four, if she has completed the first year successfully on a part-time basis. She will have to make up the missing first-year credits either by taking on extra courses during the following two years, or by going to summer school, if the university has a summer program.

CASE 6. This student will find that a law degree is an exceedingly portable commodity. Actually, most law schools don't concentrate on teaching the specific laws of the state in which they are located. They concentrate on legal principles and methodology, which can be applied to the laws of any state. So, it makes very little difference whether a potential lawyer who wishes to practice in California goes to school in Connecticut, Ohio, or California. She will, of course, wish to take her bar examination in California. For this, she will have to learn California law. However, in recent years, bar examinations in the various states have been surprisingly uniform. They do require some knowledge of the statutes of the state in which they are administered. Most law-school graduates find that they will have to take a brief cram course in that state's law, even if they went to law school there. In other words, a student at Yale University Law School or at the University of Connecticut Law School probably would learn only a minimum amount of Connecticut law, but would have acquired a method of thinking and analyzing that would make it possible for her to pass a bar examination in any state, with a minimal amount of extra study.

CASE 7. The lawyer would have to take a bar examination

in Ohio. Unlike some other professional licenses, admission to the bar of the various states is not reciprocal. But like the lawyer in Case 6, she probably would have very little trouble passing the new examination. A few weeks of study of the peculiarities and specifics of Ohio law should get her through the bar examination without any trouble.

CASE 8. The law school graduate is in an excellent position. We are now entering a period when the job market for lawyers is becoming increasingly tight. But women lawyers still have a slight edge over their male colleagues. There are considerably fewer women lawyers employed in government offices, large law firms, and business organizations than male lawyers. Most potential employers have at least a subliminal worry about Equal Opportunity Laws on the state and federal level. If they look around their offices and find that only the secretaries are women, they might be very much inclined to hire a woman lawyer.

What's more, some female clients are asking to see women lawyers, especially in divorce cases and in estate and trust matters. Old, prestigious law firms have had the experience of having a woman client walk in and ask to see a woman lawyer. If none is available, the client just may ask politely if the firm can suggest another law office that has women on its professional staff, and walk out. Increasingly, large law offices are finding that there are distinct professional and financial advantages to having women on their staffs, besides the requirements of state and federal antidiscrimination laws. So, it certainly would be worthwhile for the law-school graduate to apply to that all-male firm. She may find that they are delighted to see her. If she is hired, she also may find that she has some old prejudices to contend with. But for any woman entering what formerly was considered an almost all-masculine profession, that is an obstacle she will have to be prepared to overcome.

CASE 9. There is absolutely no reason why this would-be lawyer should not plan to go to law school. There are probably more part-time jobs in law than there are right now in teaching or social work. Many offices employ part-time lawyers, either to handle selected cases or to do legal research. Legal-assistance organizations, funded by the federal or state government, hire many part-time lawyers. In some communities, Women's Law Cooperatives are being started. These are organized to help women who may not be able to pay standard legal fees, but who also are not eligible for free legal assistance. Many of these organizations charge fees on a sliding scale, according to the client's ability to pay, and often they offer other needed services, such as psychiatric counseling, group therapy, and assistance with financial planning. The Women's Cooperative can be an especially exciting place for a young women lawyer who enjoys a challenging situation, and who went into law in the first place because she was interested in advancing the cause of her fellow women. Most of these organizations function with a full-time director and a staff of part-time lawyers (as well as part-time psychiatrists, social workers, and other assistants).

CASE 10. The forty-year-old applicant in this case will find that she may have to be very persuasive before she is accepted at a good law school. She might have exactly the same problem if she were a forty-year-old man. Many law-school deans will emphasize that she has only a limited number of years to practice, while the twenty-one-year-old applicant (whose place she is taking) has at least twenty more years of practice ahead of her or him. Ten years ago, she would have had little chance of being accepted. In the past two or three years, however, changes have taken place on the law-school scene. Admissions committees that at first reluctantly accepted older applicants have found that these more mature women (and men) were talented, dedicated students who brought an extra dimension into the classroom. They also brought their life experience into the law practice that they eventually entered. Law schools that offered part-time evening courses were the first to open their doors to older applicants. Now, even Ivy League colleges are accepting students in their forties and early fifties.

They usually require that the applicant who has taken an LSAT more than two or three years ago do so over again. They want to be sure that the would-be student has maintained her ability to concentrate and to keep up with much younger fellow students.

Although the number of women lawyers will be increasing in the coming years, as all the students who are now flooding the universities graduate, opportunities for women in law are still vast. Positions in government and industry are opening up to them. In the coming years we will see increasing numbers of women judges. Many of the female law students now in the universities are already complaining of the dearth of female faculty members. Law schools are slowly beginning to realize that they will have to employ more and more women as professors, not just to give their female students adequate role models, but their male students as well. The male student will be working with female colleagues when he graduates, and he will be at a distinct disadvantage if he has never worked with a woman lawyer before.

"Not only is our presence beneficial to our female clients, I think we are able to change the attitude of our male colleagues as well," said one young woman lawyer working for a Legal Women's Cooperative. "When I first started to practice, my male opponent often did not take me seriously. He would hold discussions with his client, even with me sitting right behind him listening to every word he said. Obviously, he assumed that I was either a spectator, or a legal secretary, or too dumb to know what he was talking about. That doesn't happen to me very often any more. Too many male lawyers have lost cases to women lawyers whose abilities they underestimated."

Another woman lawyer pointed out the ability of a young female prosecutor at the Watergate Grand Jury hearings to get answers from male defendants that male lawyers had not been able to elicit. Since many of these defendants were lawyers themselves, they obviously let their guard down when an attractive young woman asked a question. They might have been more careful had she been a man, and the American public might have missed some of the most revealing facts.

Another woman lawyer pointed out that she, too, had to

get accustomed to some new attitudes and approaches. "If I expect to be treated as an equal, I have to act like one," she said. "Often a male opponent tries to fluster or embarrass me by swearing like a marine. I have learned to let all those expletives, which certainly would have been deleted for my benefit in a social situation, float right over my head. There's absolutely nothing that anyone can say today that will shock or fluster me, except perhaps, "What she did was stupid and hurt her client," or "If she had kept her head, she might have won that legal point."

Chapter XIV

WOMEN IN POLITICS:
A GENERAL SURVEY

In the 1974 elections 1,225 women ran for office. Many were successful in their bids. Connecticut elected Ella Grasso as the first woman in United States history to win the governor's chair on her own, San Diego picked Janet Gray Hayes as the first woman to become mayor of a city with more than half a million in population, and North Carolina elected Susie Sharp as the first female chief justice of a state supreme court. Eighteen women were elected to Congress, and hundreds of others won offices at the state and local level in legislatures, on city councils, and on town boards and committees.

In several state legislatures, men who vocally and consistently had opposed ratifying the Equal Rights Amendment (especially in Florida, Illinois, and Arizona) found that they had been replaced by women who favored the amendment. Votes for women frequently crossed party lines.

One of the coauthors of this book now lives in a town—Madison, Connecticut—which has a Republican first selectwoman (the equivalent of mayor in many New England rural communities), is represented by a Democratic woman in the state senate, which is headed by a woman governor and assisted by a woman secretary of the state. In a neighboring county, the electorate picked the first woman in the state's history to be high sheriff. It's interesting to note that not one of these women is a lawyer.

Political analysts feel that 1974 was "The Year of the Woman" for some special reasons. Watergate and the economy had predisposed the public to vote against incumbents who were, of course, usually men. Political parties had designated their candidates before the dissatisfaction of the electorate with the status quo became quite so evident to the pollsters. So women, who often have been the sacrificial lambs in the political process, were nominated to candidacies that they were expected to lose. To everyone's surprise, more often than not they won.

In states where the chances of winning high office looked promising, party leaders often still preferred men. But women candidates, instead of sitting back quietly and listening to soothing words about the future, ran against their male opponents. In two notable instances, the governor's race in Connecticut and the lieutenant governor's race in New York, women won upset victories.

Of course, neither Connecticut's Ella Grasso nor New York's Mary Ann Krupsak (who ran under her maiden name) were newcomers to the political process. Governor Grasso had worked her way up through the ranks since she first ran for the legislature more than twenty years ago. She served as secretary of the state for many terms, and followed up with two terms in the U.S. House of Representatives. Lieutenant Governor Krupsak had extensive experience in her state legislature.

Is Watergate and the general distrust of established politicians the only reason why so many women won in 1974? In other words, is "The Year of the Woman" a fluke?

Another Connecticut politician, who has served in elective office in Connecticut for over a decade, doesn't think so. Gloria Schaffer became secretary of the state when Ms. Grasso decided to run for Congress. She thinks that Ella Grasso is only the first of many women governors to come. She sees more and more town governments in her state dominated by women, and in meetings with women legislators across the country finds that Connecticut is in no way unique.

"There are good reasons why we will find more women in politics in the years to come," she says. "Men have always regarded politics as a serious job. Until recently, women looked at government as a volunteer activity or even a hobby. That's no longer true. Women want to win now, just as men always have."

She points out that women may have a distinct political advantage over men in the political arena. "Most male fresh-men candidates come right out of law offices, where they have been buried in statutes on trusts and estates," she says. "Women often have a real advantage over men in the political arena. They know about pollution, consumerism, the problems of the old, education, welfare, and the neglect of the ill and the handicapped. Women have dealt with these problems as part of their everyday lives, as homemakers, in people-oriented jobs, and as volunteers. Men have to get out of that law library to learn what life in the community is all about. . . . A woman may know instinctively."

U.S. Representative Pat Schroeder of Colorado, the first Democrat in the history of her district to be elected to the House (in 1972), is just such a woman. When she was asked her first committee choice, she picked the Armed Services Committee. When legislators, surprised at her choice, asked, "That's not really where female interests lie, is it?" she had her answer ready. "Men have always told us they wage wars to protect their women and children," she said. "I want to represent those who supposedly are getting this protection. Personally, I haven't liked it very much. How did the Vietnam War protect *me?* Or my children, for that matter? Does this world really need enough dynamite and atom power to blow each of us up seven times? There are other life-enhancing matters that women and children need more: clean air and water, good medical care, a decent diet, and a good education. So I got on the Armed Services Committee to make these points." Because she has consistently opposed military expenditures that she considers wasteful, in spite of the fact that her district includes industries that manufacture military hardware, her seat was in considerable danger in 1974. She proved the pessimists in her own party wrong. Her victory margin exceeded that of 1972.

Representative Patsy Mink of Hawaii has noted a new spirit among young women in high school and college toward politics. "Many male students have given up on the system, while women are just getting ready to join in it and to lead, if possible," she says. "They think they might be able to do better than men, and they are willing to try. They tend to trust in themselves and in each other much more than women did a generation ago."

Of course, the woman who goes into politics still faces prejudices from men as well as from other women. "I tore off the cover of your latest issue and am sending it back to you because I cannot abide it in my house," one indignant subscriber wrote to *Newsweek*, which had featured Ella Grasso on the cover. "Even to think of a woman as governor of a state is insanity in its worst form." Not many of the voters are as honest in their expression of chauvinism, but under many pious, protesting phrases, they still feel that although a woman's place may not be in the home, it certainly isn't in the state house. This leads to another problem women candidates frequently encounter: lack of campaign contributions. "I don't know anyone who is really rich," one woman candidate for a state senate seat said plaintively. "My friends have done all they can. They send $15 or $20 or $25 saved from jobs and household allowances. My opponent gets checks in the thousands from his business associates." The young would-be state senator won—and has a $2,500 campaign debt. She spent a total of $4,000 to win her seat. Her losing opponent spent $25,000, and has some money left over.

In order to rise, any candidate, including a female one, has to start somewhere in the political process. How does a woman get started in politics? Certainly the old route via the women's committee of her party leads her nowhere, according to interviews with female officeholders. "Join your regular political club, your town caucus, get elected to a town or state committee," most of these women advised. "Run for every office you can, even if the outcome seems hopeless. Get your name around, find an issue with which you can identify. If you are running in a local election, the issue had best be one of local interest. Few of your constituents in a board-of-education election care very much what you think of the Middle East oil crisis. They want to know how you feel the school budget can be balanced without sacrificing quality education."

Other successful women officeholders advise that a woman will have to insist on equality from the first day she serves on a town committee. "If you are the only female in the room, you'll be asked to take minutes right away," one state senator said. "Insist that that chore be rotated every week. You'll be a good sport and do it *this* week, but next week is Sam's turn. The same goes for coffee-making and envelope-licking."

The state senator who gave this advice hasn't been on an envelope-licking committee for years. She writes position papers on pollution and unemployment for her party.

Women political leaders insist 1974 was not a fluke—they are in government to stay. Men, some of them reluctantly, agree. The National Democratic Party already has had one female chairperson, and may have one again. The Republican Party has one right now. On political committees, women are in policy-making positions at all levels. They make up more than half the population of the United States. Nobody expects them to vote as a block on all issues, but in recent years women have shown an increasing tendency to support each other. Where they are organized, they have created a real political network and they know which candidate is for job equality, against discrimination in credit, and for adequate education for their children. Often the candidate who most realistically reflects their views turns out to be another woman.

It is no longer possible to exclude women from the world of work, from recreation, from law—and it becomes increasingly difficult to exclude them from the councils of government. How well they fare there will depend on how they conduct themselves. Women probably are not intrinsically more moral or honest than men. As they gain power, they will learn that power can corrupt. They have long understood, from their own special situation at the bottom, that the powerless are unable to effect changes. As Gloria Schaffer puts it, "We're probably more equal than we think. Not worse than men . . . but not better either."

The way in which women deal with the political power they are just beginning to acquire may well change the history of this country, and along with it, the history of the world.

Appendix A

STATE FAIR EMPLOYMENT PRACTICES COMMISSIONS

ALASKA

State Commission for Human Rights

Alaska State Commission for Human Rights
2457 Arctic Blvd., Suite 3
Anchorage, Alaska 99503

ARIZONA

Civil Rights Division

Civil Rights Division
1645 West Jefferson St.
Phoenix, Arizona 85007

CALIFORNIA

Fair Employment Practice Commission

Fair Employment Practice Commission
455 Golden Gate Ave. (P.O. Box 603)
San Francisco, California 94101
Branch Offices:
Los Angeles: 322 W. First St.
Fresno: 2550 Mariposa St.
San Diego: 1350 Front St.
Sacramento: 926 J St.

COLORADO

Civil Rights Commission

312 State Services Building
1525 Sherman St.
Denver, Colorado 80203

Branch Offices:
Denver: 2300 Welton
        1312 Santa Fe
Alamosa: 815 Main St.
Colorado Springs: 27 East Vermijo
Grand Junction: 322 Main St.
Pueblo: 525 North Santa Fe

CONNECTICUT

Commission on Human Rights and Opportunities

90 Washington St.
Hartford, Connecticut 06115

DELAWARE

Division Against Discrimination

Department of Labor and Industrial Relations
506 W. 10th St.
Wilmington, Delaware 19801

DISTRICT OF COLUMBIA

District of Columbia Human Relations Commission

District Building, Room 22
14th and E Streets, N.W.
Washington, D.C. 20004

FLORIDA

Commission on Human Relations

Florida Commission on Human Relations

Howard Building
2571 Executive Center Circle East
Tallahassee, Florida 32301

HAWAII

*Department of Labor and
Industrial Relations*

Labor Law Enforcement

State Office: 825 Mililani St.
Honolulu, Hawaii 96813
District Offices:
75 Aupuni St., Hilo, Hawaii 96720
54 South High St., Wailuku, Hawaii
96793
State Office Building, Lihue, Hawaii
96766
Kealakekua, Hawaii 96750

IDAHO

Commission on Human Rights

Address correspondence to:
Linda Gonzales, Director
506 North 5th
Statehouse
Boise, Idaho 83702

ILLINOIS

*Fair Employment Practices
Commission*

189 W. Madison St.
Chicago, Illinois 60602
Branch Office:
103 Centennial Building
Springfield, Illinois 62706

INDIANA

Civil Rights Commission

319 State Office Building
Indianapolis, Indiana 46204

IOWA

Civil Rights Commission

Iowa Civil Rights Commission
State Capitol Building
Des Moines, Iowa 50319

KANSAS

Commission on Civil Rights

Kansas Commission on Civil Rights
1155 W., State Office Building
Topeka, Kansas 66612

KENTUCKY

Commission on Human Rights

Kentucky Commission on Human
Rights
828 Capitol Plaza Tower
Frankfort, Kentucky 40601
Branch Office:
600 West Walnut St.
Louisville, Kentucky 40203

MAINE

Human Rights Commission

Maine Human Rights Commission
State House
Augusta, Maine 04330

MARYLAND

Commission on Human Relations

Mt. Vernon Bldg.
701 St. Paul St.
Baltimore, Maryland 21202

MASSACHUSETTS

*Massachusetts Commission Against
Discrimination*

120 Tremont St.
Boston, Massachusetts 02108

MICHIGAN

*Michigan Civil Rights
Commission*

117 W. Allegan St.
Lansing, Michigan 48933

1000 Cadillac Square Building
Detroit, Michigan 48226

Regional Offices:

Lansing Region
703 E. Michigan
Lansing, Michigan 48933

Detroit Region
1000 Cadillac Square Building
Detroit, Michigan 48226

Grand Rapids Region
1214 Madison S.E.
Grand Rapids, Michigan 49507

District Offices:

Detroit-East Office
6362 Gratiot Ave.
Detroit, Michigan 48207

Detroit-West Office
8243 Linwood
Detroit, Michigan 48206

Battle Creek Office
132 West Van Buren
Battle Creek, Michigan 49014

Benton Harbor Office
Suite 402 Fidelity Building
Benton Harbor, Michigan 49022

Flint Office
328 South Saginaw St.
810 Citizens Bank Building
Flint, Michigan 48502

Grand Rapids Office
1214 Madison, S.E.
Grand Rapids, Michigan 49507

Jackson Office
1224 Francis St.
Jackson, Michigan 49203

Lansing Office
703 East Michigan
Lansing, Michigan 48933

Muskegon Office
10 East Sherman
Muskegon Heights, Michigan 49444

Pontiac Office
Suite 2 Auburn Building
84 Auburn
Pontiac, Michigan 48058

Saginaw Office
126 North Franklin
Saginaw, Michigan 48606

MINNESOTA

Board of Human Rights

Department of Human Rights
200 Capitol Square Building
St. Paul, Minnesota 55101

MISSOURI

*Missouri Commission on Human
Rights*

314 East High St.
Jefferson City, Missouri 65101

Regional Offices:

508 N. Grand Blvd.
St. Louis, Missouri 63103

615 East 13th St.
Kansas City, Missouri 64106

103 Center St.
Sikeston, Missouri 63736

NEBRASKA

*Nebraska Equal Opportunity
Commission*

233 South 14th St.
Lincoln, Nebraska 68508

Branch Office:
416 Karbach Building

209 South 15th St.
Omaha, Nebraska 68102

NEVADA

*Commission on Equal Rights of
   Citizens*

Nevada Commission on Equal
   Rights of Citizens
215 East Bonanza Rd.
Las Vegas, Nevada 89101

NEW HAMPSHIRE

*New Hampshire Commission for
   Human Rights*

66 South St.
Concord, New Hampshire 03301

NEW JERSEY

*Division on Civil Rights,
   Department of Law and Public
   Safety*

Branch Offices:
436 East State St.
Trenton, New Jersey 08608
530 Cooper St.
Camden, New Jersey 08102
370 Broadway
Paterson, New Jersey 07501

NEW MEXICO

*Human Rights Commission of
   New Mexico*

121 Villagra Building
Santa Fe, New Mexico 87501

NEW YORK

State Division of Human Rights

270 Broadway
New York, New York 10007
Branch Offices:
Albany, 217 Lark St.

Binghamton, State Office Building,
44 Hawley St.
Bronx, 1022 E. 163rd St.
Brooklyn, 16 Court St.
Buffalo, 295 Main St.
Long Island (Nassau), Hempstead,
183 Fulton St.
Long Island (Suffolk), Brentwood, 24
Wicks Rd.
New York City—Lower Manhattan,
270 Broadway
New York City—Upper Manhattan,
163 W. 125th St.
Queens, Jamaica, 89–14 Sutphen
Blvd.
Rochester, 65 Broad St.
Staten Island, 25 Hyatt St.
Syracuse, 100 New St.
White Plains, 222 Mamaroneck Ave.

OHIO

Ohio Civil Rights Commission

220 Parsons Ave.
Columbus, Ohio 53215
Branch Offices:
Cleveland, Rockefeller Building,
   614 Superior Ave.
Cincinnati, 100 East Eight St.
Columbus, 240 Parsons Ave.
Toledo, 506 Madison Ave.
Akron, 5 E. Buchtel Ave.

OKLAHOMA

Human Rights Commission

State Capitol Building, Rm. 111A
P.O. Box 52945
Oklahoma City, Oklahoma 73105
Branch Office:
Room 212 Court Arcade Building
524 South Boulder
Tulsa, Oklahoma 74103

OREGON

Civil Rights Division, Bureau of Labor

Civil Rights Division
Oregon Bureau of Labor
Room 479, State Office Building
1400 S. W. Fifth Ave.
Portland, Oregon 97201
Branch Office:
Civil Rights Division
Oregon Bureau of Labor
Room 301, State Office Building
Eugene, Oregon 97401

PENNSYLVANIA

Pennsylvania Human Relations Commission

Governor's Office
Commonwealth of Pennsylvania
100 N. Cameron St.
Harrisburg, Pennsylvania 17101
Branch Offices:
301 Muench St.
Harrisburg, Pennsylvania 17102
101 State Office Building
Broad and Spring Garden Sts.
Philadelphia, Pennsylvania 19130
4 Smithfield St., Room 810
Pittsburgh, Pennsylvania 15222

RHODE ISLAND

Rhode Island Commission for Human Rights

244 Broad St.
Providence, Rhode Island 02903

SOUTH CAROLINA

State Human Affairs Commission

Post Office Drawer 11528
Columbia, South Carolina 29211

SOUTH DAKOTA

Commission on Human Rights

South Dakota Commission on Human Rights
Department of Commerce and Consumer Affairs
State Capitol Building
Pierre, South Dakota 57501

UTAH

Anti-Discrimination Division, Industrial Commission

350 East 500 South
Salt Lake City, Utah 84111

WASHINGTON

Washington State Human Rights Commission

319 Seventh Ave. East
Olympia, Washington 98504
Branch Offices:
Seattle, 1411 Fourth Ave. Building 98101
Pasco, 112 South Fourth, Rm. 7, 99301
Spokane, 715 Old National Bank Building 99201
Yakima, 1211 S. 7th St., 98901
Tacoma, Tacoma Public Service Building, 13th and Tacoma 98402
Vancouver, Y.W.C.A. Building, 917 "Z" St., 98661

WEST VIRGINIA

Human Rights Commission

West Virginia Human Rights Com-
    mission
1591 Washington St. East
Charleston, West Virginia 25305

WISCONSIN

*Department of Industry, Labor
    and Human Relations*

201 E. Washington Ave.
Madison, Wisconsin 53702
Equal Rights Division:
201 E. Washington Ave.
Madison, Wisconsin 53702

WYOMING

Fair Employment Commission

304 Capitol Building
Cheyenne, Wyoming 82001

Appendix B

GROUNDS FOR DIVORCE

ALABAMA

1. Incurable physical incapacity for entering into marriage state at time of marriage
2. Adultery
3. Voluntary abandonment for one year
4. Imprisonment for two years under sentence of seven or more years
5. Commission of crime against nature
6. Postmarital habitual drunkenness or habitual use of narcotics
7. Hopeless insanity and confinement for five successive years
8. Incompatibility of temperament
9. Irretrievable breakdown

ALASKA

1. Impotency continuing since marriage
2. Adultery
3. Conviction for felony
4. Willful desertion for one year
5. Cruel and inhuman treatment, personal indignities or incompatibility
6. Habitual drunkenness for one year, occurring after marriage
7. Willful neglect by husband to support wife for twelve months
8. Continuing incurable insanity and confinement for eighteen months
9. Narcotic addiction after marriage

ARIZONA

1. Irretrievable breakdown

ARKANSAS

1. Impotency continuing since marriage
2. Willful desertion for one year
3. Bigamy

4. Conviction of felony or infamous crime
5. Habitual drunkenness for one year or cruelty or personal indignities
6. Adultery
7. Three years' living apart
8. Living apart for three years because of incurable insanity
9. Willful nonsupport by able spouse

CALIFORNIA

1. Irreconcilable differences caused by irremediable breakdown
2. Irreconcilable differences

COLORADO

1. Irretrievable breakdown

CONNECTICUT

1. Irretrievable breakdown
2. Living apart for eighteen months
3. Adultery
4. Fraudulent contract
5. Willful desertion for one year with total neglect of duty
6. Seven years' absence without being heard from
7. Habitual intemperance
8. Intolerable cruelty
9. Sentence to prison for life or commission of infamous crime, punishable by imprisonment for over one year
10. Legal confinement in an institution because of mental illness for a total of five out of prior six years

DELAWARE

1. Adultery
2. Bigamy
3. Imprisonment for two years or one year of an indeterminate sentence
4. Extreme cruelty
5. Habitual drunkenness for two years
6. Willful desertion for one year
7. By wife, if she was under sixteen at marriage
8. By husband, if he was under eighteen at marriage
9. Husband's inability to support family of which wife was unaware at marriage
10. Mental retardation, epilepsy, or chronic or recurrent mental illness of five years' duration

11. Eighteen months' living apart
12. Incompatibility of two years' duration

FLORIDA

1. Irretrievable breakdown
2. Adjudication of mental incompetence three years prior to suit

GEORGIA

1. Incestuous marriage
2. Mental incapacity at time of marriage
3. Impotency at time of marriage
4. Force, duress, menace, or fraud in obtaining marriage
5. Pregnancy at time of marriage of which husband is unaware
6. Adultery
7. Willful desertion for one year
8. Conviction of crime involving moral turpitude and imprisonment for two years
9. Habitual intoxification
10. Physical or mental cruelty
11. Incurable insanity and confinement for two years
12. Habitual drug addiction
13. Irretrievable breakdown

HAWAII

1. Irretrievable breakdown
2. Expiration of decree of separation without reconciliation
3. Living apart under decree of separate maintenance for two years without reconciliation
4. Two years' separation

IDAHO

1. Adultery
2. Extreme cruelty
3. Willful desertion
4. Willful neglect
5. Habitual intemperance
6. Conviction of a felony
7. Permanent insanity and confinement for three years
8. Irreconcilable differences

ILLINOIS

1. Impotency continuing since marriage
2. Bigamy

3. Adultery
4. Drug addiction for two years
5. Willful desertion for one year
6. Habitual drunkenness for two years
7. Attempted murder of spouse
8. Extreme physical or mental cruelty
9. Conviction of felony or infamous crime
10. Infection of spouse with venereal disease

INDIANA

1. Irretrievable breakdown
2. Conviction of infamous crime
3. Impotency at marriage
4. Incurable insanity and confinement for two years

IOWA

1. Irretrievable breakdown

KANSAS

1. Abandonment for one year
2. Adultery
3. Extreme cruelty
4. Habitual drunkenness
5. Gross neglect of duty
6. Conviction of felony and imprisonment after marriage
7. Confinement for mental illness for three years and poor prognosis
8. Incompatibility

KENTUCKY

1. Irretrievable breakdown

LOUISIANA

1. Adultery
2. Conviction of felony and sentence to death or imprisonment at hard labor
3. Separation for two years
4. Separation under divorce from bed and board for one year without reconciliation

MAINE

1. Adultery
2. Impotence

3. Extreme cruelty
4. Utter desertion for three years
5. Habitual intoxication or drug use
6. Inability of husband to support
7. Irreconcilable differences

MARYLAND

1. Impotency
2. Any cause rendering marriage void *ab initio*
3. Adultery
4. Abandonment for one year without expectation of reconciliation
5. Separation for one year because of irreconcilable differences
6. Conviction of felony or misdemeanor, sentence of three years, eighteen months having been served
7. Living apart for three years
8. Incurable insanity and confinement for three years

MASSACHUSETTS

1. Adultery
2. Impotency
3. Utter desertion for two years
4. Habitual drunkenness or drug use
5. Cruel and abusive treatment
6. Habitual neglect of husband to support wife
7. Sentence to penal institution for five years

MICHIGAN

1. Irretrievable breakdown

MINNESOTA

1. Irretrievable breakdown by reason of:
   a. conduct detrimental to relationship
   b. imprisonment
   c. alcoholism or chemical dependency for one year
   d. mental illness
   e. separation under decree of limited divorce or separation for one year

MISSISSIPPI

1. Natural impotency
2. Adultery

3. Sentence to prison
4. Willful desertion for one year
5. Habitual drunkenness or drug abuse
6. Habitual cruel and inhuman treatment
7. Insanity or idiocy unknown to other party at time of marriage
8. Bigamy
9. Pregnancy by another man at time of marriage, unknown to husband
10. Incestuous marriage
11. Incurable insanity and confinement for three years

MISSOURI

1. Irretrievable breakdown

MONTANA

1. Incurable insanity and confinement for five years
2. Adultery
3. Extreme cruelty
4. Willful desertion
5. Willful neglect
6. Habitual intemperance
7. Conviction of felony
8. Irreconcilable differences for six months

NEBRASKA

1. Irretrievable breakdown

NEVADA

1. Insanity for two years
2. One year's separation
3. Incompatibility

NEW HAMPSHIRE

1. Impotency
2. Adultery
3. Extreme cruelty
4. Conviction of crime and imprisonment for one year
5. Treatment injurious to health or reason
6. Two years' absence without communication
7. Habitual drunkenness for two years
8. Membership in sect professing that relationship of husband and wife unlawful and refusal to cohabit for six months

9. Abandonment and refusal to cohabit for two years
10. Husband willingly absent for two years without supporting wife
11. Wife willingly absent without husband's consent for two years
12. Wife leaving state and remaining away ten years without husband's consent
13. Husband leaving country to become foreign citizen for two years without supporting wife
14. Irreconcilable differences

New Jersey

1. Adultery
2. Willful desertion for twelve months
3. Extreme cruelty
4. Separation for eighteen months
5. Drug addiction or habitual drunkenness for twelve consecutive months
6. Institutionization for mental illness for twenty-four consecutive months
7. Imprisonment for eighteen months
8. Deviant sexual conduct

New Mexico

1. Abandonment
2. Adultery
3. Cruel and inhuman treatment
4. Incompatibility

New York

1. Mental or physical cruelty
2. Abandonment for one year
3. Adultery
4. Imprisonment for three years
5. Separation under decree or agreement for one year

North Carolina

1. Adultery
2. Impotence
3. Concealed pregnancy at time of marriage
4. Separation (if by reason of criminal act, for one year)
5. Unnatural or abnormal sex
6. Incurable insanity and confinement for three continuous years

NORTH DAKOTA

1. Adultery
2. Extreme cruelty
3. Willful desertion
4. Willful neglect
5. Habitual intemperance
6. Conviction of felony
7. Institutionalization for five years because of insanity
8. Irreconcilable differences
9. Decree of separate maintenance after four years without reconciliation

OHIO

1. Bigamy
2. Willful absence for one year
3. Adultery
4. Impotence
5. Extreme cruelty
6. Fraudulent contract
7. Gross neglect of duty
8. Habitual drunkenness
9. Imprisonment
10. Out-of-state divorce
11. Separation for two years

OKLAHOMA

1. Abandonment for one year
2. Adultery
3. Impotence
4. Pregnancy by another man at time of marriage
5. Extreme cruelty
6. Fraudulent contract
7. Incompatibility
8. Habitual drunkenness
9. Gross neglect of duty
10. Imprisonment for a felony
11. Out-of-state divorce
12. Incurable insanity for five years and confinement

OREGON

1. Irreconcilable differences

PENNSYLVANIA

1. Impotence or sterility at marriage
2. Bigamy
3. Adultery
4. Desertion for two years
5. Cruelty or personal indignities
6. Fraud, force, or coercion in obtaining marriage
7. Conviction of certain crimes and sentence to two years in prison
8. Incestuous marriage
9. Remarriage after two years of supposed death of other spouse
10. Institutionalization for three years because of mental illness

RHODE ISLAND

1. Marriage void or voidable
2. Impotence
3. Adultery
4. Extreme cruelty
5. Willful desertion for five years
6. Continued drunkenness
7. Habitual and excessive drug use
8. Neglect to support for one year
9. Gross misbehavior
10. Separation for five years

SOUTH CAROLINA

1. Adultery
2. Desertion for one year
3. Physical cruelty
4. Habitual drunkenness or narcotic addiction
5. Three years' separation

SOUTH DAKOTA

1. Adultery
2. Extreme cruelty
3. Willful desertion
4. Willful neglect
5. Habitual intemperance
6. Conviction of felony
7. Confinement of five years for mental illness

TENNESSEE

1. Impotence and sterility
2. Bigamy
3. Adultery
4. Willful desertion for one year
5. Conviction of infamous crime or felony and sentence to prison
6. Attempted murder of spouse
7. Refusal of wife to move with husband to Tennessee without reasonable cause and absence for two years
8. Pregnancy by another at marriage unknown to husband
9. Habitual drunkenness or drug addiction
10. No reconciliation after two years under decree of divorce from bed and board or separate maintenance

TEXAS

1. Insupportability
2. Cruelty
3. Adultery
4. Conviction of felony and imprisonment for one year
5. Abandonment for one year
6. Separation for three years
7. Confinement to mental hospital for three years

UTAH

1. Impotence
2. Adultery
3. Desertion for one year
4. Neglect of support
5. Habitual drunkenness
6. Conviction of felony
7. Cruel treatment
8. Separation under decree for three years
9. Adjudication of incurable insanity

VERMONT

1. Adultery
2. Sentence to prison for three years and incarceration
3. Intolerable severity
4. Willful desertion
5. Refusal to support
6. Incurable insanity and confinement for five years
7. Living apart for six months

VIRGINIA

1. Adultery, sodomy, or buggery
2. Impotence
3. Sentence to prison and cohabitation not resumed
4. Without knowledge of spouse, conviction of infamous offense
5. Desertion for one year
6. Wife pregnant by another without husband's knowledge at marriage
7. Wife a prostitute before marriage without husband's knowledge
8. Separation for two years

WASHINGTON

1. Irretrievable breakdown

WEST VIRGINIA

1. Adultery
2. Imprisonment for a felony
3. Willful abandonment for one year
4. Cruel and inhuman treatment
5. Habitual drunkenness
6. Narcotic addiction
7. Separation for two years
8. Permanent and incurable insanity

WISCONSIN

1. Adultery
2. Imprisonment for three years
3. Willful desertion for one year
4. Cruel and inhuman treatment
5. Habitual drunkenness for one year
6. Living apart for one year
7. Failure of able husband to support wife
8. Involuntary commitment to mental institution for one year

WYOMING

1. Adultery
2. Impotence
3. Sentence to prison for felony
4. Willful desertion for one year
5. Habitual drunkenness
6. Extreme cruelty

7. Failure of husband to support wife for one year
8. Indignities
9. Husband guilty of crime constituting vagrancy
10. Commission of felony or infamous crime prior to marriage unknown to spouse
11. Concealed pregnancy by another man before marriage
12. Incurable insanity and commitment for two years
13. Separation for two years without fault on plaintiff's part

Appendix C

INFORMATION ON LAW SCHOOLS IN THE UNITED STATES

All tuition charges were correct at the time the book was written. However, tuition costs are rising rapidly and any student planning to go to law school at the time the book is published should check for the correct amount of the tuition payment at the school of her choice.*

THE UNIVERSITY OF AKRON SCHOOL OF LAW, Akron, Ohio
Enrollment: Is relatively small.
Admission: Although applications may be accepted through August, this is contingent upon availability of space. It is recommended that applicants for the day division apply before March 1, evening division applicants should apply prior to June 1. Applications should be sent to Director of Admissions, School of Law, The University of Akron, Akron, Ohio 44325.
Tuition: For Ohio Residents, $23 per credit hour; for nonresidents, $29 per credit hour. Application fee $20.
Correspondence should be sent to Associate Dean, School of Law, same address.

THE UNIVERSITY OF ALABAMA SCHOOL OF LAW, University, Alabama
Enrollment: The last available figure was 485 students, including 170 first-year students.
Admission: For admission in fall term, application materials are available the preceding October. Application should be made as soon as possible after October 1, and should be sent to: Director of Admissions.
Tuition: For Alabama residents, $355 per semester; for nonresidents $610 per semester.

*In some instances enrollment figures are not available.

Correspondence should be sent to Admissions Office, U. of Alabama School of Law, P.O. Box 1435, University, Alabama 35486.

ALBANY LAW SCHOOL, Albany, New York
Enrollment: 640 students.
Admission: Application fee, $10. For the last two years applications were returned to students who had not taken the Law School Admission Test (LSAT) at or before the February administration. Students are admitted only in the fall semester and only for full-time study. Applications should be sent to: Director of Admissions.

Correspondence and requests for applications should be directed to: Albany Law School, 80 New Scotland Avenue, Albany, New York 12208.

WASHINGTON COLLEGE OF LAW, THE AMERICAN UNIVERSITY, Washington, D.C.
Enrollment: Since the size of the entering class is limited to about 190 for an optimum student body of about 600, admission is highly selective.
Admission: All applicants should take the Law School Admission Test (LSAT) on or before the February administration of the test. Most applications are acted on prior to April 1. Applications that are not complete with a transcript analysis by that time will be considered after April 1 only if space is still available. Applications that are not complete by May 31 are not likely to be considered.
Tuition: Full-time students, $1,160 a semester; part-time students, $87 a credit. However, given the current economic conditions and the growth of the university, tuition and fee increases of about 10 percent each year can be expected.

All correspondence and applications should be sent to: Director of Admissions, Washington College of Law, The American University, Washington, D.C. 20016.

ANTIOCH SCHOOL OF LAW, Washington, D.C.
Enrollment: In the first year was limited to 155 students. Total enrollment is expected to reach 500 when all programs of the School of Law are in full operation. Minority students comprise nearly 30 percent of the present student body. Approximately 27 percent are women.

Admission: Applications may be obtained as early as a year before the anticipated date of enrollment. The application deadline last year was March 15, but they should be filed as early as possible in the admissions year.

Tuition: $2,900 for academic year.

Correspondence and requests for applications should be directed to: Director of Admissions, Antioch School of Law, 1624 Crescent Place, N.W., Washington, D.C. 20009.

UNIVERSITY OF ARIZONA COLLEGE OF LAW, Tucson, Arizona

Enrollment: About 80 percent of the 465 law students are residents of Arizona; the rest come from many other states. Eleven percent are women and five percent are members of minority groups.

Admission: Applications should be received by the Director of Admissions by March.

Tuition: Annual tuition fees of last available date were $481 annually for residents and $1,371 for nonresidents.

Correspondence should be sent to: College of Law (Room 405), University of Arizona, Tucson, Arizona 85721.

ARIZONA STATE UNIVERSITY COLLEGE OF LAW, Tempe, Arizona

Enrollment: The full-time student body numbers about 400, with a substantial number of minority students including Chicanos, Indians, and blacks.

Admission: The deadline for completed applications including college transcripts and the Law School Admission Test (LSAT) score is April 1.

Tuition: Residents, $384 a year; nonresidents, $1,274 a year.

Correspondence and requests for the "Bulletin" of the College of Law and for application forms should be addressed to: Law Admissions, College of Law, Arizona State University, Tempe, Arizona 85281.

UNIVERSITY OF ARKANSAS SCHOOL OF LAW, Fayetteville, Arkansas

Enrollment: No information given regarding the number of students.

Admission: Deadline May 1.

Tuition: Arkansas residents paid a registration fee of $400 (last

available date); out-of-state students paid a total of $930 in tuition
and registration fees.

Correspondence for registration forms, medical report forms, etc.
should be addressed to: Registrar's Office, University of Arkansas,
Fayetteville, Arkansas 72701.

UNIVERSITY OF BALTIMORE SCHOOL OF LAW, Baltimore, Maryland

Enrollment: Last available figures show 150 day-division students
and 150 evening-division students.

Admission: Beginning students are admitted to the School of Law
at the commencement of the fall or spring semester. However,
since there is no formal program beginning in the spring semester,
the spring entrant is unable to take a full course load.

Tuition: For the full-time day division (12 to 18 credit hours a
semester) is $600 for each semester. If fewer than 12 hours are
taken in the semester, the day tuition is $50 a credit hour. Tuition
in the evening division is $36 a semester hour.

Correspondence and applications should be sent to: Director of
Law School Admissions, University of Baltimore School of Law,
1420 North Charles Street, Baltimore, Maryland 21201.

BAYLOR UNIVERSITY SCHOOL OF LAW, Waco, Texas

Enrollment: About 75 percent of the 350 students are residents
of Texas; the rest come from many states.

Admission: Entering classes are accepted three times annually.
Application deadline for the class entering in the spring quarter is
November 1; for the summer class, February 1; and for the fall class,
March 1. Applications received after these dates may be considered, but the late applicant will be at a disadvantage in obtaining
admittance. Transfers from other law schools are accepted only if
the student has a better-than-average record at the previous law
school.

Tuition: For law students taking a full course load (10 quarter
hours or more a quarter) is $350 a quarter. Students taking less than
a full load will be charged $35 a quarter hour.

Address all correspondence to: Baylor University School of Law,
Waco, Texas 76703.

BOSTON COLLEGE LAW SCHOOL, Brighton, Massachusetts

Enrollment: The entering class numbers approximately 230 out of a total enrollment of approximately 700. About 28 percent of the present freshmen class is female, and a higher percentage is expected with the present increase in applications from women.

Admission: Applications must be received by the school prior to March 1, preceding the September in which enrollment is desired. Applications received after that date will be returned.

Tuition: For the last available year was $2,550.

Correspondence and admissions should be sent to: Director of Admissions, Admissions Office, Boston College Law School, Brighton, Massachusetts 02135.

BOSTON UNIVERSITY SCHOOL OF LAW, Boston, Massachusetts

Enrollment: Number in student body not given. A growing percentage of the student body, however, presently over 25 percent, is female.

Admission: With only a few exceptions, applications received after March 1 were returned unprocessed. Over 5,000 applications were received for the 350 positions allocated for the class of 1976.

Tuition and Fees: $2,825.

Correspondence and requests for application materials should be sent to: Boston University School of Law, 765 Commonwealth Avenue, Boston, Massachusetts 02215.

BROOKLYN LAW SCHOOL, Brooklyn, N.Y.

Enrollment: No information available on student body.

Admission: Applications should be submitted between November 1 and April 1 of the year preceding admission. Transfer students are not accepted.

Tuition: For the last date available was $1,800 a year. Full-time students pay $900 for each of six semesters and part-time evening students $675 for each of eight semesters. A fee of $15 is required on filing application. Upon notice of acceptance the applicant is required to deposit $100. The deposit fee, which may not be refunded, will be applied toward the first semester's tuition.

Correspondence should be sent to: Admissions Office, Brooklyn Law School, 250 Jorelemon Street, Brooklyn, New York 11201. Applications should be sent to: Director of Admissions, same address.

UNIVERSITY OF CALIFORNIA, BOALT HALL SCHOOL OF LAW, Berkeley, California

Enrollment: The School of Law has a population of approximately 880 students and annually seeks to admit a first-year class of approximately 290. Women presently comprise 25 percent of the student body, and their representation is increasing each year.

Admission: Applications for September and all supporting materials must be filed no later than March 1, preceding September in which enrollment is desired. An evaluation fee of $20 must accompany the application. Admissions are highly selective.

Tuition: California residents, $708.26; nonresidents paid an additional tuition fee of $1,500. A nonresident student who is over 21 may, however, acquire California residence after one year, even while enrolled as a student. Address application to: Director of Admissions.

Correspondence should be sent to: Admissions Office, Boalt Hall School of Law, University of California, Berkeley, California 94720.

UNIVERSITY OF CALIFORNIA, DAVIS SCHOOL OF LAW, Davis, California

Enrollment: Student body of 482 (last available figure). The school is fast approaching its goal of 500. Over 25 percent were women and over 30 percent were from ethnic minority groups.

Admission: Applications must be received by March 1.

Tuition: California residents $223.50 a quarter for three academic quarters each year. Nonresidents pay an additional fee of $500 a quarter.

Correspondence should be sent to: Admissions Office, School of Law, University of California, Davis, California 95616.

UNIVERSITY OF CALIFORNIA, SCHOOL OF LAW, Los Angeles, California

Enrollment: No information available on student body.

Admission: Application deadline is March 1 of the year in which the fall quarter admission is sought.

Tuition: Resident tuition and fees (last available figures) were $696 ($232 a quarter). Nonresident tuition and fees were $2,196, which includes the $500 a quarter nonresident fee.

Correspondence: Application materials are available after Sep-

ember 1 from: Admissions and Records Office, UCLA School of
Law, 405 Hilgard Ave., Los Angeles, California 90024.

UNIVERSITY OF CALIFORNIA, HASTINGS COLLEGE OF THE LAW,
San Francisco, California

Enrollment: 1500 students currently enrolled in the law school.
Of these approximately 17 percent are women.

Admission: Students are admitted only in the fall semester. Prospective students may submit applications after October 1 for the
following academic year. This past year, applications were closed
March 1.

Tuition: Students at Hastings pay a $150 registration fee a semes-
ter. In addition, residents of California pay a $180 educational (or
tuition) fee a semester, and nonresidents pay $750. Incidental fees
total $26.

Requests for information materials should be addressed to: Office
of Admission, University of California, Hastings College of the Law,
198 McAllister Street, San Francisco, California 94102. Applications
should be sent to: Director of Admissions, same address.

UNITED STATES INTERNATIONAL UNIVERSITY, CALIFORNIA WEST-
ERN SCHOOL OF LAW, San Diego, California

Enrollment: The current enrollment of 465 students represents
38 states, 3 foreign countries, and 111 colleges and universities. At
last available date, the entering class numbered 178. Women comprise approximately 8 percent of the total student population, and
represented 12 percent of the first-year class.

Admission: Students are admitted only in the fall. Application
deadline is May 15.

Tuition: $1,800 a year.

Correspondence and applications should be sent to: Admissions
Office, California Western School of Law, 350 Cedar, San Diego,
California 92101.

CAPITAL UNIVERSITY LAW SCHOOL, Columbus, Ohio

Enrollment: The student body is comprised of approximately 450
students divided equally between the day and evening divisions.
About 7 percent are female.

Admission: It is recommended that applications be filed at leas six months before expected entry into the law school. Since ne students are accepted only in the fall, the law school recommend that beginning students apply no later than March 1 of the year c entry.

Tuition: $2,160 a year for all applicants for day division; evenin tuition is $75 per credit hour.

Correspondence and applications should be sent to: Dean, Capi tal University Law School, 2199 East Main Street, Columbus, Ohi 43209.

CASE WESTERN RESERVE UNIVERSITY–FRANKLIN T. BACKU SCHOOL OF LAW, Cleveland, Ohio

Enrollment: No information available on current enrollment.

Admission: Application deadline is May 1. Applications are re viewed on a continuous basis and decisions communicated as earl as possible.

Tuition: Full-time students, $2,600 per year, one-half of which i payable each semester.

Correspondence and applications should be sent to: Admission Office, Case Western Reserve Law School, 11075 East Boulevard Cleveland Ohio, 44106.

THE CATHOLIC UNIVERSITY OF AMERICA–THE COLUMBUS SCHOO OF LAW, Washington, D.C.

Enrollment: At last available date, the full-time student body numbered about 400, including 126 first-year students. The part time enrollment was about 225, including 63 in the first year.

Admission: Applicants are encouraged from all parts of the coun try and from all racial, religious, and ethnic backgrounds. Th School of Law admits beginning students only in August for bot full- and part-time programs. Applications and supporting docu ments must be filed by April 1. Applications received thereafte may be processed, but only students with exceptional credential may be accepted.

Tuition: $2,325 annually for full-time students, and $87 a semes ter hour for part-time students.

Correspondence and applications should be sent to: The Dean'

Office, The Columbus School of Law, The Catholic University Of America, Washington, D.C. 20017.

THE UNIVERSITY OF CHICAGO LAW SCHOOL, Chicago, Illinois
    Enrollment: There are about 160 students in each entering class.
    Admission: Since applications are considered as soon as completed, candidates are urged to have all their material submitted by January 1. Applications received after March 1 are considered only in exceptional circumstances.
    Tuition: $3,000 a year.
    Correspondence and applications should be sent to: Admissions Office, The Law School, The University of Chicago, 1111 E. 60th Street, Chicago, Illinois 60637.

ILLINOIS INSTITUTE OF TECHNOLOGY–CHICAGO-KENT COLLEGE OF LAW, Chicago, Illinois
    Enrollment: Approximately 700 students enrolled, about 310 of whom were in the evening division.
    Admission: Only a limited number of students are admitted in January. Applications should be filed by April for fall admission, and by October 15 for spring.
    Tuition: $55 a semester hour for programs over seven hours, $60 an hour for programs seven hours or less.
    Correspondence and applications should be sent to: Registrar, IIT/Chicago-Kent, 10 North Franklin Street, Chicago, Illinois 60606.

UNIVERSITY OF CINCINNATI COLLEGE OF LAW, Cincinnati, Ohio
    Enrollment: At the last available date, the student body numbered approximately 350 students.
    Admission: Applications are reviewed only within the year preceding the September in which the student wishes to enroll. Applications received after April 1 may be approved under special circumstances.
    Tuition: At the last available date, tuition for year was $1,050 for Cincinnati residents, $1,200 for other residents of Ohio, and $2,100 for nonresidents.
    Correspondence and applications should be sent to: Secretary of

Admissions, College of Law, University of Cincinnati, Cincinnati, Ohio 45221.

CLEVELAND STATE UNIVERSITY COLLEGE OF LAW, Cleveland Ohio

Enrollment: Out of 343 students in an entering class, 51 were women. The largest number of students come from the state of Ohio, but an increasing number are enrolling from out of state— approximately 1 in 4 in the full-time day division class.

Admission: A baccalaureate degree from an accredited college or university is required. Students must take the Law School Admission Test and register with the Law School Data Assembly Service. Applications should be submitted by May 1.

Tuition: For full-time day program, $330 a quarter for resident students, and $660 for nonresidents.

Correspondence and applications should be addressed to: Assistant Dean for Admissions, The Cleveland State University College of Law, Cleveland, Ohio 44115.

UNIVERSITY OF COLORADO SCHOOL OF LAW, Boulder, Colorado

Enrollment: At the last available date the students enrolled in the School of Law totaled 465. In that class 16 percent were women; 15 percent were from minority groups.

Admission: Applications must be received by January 15, and credentials completed by February 15.

Tuition: Colorado residents, $596 for an academic year; nonresidents, $1,915 (per last available year's information).

Correspondence and applications should be sent to: University of Colorado School of Law, Fleming Law Building, Admissions Office, Boulder, Colorado 80302.

COLUMBIA UNIVERSITY SCHOOL OF LAW, New York, New York

Enrollment: An entering class generally consists of about 275 students from more than 100 undergraduate institutions.

Admission: Applications should be received after September 15 and preferably before March 1.

Tuition: Tuition and fees were $3,280 for the last year for which we have information.

Address correspondence and applications to: School of Law Admissions Office, Columbia University, 435 W. 116th Street, New York, New York 10027.

UNIVERSITY OF CONNECTICUT SCHOOL OF LAW, West Hartford, Connecticut

Enrollment: Thirty-eight percent of the freshman class are women.

Admission: Applications are accepted commencing October 1 for the following September and applicants are encouraged to file as early as possible. Selected admission of outstanding applicants begins as early as December, although most applicants receive notifications sometime after April 1. The application form and fee must be filed before February 1 for the day division and April 1 for the evening division to ensure equal consideration. Students are admitted only in September of each year.

Tuition: Estimated expenses are $3,000 for single students and $3,400 for married students. This includes tuition, which is $650 a year for residents. Nonresidents are charged an additional fee of $500 a year.

Applications and catalogs may be obtained by writing to: Director of Admissions, The University of Connecticut School of Law, Greater Hartford Campus, West Hartford, Connecticut 06117.

CORNELL UNIVERSITY SCHOOL OF LAW, Ithaca, New York

Enrollment: The Cornell Law School wishes to increase its minority student enrollment and toward that end allocates special energies and resources to the recruitment and support of minority students. Applications from minority students are given special consideration by the admissions committee.

Admission: Beginning students are accepted only in the fall, at which time 155 new students are enrolled. The recommended date for completion of the application for admission is January 1 and the deadline is February 28.

Tuition: The normal expense for a single student (not including travel and registration deposit) is about $5,400 for one academic year. A total of about $6,700 should be projected for a married student without children, and $7,000 for a married student with one child.

Send correspondence to: Admissions Office, Cornell Law School, Ithaca, New York 14850.

CREIGHTON UNIVERSITY SCHOOL OF LAW, Omaha, Nebraska
Admission: Applications should be submitted as early as possible and in any event by March 15.
Tuition: $1,050 a semester.
Inquiries concerning the School of Law should be addressed to: Dean, Creighton University School of Law, Omaha, Nebraska 68131. Requests for catalogs and application forms should be addressed to: Admissions Office of the School of Law.

SAMFORD UNIVERSITY–CUMBERLAND SCHOOL OF LAW, Birmingham, Alabama
Admission: Applicants for admission must earn a baccalaureate degree from an accredited college or university and a cumulative grade-point average which, when considered with the score on the Law School Admission Test and other relevant data, indicates a reasonable probability of success in the study of law.
Tuition: The basic tuition is $46 a semester hour, exclusive of such variable expenses as books, supplies, and special charges for late registration and change of schedule. All student charges are payable at the beginning of the semester.
Inquiries concerning the Cumberland School of Law may be addressed to: Dean of Admissions, Cumberland School of Law, Samford University, 800 Lakeshore Drive, Birmingham, Alabama 35200.

UNIVERSITY OF DENVER COLLEGE OF LAW, Denver Colorado
Enrollment: A total of 839 students were enrolled for the last available date. Of these 602 were enrolled in the day division and 237 in the evening division. The 188 first-year students in the day division and 108 freshmen from the evening division came from 38 states and 4 foreign countries. Only 15 percent of the student body were from the state of Colorado.
Admission: The admissions committee ordinarily begins its evaluation of applicants during the first week of January for students seeking admission in the following autumn. While there is no formal

closing date for admissions, those received after May 1 may be subject to more stringent scrutiny because of prior acceptances and space limitations.

Tuition: As of the fall quarter of 1973 was $900 per quarter for full-time students—those taking more than 12 credit hours a quarter. Students taking fewer credits are assessed at the rate of $60 a quarter hour.

Address correspondence to: Committee on Admissions, University of Denver College of Law, 200 West 14th Avenue, Denver, Colorado 80204.

DE PAUL UNIVERSITY COLLEGE OF LAW, Chicago, Illinois

Enrollment: 900 students were enrolled in the College of Law at the last available date. Full-time day division students constitute approximately two-thirds of that total. Each fall, 225 to 250 freshmen are admitted. The student body is drawn from colleges and universities throughout the nation, as well as Chicago. Approximately 20 percent of the student body are women. Freshman classes are limited to 75 students.

Admission: It is extremely doubtful that an applicant could be admitted whose application and supporting documents were not received by March 1 of the year in which admission is sought.

Tuition: Is $1,900 an academic year for day-division students and $1,350 an academic year for evening division students.

Correspondence should be sent to: Director of Admissions, College of Law, De Paul University, 25 East Jackson Blvd., Chicago, Illinois 60604.

UNIVERSITY OF DETROIT SCHOOL OF LAW, Detroit, Michigan

Enrollment: The entering class size is 250—equally divided between the day and evening divisions.

Admission: Entering classes begin in the fall term. Applications should be submitted by March 15 for the term beginning the following fall. Applications received after that date will be evaluated and considered, but acceptance will occur only if vacancies exist.

Tuition: Day students, $950 a semester; evening students, $650 a semester.

Address correspondence to: The Assistant Dean, University of Detroit School of Law, 651 E. Jefferson, Detroit, Michigan 48226.

DETROIT COLLEGE OF LAW, Detroit, Michigan
Enrollment: The last enrollment figure available was 910, representing 145 educational institutions.

Admission: Application deadline for the fall semester is January 1, and for the spring semester June 1. An application fee of $20 is required with the filing of all applications.

Tuition: $1,200 for full-time study and $900 for part-time study.

Address correspondence to: Admissions Office, Detroit College of Law, 136 East Elizabeth, Detroit, Michigan 48201.

DICKINSON SCHOOL OF LAW, Carlisle, Pennsylvania
Enrollment: The student body comprises approximately 430 students from 128 colleges and 13 states. The entering class in recent years has approximated 140.

Admission: Applications for acceptance in the first-year class must be received no later than February 15 and preferably in the fall for the following year.

Tuition: $1,300 for residents of Pennsylvania; $1,500 for nonresidents. The student activity fee is $30.

Requests for applications and all inquiries should be addressed to: Director of Admissions, Dickinson School of Law, Carlisle, Pennsylvania 17013.

DRAKE UNIVERSITY LAW SCHOOL, Des Moines, Iowa
Enrollment: Approximately 400 students are enrolled in Drake Law School, including 150 freshmen.

Admission: Applications must be received by March 1.

Tuition: $1,160 a semester (all students).

For further information write to: Director of Admissions, Drake University Law School, Des Moines, Iowa 50311.

DUKE UNIVERSITY SCHOOL OF LAW, Durham, North Carolina
Enrollment: A typical class consists of about 150 students. Women comprise about 13 percent of recent classes, and that percentage is increasing.

Admission: While for many years Duke firmly resisted imposing formal deadlines for submission of applications, now it is strongly suggesting that applications be filed no later than January 1 of the year in which admission is desired and that the admission file be completed prior to February 1 of that year. Applicants who file in the fall and complete their files prior to January 1 will receive decisions by March 15.

Tuition: $2,500 a year; books and supplies approximately $200 a year.

Correspondence should be sent to: Brenda F. Parnell, Admissions Officer, Duke University School of Law, Durham, North Carolina 27706.

DUQUESNE UNIVERSITY SCHOOL OF LAW, Pittsburgh, Pennsylvania

Admission: Applications will be accepted after September 1 for the class entering the following September. Applications received after April 1 will be processed only if space is available.

Tuition: $900 a semester for day division; $650 a semester for evening division.

For further information on the School of Law, write to: Office of Admissions, Duquesne University School of Law, 600 Forbes Avenue, Pittsburgh, Pennsylvania 15219.

EMORY UNIVERSITY SCHOOL OF LAW, Atlanta, Georgia

Enrollment: The student body has approximately 650 students, the first-year class numbers 250, and approximately 20 percent are women.

Admission: The school admits only full-time students and only in September. Applications should be submitted in the fall preceding admission. Applications received after March 1 may be returned without processing unless the applicant shows unusually good credentials.

Tuition: $750 a quarter.

With regard to admission, write to: Director of Admissions, School of Law, Emory University, Atlanta, Georgia 30322.

FLORIDA STATE UNIVERSITY COLLEGE OF LAW, Tallahassee, Florida

Enrollment: There are approximately 150 students in the entering class. Of the total enrollment of about 540, more than 50 are women.

Admission: Freshman students are accepted for the fall quarter only.

Tuition and Fees: For Florida residents as of last available date were $240 a quarter. For nonresidents they were $590 a quarter.

For information write to: College of Law, Florida State University, Tallahassee, Florida 32306.

FORDHAM UNIVERSITY SCHOOL OF LAW, New York, New York

Enrollment: Approximately 75 percent of the student population of 1,072 are residents of New York State. The remaining 25 percent come from some 25 other states and 10 foreign countries. Women comprise 10 percent of the student body and 13 percent of the entering class.

Admission: Applications should be submitted during the period from October 15 to April 1.

Tuition: $2,400 for the day division (at last available date) and $1,800 for the evening division.

Send correspondence to: Admissions Office, Fordham University School of Law, 140 West 62nd Street, New York, New York 10023.

GEORGE WASHINGTON UNIVERSITY, NATIONAL LAW CENTER, Washington, D.C.

Enrollment: The National Law Center enrolls more than 1,800 students in both day and evening divisions, making it one of the largest law schools in the nation.

Admission: At last available date, 6,000 applications were received for approximately 300 places in the entering day class and the 100 places in the entering evening class. Students are admitted only in September.

Tuition: $2,350, plus $75 in fees.

Correspondence should be sent to: Office of Admissions, The George Washington University National Law Center, 305 Bacon Hall, 2000 H Street, N.W., Washington, D.C. 20006.

GEORGETOWN UNIVERSITY, THE LAW CENTER, Washington, D.C.

Enrollment: The student body numbers approximately 2,000, including approximately 240 postgraduate students. Women comprise 15 percent.

Admission: The deadline for application to the day program is March 1; for the evening program, May 15.

Tuition: $2,500 for full-time students; $88 a credit hour for part-time students.

Application forms and catalogues may be obtained by writing to: Admissions Office, Georgetown University Law Center, 600 New Jersey Avenue, N.W., Washington, D.C. 20001.

UNIVERSITY OF GEORGIA, SCHOOL OF LAW, Athens Georgia

Enrollment: Approximately 240 first-year students have been admitted to each class in the past few years. Total enrollment is approximately 650. It is anticipated that first-year admissions may be reduced slightly to maintain the enrollment above 600.

Admission: First-year students are admitted only in September. The application deadline is April 1.

Tuition: For the last available year was $639 for residents and $1,359 for nonresidents.

Address correspondence to: University of Georgia, School of Law, Athens, Georgia 30601.

GOLDEN GATE UNIVERSITY SCHOOL OF LAW, San Francisco, California

Enrollment: About 50 percent of the student body is from California. The current student body is about 650.

Admission: The application deadline is May 1; late applicants will be admitted only with extremely strong credentials, a reasonable explanation for lateness, and availability of room.

Tuition: $60 a unit (for last available year).

Correspondence should be sent to: Golden Gate University, School of Law, 536 Mission, San Francisco, California 94105.

GONZAGA UNIVERSITY SCHOOL OF LAW, Spokane, Washington

Admission: Because the number of qualified applicants exceeds available space, application in the fall or early winter prior to expected entrance is advisable.

Tuition: $60 a credit hour for residents and nonresidents, plus university fees of approximately $50 a semester.

Correspondence should be addressed to Gonzaga Law School, 600 East Sharp Avenue, Spokane, Washington 99202.

HARVARD UNIVERSITY LAW SCHOOL, Cambridge, Massachusetts

Admission: The large volume of applications for admission makes the admissions process highly selective. More than 6,500 applications are received for approximately 525 places in the first-year class entering in September. There are no absolute standards for admission. The faculty admissions committee weighs a wide variety of factors and attempts to obtain a broad diversity among student backgrounds and points of view. But clear, careful evaluation of individual excellence and accomplishment is the heart of the selection process. Most applicants to Harvard know that the competition for admission is keen, and few apply without strong qualifications.

Tuition and Fees: For the last available year were approximately $2,560.

All correspondence should be sent to: Admissions Office, Harvard Law School, Cambridge, Massachusetts 02138.

HOFSTRA UNIVERSITY SCHOOL OF LAW, Hempstead, New York

Enrollment: The school's 393, first-, second-, and third-year students are graduates of more than 100 colleges and universities across the country. Approximately 20 percent of the student body are women.

Admission: Deadline for receipt of applications is April 15. Admission is very competitive.

Tuition: $2,300 a year, payable in two equal installments prior to the start of each semester.

Correspondence should be sent to the School of Law, Hofstra University, Hempstead, New York 11550.

UNIVERSITY OF HOUSTON COLLEGE OF LAW, Houston, Texas

Enrollment: The student body consists of approximately 800 persons from across the United States and foreign countries. Of that number approximately 600 are day students and the remainder attend at night.

Admission: A completed application must be sent to the college before May 1.

Tuition: At the time of this writing, tuition for full-time Texas residents is only $60 a semester and for nonresidents only $600, but it may change soon.

Inquiries concerning the college should be addressed to: Admissions Office, University of Houston, College of Law, Cullen Boulevard, Houston, Texas 77004.

HOWARD UNIVERSITY, SCHOOL OF LAW, Washington, D.C.
Admission: While the School of Law does not require applicants to take the Law School Admission Test (LSAT), it suggests that they do so. An applicant must submit: an application for admission upon a standard form; two written testimonials as to his or her character obtained from persons not related to the applicant; an autobiographical sketch of not more than two pages; and transcripts of the college record. Applications should be submitted no later than June 1. Questions concerning U.S. Immigration and Naturalization Service regulations should be directed to: Office of Foreign Student Service, second floor, Administration Building. Students who make formal application to the university are required to pay a fee of $10. Those who enter the university also pay an enrollment fee of $60; these are not refundable.
Tuition: At time of this writing $1,043 for full-time students.
Correspondence should be sent to: Office of Admissions, Howard University, 2370 Sixth Street, N.W., Washington, D.C. 20001.

UNIVERSITY OF IDAHO, COLLEGE OF LAW, Moscow, Idaho
Enrollment: Although the College of Law is quite small in total enrollment, the 253 students enrolled at last available date held degrees from 61 colleges and universities.
Admission: Applications are not accepted until late in the September preceding the year in which enrollment is desired. Entering students are admitted only for the fall semester. Application blanks can be secured from the College of Law. Late-fall or early-winter application is recommended. The entering class usually is completely filled by early to mid-March.
Tuition: Idaho residents do not pay any tuition but presently are charged mandatory fees for such items as health services and activities in the amount of about $550 a year. Nonresident students are charged tuition in addition to the mandatory fees. Tuition is expected to approximate $800, bringing the total educational cost for nonresident students to around $1,350.
Correspondence should be sent to: Dean, College of Law, University of Idaho, Moscow, Idaho 83843.

UNIVERSITY OF ILLINOIS, COLLEGE OF LAW, Champaign, Illinois

Enrollment: At the last available year, approximately 10 percent of the entering class were members of minority groups, and 15 percent were women. Approximately 700 professional students and 30 graduate law students were in attendance, according to last available figures.

Admission: Freshmen are admitted only in the fall. Applications are available the preceding September and must be submitted before March 15. Applicants must register with the Law School Data Assembly Service, and a Law School Admission Test score is required.

Tuition and Fees: For Illinois residents are $343 a semester, and $838 for nonresidents.

Correspondence should be sent to: Office of the Dean, University of Illinois College of Law, Champaign, Illinois 61820.

INDIANA UNIVERSITY, SCHOOL OF LAW, Bloomington, Indiana

Enrollment: The entering class numbers about 190 students. About three-quarters of the students are residents of Indiana. For the past few years, over 10 percent of the entering class have been women.

Admission: Written recommendations or interviews are not required, but they are granted on request. There is no application deadline, but candidates whose completed applications are received after March 1 will be at a disadvantage because a portion of the class will already be filled at that time. Applicants who are admitted may begin in either the summer or fall term. Only full-time students are admitted.

Tuition: Depending on electives, Indiana residents paid between $702 and $783 for tuition, according to figures for last available year. The figure for nonresidents was $1,612–$1,798. The minimum academic-year expenses are estimated at $1,500.

All correspondence should be sent to: Admissions Office, Indiana University School of Law, Bloomington, Indiana 47401.

INDIANA UNIVERSITY, INDIANAPOLIS LAW SCHOOL, Indianapolis, Indiana

Enrollment: Approximately 450 are enrolled in the full-time division and 500 in the part-time division, of which 65 were women. The entering class had 155 full- and 110 part-time students during this same year. Approximately 85 percent of the students are residents of Indiana.

Admission: Applicants are required to take the LSAT no later than the April test date of the year of entrance. Application forms are available from: Office of Admissions. An application fee of $15 is required except for applicants who have attended Indiana University as regular students or who have completed 12 or more semester hours at another Indiana University campus. Each applicant must furnish an official transcript of his record from all colleges or universities attended.

Tuition: Indiana residents pay $27 a credit hour for regular semesters and summer sessions. The rate for nonresidents if $62 a credit hour. Book costs approximate $100 a semester. A full-time student (single) can anticipate spending $3,500 a year.

Correspondence should be sent to: Office of Admissions, Indianapolis Law School of Indiana University, 735 West New York Street, Indianapolis, Indiana 46202.

UNIVERSITY OF IOWA COLLEGE OF LAW, Iowa City, Iowa

Enrollment: The student body is approximately 580. Approximately 12 percent of the student body is female.

Admission: Beginning students may enter either in the fall or in the summer and must file their application no later than April 1. An applicant normally does not receive serious consideration if he or she does not have a grade-point average near 3.0 on a 4.0 scale and a LSAT score near 600.

Tuition: The present fee schedule is $710 a year for residents of Iowa and $1,270 a year for nonresidents (as of last figures available). Books and supplies average about $140 a year.

Correspondence should be sent to: Dean, College of Law, The University of Iowa, Iowa City, Iowa 52242.

THE JOHN MARSHALL LAW SCHOOL, Chicago, Illinois

Enrollment: While the school received more applications from students who expect to practice law in the Great Lakes area, its student body of over 1,600 is derived from 28 states. As of last available date, 625 freshmen were admitted.

Admission: Letters of recommendation are carefully weighed and should come from members of the legal profession.

Tuition: $60 a semester hour. Books, minimum of $100 a year.

All correspondence should be sent to: Helen M. Thatcher, Assistant Dean, The John Marshall Law School, 315 S. Plymouth Court, Chicago, Illinois, 60604.

UNIVERSITY OF KANSAS SCHOOL OF LAW, Lawrence, Kansas

Enrollment: Approximately 500 students are enrolled in an academic year.

Admission: A completed School of Law application accompanied by a $10 filing fee is necessary. The deadlines for completed files are March 15 for summer admission and May 15 for fall admission. Applicants for fall admission whose completed files reach the Admissions Committee by April 1 will have a greater chance of admission than those received after April 1.

Tuition and Fees: For resident students approximately $317 a semester and for nonresidents $712. Books and supplies average an additional $70 to $100 a semester.

All inquires should be directed to: Admissions Office, University of Kansas School of Law, Green Hall, Lawrence, Kansas 66044.

UNIVERSITY OF KENTUCKY COLLEGE OF LAW, Lexington, Kentucky

Admission: Is considered and granted based on the cumulative undergraduate grade record and the LSAT score. Personal interviews are not required. Applications should be submitted as early as possible. March 1 is the deadline for receipt of an application and March 31 for all supporting credentials. Applicants are admitted generally for the fall term only. Those who are members of minority groups are considered specially by the admissions committee.

Tuition: Approximately $480 ($240 a semester) for Kentucky residents and $1,210 ($605 a semester) for nonresidents.

Correspondence should be sent to: University of Kentucky Admissions Office, Administration Annex, University of Kentucky, Lexington, Kentucky 40506.

LEWIS AND CLARK COLLEGE, NORTHWESTERN SCHOOL OF LAW, Portland, Oregon

Enrollment: Is approximately 600.

Admission: The admissions process is designed to leaven the student body and the legal profession with competent representation from all groups, particularly those who have been traditionally underrepresented in the legal process. No deadline has been given for applicants but it is suggested that these be submitted as early as possible.

Tuition and Fees: Approximately $2,000 a year in the day division and $1,1200 in the evening division. Additional fees total $65.

For further information write to: Dean of Admissions, Northwestern School of Law of Lewis and Clark College, 10015 Southwest Terwilliger Boulevard, Portland, Oregon 97219.

LOUISIANA STATE UNIVERSITY LAW SCHOOL, Baton Rouge, Louisiana

Admission: The law school admits students only in the fall and only for full-time study. There are no night courses offered. Applications are available only in the fall preceding the year of desired admission.

Tuition: For the last available year was $255 a semester for a full-time student, $570 per semester for nonresidents.

Further information may be obtained by writing to: Admissions Office, Room 102, LSU Law School, Baton Rouge, Louisiana 70803.

UNIVERSITY OF LOUISVILLE SCHOOL OF LAW, Louisville, Kentucky

Enrollment: Approximately three-quarters of the law students are residents of Kentucky. The day division has approximately 450 students, of whom approximately 150 were freshmen, and the evening division has approximately 180 students.

Admission: Applicants are admitted only at the beginning of the fall semester and applications should be in by January 15.

Tuition: For Kentucky residents approximately $1,000 for day-division students and $750 for evening-division students; nonresidents, for academic year approximately $2,000 and $1,500 for evening division.

Send inquiries to: School of Law Admissions Office, University of Louisville, Louisville, Kentucky 40208.

LOYOLA UNIVERSITY SCHOOL OF LAW, Chicago, Illinois

Enrollment: As of last available year was 590, of which 375 were full-time students.

Admission: The number of applicants far exceeds the number of available spaces every year. Therefore, applicants are encouraged to apply early in the academic year preceding their expected date of enrollment. March 1 is the deadline for those who expect serious consideration.

Tuition: Approximately $950 a semester for day students and $713 a semester for evening students.

For applications and information concerning admission write to: Admissions Office, Loyola University School of Law, 41 East Pearson Street, Chicago, Illinois 60611.

LOYOLA UNIVERSITY SCHOOL OF LAW, Los Angeles, California

Enrollment: There are about 1,200 students with almost 650 in the day division.

Admission: Applicants should file admission forms with the Office of the Registrar, and in addition, an official transcript of all undergraduate work must be sent either to the Law School Data Assembly Service or directly to the Office of the Registrar at the School of Law.

Tuition: $60 a unit for both day and evening divisions.

For information write to: Office of the Registrar, Loyola University School of Law, 1440 West Ninth Street, Los Angeles, California 90015.

LOYOLA UNIVERSITY SCHOOL OF LAW, New Orleans, Louisiana

Enrollment: The student body numbers over 600, of which almost two-thirds come from Louisiana.

Admission: Applications must be received prior to April 1 for full-time curriculum and prior to May 1 for part-time curriculum. The applicant's file must be completed prior to June 15.

Tuition and Fees: For full-time students, $850 a semester; for part-time students, $615 a semester. Fees amount to $25 a semester.

All correspondence concerning admission and information should be addressed to: Assistant Dean for Admissions, Loyola University School of Law, New Orleans, Louisiana 70118.

UNIVERSITY OF MAINE SCHOOL OF LAW, Portland, Maine

Enrollment: As of last available information, the student body numbered 195 students, of whom 24 were women.

Admission: Beginning students are admitted only in September. The deadline for applications is February 15.

Tuition and Fees: Residents of New England were charged $550 a year for tuition and fees; nonresidents, $1,650, according to last available information.

Correspondence should be sent to: Registrar, University of Maine School of Law, 246 Deering Avenue, Portland, Maine 04102.

MARQUETTE UNIVERSITY SCHOOL OF LAW, Milwaukee, Wisconsin

Enrollment: Has a program for recruiting and retaining members of minority groups. There is a student bar association, to which all students belong, and a chapter of the Black American Law Students Association.

Admission: We have no available information on deadline for applications, so suggest that they be sent in as soon as possible.

Tuition and Fees: For full-time students $1,049 a semester with a nonrefundable application fee of $20, a tuition deposit of $100 credited to the first semester's tuition, and a graduation fee of $17.

Write to: Admissions Officer, Marquette University Law School, 1103 West Wisconsin Avenue, Milwaukeee, Wisconsin 53233, for further information.

UNIVERSITY OF MARYLAND SCHOOL OF LAW, Baltimore, Maryland

Enrollment: Approximately 550 full-time students are enrolled in the school.

Admission: Each applicant is required to file an application for admission, obtainable from the law school; to take the Law School Admission Test; and to have transcripts sent to the Law School Data Assembly Service. First-year students are admitted only in September and are urged to file applications as early as possible after October 1 of the year preceding enrollment, and in any case prior to March 1.

Tuition and Fees: Annually are approximately $631 for Maryland residents and $1,631 for nonresidents.

For further admission information write to: Committee on Admissions, University of Maryland School of Law, 500 West Baltimore Street, Baltimore, Maryland 21201.

MEMPHIS STATE UNIVERSITY SCHOOL OF LAW, Memphis, Tennessee

Enrollment: Graduates of 92 colleges and universities are presently represented in the student body; the female enrollment is 5 percent.

Admission: Is selective. Students are admitted only in September and day students are admitted only for full-time study. A part-time night-school program is available. Applications have to be submitted prior to January 1 for admission the following September.

Tuition and Fees: For Tennessee residents were $189 a semester and $480 for nonresidents as of the last available year.

Correspondence should be sent to: Committee for Law School Admissions, Office of Admissions and Records, Memphis State University, Memphis, Tennessee 38152.

MERCER UNIVERSITY, THE WALTER F. GEORGE SCHOOL OF LAW, Macon, Georgia

Enrollment: In the last year for which we have enrollment figures there were 241 students for the fall quarter, of whom two were women and five were minority-group members. The entering class was limited to 87, since the law school wishes to retain the distinction of moderate size to have the ability of offering the student more individualized instruction.

Admission: The most frequently found deficiency in the law-school student, this school claims, is the inability to use the English language concisely and accurately. A thorough background in English grammar and composition therefore is indispensable for prospective law students. It is strongly recommended that the applicant take the LSAT by January 1 of the year in which he seeks admission. Letters of recommendation are required. Students are accepted only for entrance in the fall quarter. A $10 application fee is required.

Tuition: Approximately $600 a quarter.

For further information write to: Dean's Office, Walter F. George School of Law, Mercer University, Macon, Georgia 31207.

UNIVERSITY OF MIAMI SCHOOL OF LAW, Coral Gables, Florida

Enrollment: The total law-school student enrollment is 1,051.

Admission: Because the number of applications received each year far exceeds the number the School of Law can accommodate, the school is highly selective. Entering students are admitted only in the fall semester and applicants are urged to apply for admission as early as possible after September 1 for the next year's fall term.

Tuition and Fees: $1,300 a semester for 12 to 16 credit hours. Less than 12 credits or in excess of 16 credits are charged $100 a credit. The same rate applies to the summer session. There is an auditing charge of $60 a course for part-time students with no auditing charge for full-time students enrolled for 12 to 18 hours.

For more information write to: Director of Law Admissions, University of Miami, P.O. Box 8087, Coral Gables, Florida 33124.

THE UNIVERSITY OF MICHIGAN LAW SCHOOL, Ann Arbor, Michigan

Enrollment: As a state-affiliated school with substantial private endowment, Michigan is a strange hybrid. The tuition schedule ensures that most state residents can afford to attend the Law School. Residents make up about one-half of the entering class. There are approximately 1,170 law students.

Admission: An application form must be submitted by April 1. Black students and persons from disadvantaged backgrounds are given special consideration. Applicants should specify whether they prefer to begin in June or August.

Tuition and Fees: For Michigan residents approximately $475 a full term or $950 a year; for nonresidents, $1,200 a term or $2,400 a year. Rates for a full summer term are $300 for residents and $760 for nonresidents. Books cost about $200.

For further information write to: Admissions Office, The University of Michigan Law School, Ann Arbor, Michigan 48104.

UNIVERSITY OF MINNESOTA LAW SCHOOL, Minneapolis, Minnesota

Enrollment: Approximately 750 with roughly 80 percent from Minnesota.

Admission: The Law School admits only full-time day students and only in September of each year. Application deadline is March 1 and early applications are encouraged.

Tuition and Fees: Annually are approximately $766 for residents and $1,651 for nonresidents, according to last available figures.

For further information and applications write to: Admissions Office, University of Minnesota Law School, Minneapolis, Minnesota 55455.

THE UNIVERSITY OF MISSISSIPPI LAW SCHOOL, University, Mississippi

Admission: Students are admitted in June or August. The same requirements apply for summer and fall admission. Application deadlines: For the summer term, March 1 for nonresidents and April 1 for Mississippi residents; for the fall term, March 1 for nonresidents and June 15 for Mississippi residents.

Tuition and Fees: Approximately $353 a semester for state residents. Nonresidents pay an additional $300 a semester. Fees are $8 a semester. Books cost from $60 to $80 per semester.

Prospective applicants should write to: Director of Admissions, School of Law, The University of Mississippi, University, Mississippi 38677.

UNIVERSITY OF MISSOURI–COLUMBIA SCHOOL OF LAW, Columbia, Missouri

Admission: Beginning students will be admitted at the opening of the fall semester only. Because this is a state-supported institution, preference is given to Missouri residents, with the result that admission criteria are somewhat higher for nonresidents. The admissions process is selective. It is recommended that students make application very early in the year; ordinarily, applications filed after March 31 will not be considered for the following fall.

Tuition and Fees: For Missouri residents $230 a semester at the last available date; for nonresidents, $460 a semester.

All inquiries pertaining to admission to the School of Law should be addressed to: Admissions Committee, 114 Tate Hall, University of Missouri–Columbia, Columbia, Missouri 65201.

UNIVERSITY OF MISSOURI–KANSAS CITY SCHOOL OF LAW, Kansas City, Missouri

Enrollment: About three-quarters of the student body are Missouri residents, with a student body numbering approximately 660.

Admission: No deadline was available for filing applications but it is suggested that these be submitted as early as possible.

Tuition: For resident of Missouri students approximately $800 a year; nonresidents, $1,700.

Information requests and applications should be sent to: Associate Dean, School of Law, University of Missouri–Kansas City, 5100 Rockhill Road, Kansas City, Missouri 64110.

UNIVERSITY OF MONTANA SCHOOL OF LAW, Missoula, Montana
Admission: No deadline was available for submitting applications but it is suggested that these be submitted as early as possible.

Tuition and Fees: Montana residents paid $446 in fees for the last year for which we have information and nonresidents $1,293.50.

Inquiries concerning the school should be addressed to: Admissions Office, School of Law, University of Montana, Missoula, Montana 59801.

UNIVERSITY OF NEBRASKA COLLEGE OF LAW, Lincoln, Nebraska
Admission: Applications are accepted one year in advance of the intended month of entry. Classes normally are filled by March. Only full-time students are enrolled at the College of Law.

Tuition and Fees: For Nebraska residents were $267.50 a semester; for nonresidents, $630.50 for the last available year for which we have this information.

Address all inquiries concerning the college to: Office of The Dean, University of Nebraska, College of Law, Lincoln, Nebraska 68508.

NEW ENGLAND SCHOOL OF LAW, Boston, Massachusetts
Admission: A completed application form, and two letters of recommendation, one from a professor, must be received by the registrar by April 1 of the year of entry. Applicants must take the Law School Admission Test and register with the Law School Data Assembly Service before this date. Admission is competitive. The school is forced to turn down considerably more applicants than it can accept.

Tuition and Fees: $1,700 for the day division and $1,275 for the evening division. There is about $45 additional required for other fees.

Requests for catalogs and applications should be sent to: Registrar's Office, New England School of Law, 126 Newbury Street, Boston, Massachusetts 02116.

UNIVERSITY OF NEW MEXICO SCHOOL OF LAW, Albuquerque, New Mexico

Enrollment: While about 90 percent of the School of Law's students are New Mexico residents, the entering class represents approximately 93 colleges. Women comprise about 22 percent of the class with 21 percent from minority groups. The student body numbers a little over 300.

Admission: Beginning students will be admitted in the fall semester only and only on a full-time basis.

Tuition: For New Mexico residents for the last available year $227 a semester and $624 for nonresidents.

Inquiries should be directed to: Assistant Dean, University of New Mexico School of Law, Albuquerque, New Mexico 87106.

STATE UNIVERSITY OF NEW YORK AT BUFFALO SCHOOL OF LAW, Buffalo, New York

Enrollment: About three-quarters of the students are residents of New York. The increasing population of women in the school was up to almost 25 percent of the total class. A minority student program recruits and assists law students from minority groups. The school welcomes applications from others who are educationally or culturally deprived.

Admission: The application deadline is February 15.

Tuition and Fees: New York residents paid $1,600 for last available year; nonresidents $2,000.

Send any inquiries to: Admissions Office, SUNY at Buffalo, School of Law, 77 West Eagle Street, Buffalo, New York 14202.

NEW YORK LAW SCHOOL, New York, New York

Enrollment: The student body is comprised of 800 students, of which about 20 percent are women, and there are proportionally more women in each entering class.

Admission: In the fall semester only. Summer school is provided only to lighten the future year's program; it does not allow acceleration of the entire program.

Tuition: At present $1,600 a year for the day division and $1,200 a year for the evening division.

For further information write to: Secretary of the School, New York Law School, 57 Worth Street, New York, New York 10013.

NEW YORK UNIVERSITY SCHOOL OF LAW, New York, New York

Enrollment: Graduates of over 200 colleges and universities are currently enrolled in the J.D. (Doctor of Laws) program, of which 25 percent are women.

Admission: Students are admitted only in September and on a full-time basis.

Tuition: Approximately $2,800 for the two semesters.

For further information and applications write to: Admissions Office, New York University School of Law, 40 Washington Square South, New York, New York 10012.

UNIVERSITY OF NORTH CAROLINA SCHOOL OF LAW, Chapel Hill, North Carolina

Enrollment: The school endeavors to maintain a balance of about 20 percent nonresidents. Females comprise about 17 percent of the first-year class and 12 percent of the total enrollment. The school tries to hold the incoming class to 225–235.

Admission: Only full-time study students are admitted and admission is offered for the fall semester only. Application materials are available the preceding fall. All elements of an application must be submitted by March 31. Applications will be processed on the basis of three years of college work. Written recommendations are not required, and personal interviews are not encouraged.

Tuition and Fees: Presently $450 a year for residents and $2,015 for nonresidents.

For further information write to: Admissions Office, University of North Carolina School of Law, Chapel Hill, North Carolina 27514.

NORTH CAROLINA CENTRAL UNIVERSITY SCHOOL OF LAW, Durham, North Carolina

Admission: Applications and admission files must be submitted by March 1. Requirements for completion of an applicant's file include transcripts from all schools attended, at least two letters of recommendation (preferably from former instructors), and LSAT score. No applications will be accepted for enrollment in the spring semester.

Tuition and Fees: For residents, $1,227; for out-of-state residents, $2,827.

Inquiries on admission and requests for catalogs and applications should be sent to: Office of the Dean, School of Law, North Carolina Central University, Durham, North Carolina 27707.

UNIVERSITY OF NORTH DAKOTA SCHOOL OF LAW, Grand Forks, North Dakota

Admission: Students are admitted only in August and only for full-time study. Applications are available as of the September preceding admission. Application deadline is April 15. Personal interviews are not encouraged.

Tuition and Fees: Semester fees for a resident law student were $232 for the last available year, for a nonresident, $596. Additional fees total $51 a semester.

For additional information and application forms write to: Office of the Dean, School of Law, University of North Dakota, Grand Forks, North Dakota 58201.

NORTHEASTERN UNIVERSITY SCHOOL OF LAW, Boston, Massachusetts

Enrollment: The student body is approximately 350 full-time students. The school offers a favorable climate for women and persons several years out of college. Almost half the student body is female.

Admission: The entering class is limited to 125 students. The deadline for applications is March 1, but early application is recommended. The school follows a "rolling admissions" policy and makes decisions on applications as soon as possible after receipt.

Tuition: For first-year students is currently $775 an academic quarter, which amounts to $2,325 a year for first-year students, and $1,600 for second- and third-year students.

For additional information and application forms write to: Registrar, School of Law, Northeastern University, 400 Huntington Avenue, Boston, Massachusetts 02115.

NORTHERN KENTUCKY STATE COLLEGE, SALMON P. CHASE COLLEGE OF LAW, Covington, Kentucky

Enrollment: The student body is approximately 550 with an entering freshman class of 200. Approximately 60 percent of the students are from the greater Cincinnati area.

Admission: The College of Law admits students only in September and only for full-time study. Application deadline is April 1; applications thereafter will not be processed.

Tuition and Fees: For first-year students is approximately $428 a semester for residents and $478 for nonresidents.

For further information or applications write to: Admissions Office, Salmon P. Chase College of Law, Northern Kentucky State College, 1404 Dixie Highway, Covington, Kentucky 41011.

NORTHWESTERN UNIVERSITY SCHOOL OF LAW, Chicago, Illinois

Enrollment: Each year the School of Law enrolls a class of 175 from among 3,000 applicants. These numbers necessarily make admissions highly competitive and the decision process very selective.

Admission: Application forms may be obtained from the school after September 15, and will be accepted starting on October 1. The deadline for applications of those students applying for financial aid is February 1, and March 1 for all other applicants.

Tuition: Approximately $3,180, for the academic year.

For further information and applications write to: Office of Admissions, Northwestern University School of Law, 357 East Chicago Avenue, Chicago, Illinois 60611.

UNIVERSITY OF NOTRE DAME LAW SCHOOL, Notre Dame, Indiana

Admission: Admissions are made by a faculty committee, which considers each application separately. The school endeavors to give special consideration to disadvantaged students, efforts that have resulted in a 10 to 15 percent representation of minority groups.

Inquiries may be directed to: Notre Dame Law School, Box R, Notre Dame, Indiana 46556.

OHIO NORTHERN UNIVERSITY COLLEGE OF LAW, Ada, Ohio

Enrollment: One of the assets of the College of Law is the relatively small student body, enabling personal contact between students and faculty. The total enrollment is approximately 360, with 150 first-year students. Approximately 70 percent of the student body comes from Ohio.

Admission: No application deadline has been set, but students are encouraged to apply as early as possible.

Tuition and Fees: Total approximately $742 a quarter.

For further information write to: Office of the Dean, College of Law, Ohio Northern University, Ada, Ohio 45810.

THE OHIO STATE UNIVERSITY COLLEGE OF LAW, Columbus, Ohio

Enrollment: Total enrollment is approximately 600 students with each class consisting of roughly 200 students. Thirty-one full-time faculty members comprise the teaching staff, providing a faculty-student ratio of approximately 20 to 1.

Admission: First-year students are admitted only in the fall semester and completed applications are accepted from September 1 to April 1 of the year preceding enrollment.

Tuition: Approximately $930 a year for Ohio residents and $1,980 for nonresidents.

For further information write to: Admissions Office, The Ohio State University, 190 N. Oval Drive, Columbus, Ohio 43210.

UNIVERSITY OF OKLAHOMA COLLEGE OF LAW, Norman, Oklahoma

Enrollment: This college is a medium-sized law school with an enrollment of about 550. By regulation of the State Regents for Higher Education the college must give preference to Oklahoma residents where it is not possible to admit all applicants to a particular class. This limitation results in the first-year class having a nonresident enrollment of approximately 15 percent.

Admission: New students are admitted only in the fall semester. Applications, including LSAT scores, must be received prior to April 15 of the year in which admission is sought.

Tuition: Currently fees are $16 a semester hour for Oklahoma residents and $42 a semester hour for nonresidents.

For further information write to: Admissions, College of Law, University of Oklahoma, 630 Parrington Oval, Norman, Oklahoma 73069.

OKLAHOMA CITY UNIVERSITY SCHOOL OF LAW, Oklahoma City, Oklahoma

Enrollment: The student body numbers approximately 470 students. First-year enrollment, which had been limited to 150

tudents, was increased to 225 with the addition of a day divi-
ion.

Admission: New students are admitted only in the fall term.
There is no deadline for the filing of applications, but it is suggested
hey be submitted as early as possible.

Tuition: $52.50 a semester hour.

For additional information write to: Office of the Dean, Okla-
oma City University School of Law, 2501 N. Blackwelder, Okla-
oma City, Oklahoma 73106.

UNIVERSITY OF OREGON SCHOOL OF LAW, Eugene, Oregon

Enrollment: This school has over 400 students from diverse backgrounds. The entering class of 150 normally represents some 50
olleges and universities. About 16 percent of the student body are
women.

Admission: Since the number of students that can be accepted is
imited, admissions are competitive. The school encourages applica-
ions from women and persons from disadvantaged backgrounds.
Applications and supporting documents must be filed between Oc-
ober 1 and March 15 for the class entering the following fall.

Tuition and Fees: $754.50 for both residents and nonresidents for
he last academic year for which we have information. However,
uition charges are subject to change.

Send all inquiries and requests for applications to: School of Law,
University of Oregon, Eugene, Oregon 97403.

UNIVERSITY OF THE PACIFIC, McGEORGE SCHOOL OF LAW, Sac-
amento, California

Enrollment: Of the nearly 1,000 students enrolled, about 55 per-
ent are evening-division students. About one-third come from
chools outside California, including a significant number from
Nevada.

Admission: Three written recommendations are required but
ersonal interviews are not encouraged. The deadline for applica-
ions for day division is May 31.

Tuition: Approximately $730 a quarter for the day division and
430 a quarter for the evening division.

For further information and applications write to: Admissions
Office, McGeorge School of Law, University of the Pacific, 3200
Fifth Avenue, Sacramento, California 95817.

UNIVERSITY OF PENNSYLVANIA LAW SCHOOL, Philadelphia, Pennsylvania

Enrollment: The student body is drawn from all sections of the country. There are approximately 600 J.D. (Doctor of Laws) candidates plus a small group of graduate students in a full-time day session. Enrollment of women and members of minority groups is substantial and increasing.

Admission: Is highly selective. Some 200 places are filled from a total of approximately 3,000 applicants. The deadline for admission applications is February 1. The school admits students only in September and only for full-time study.

Tuition and Fees: Approximately $3,050 for the academic year.

For further information and applications write to: Admissions Office, University of Pennsylvania Law School, 3400 Chestnut Street, Philadelphia, Pennsylvania 19104.

PEPPERDINE UNIVERSITY SCHOOL OF LAW, Anaheim, California

Enrollment: There are approximately 500 in the student body, with more than half in the full-time division.

Admission: Students are admitted only in the fall. While there is no formal closing date for admissions, those received after April 1 will be evaluated and considered but will be at a considerable disadvantage.

Tuition and Fees: For a full-time student about $1,150 a semester, in the evening division, approximately $800.

For further information and applications write to: Admissions Office, Pepperdine University School of Law, 1520 South Anaheim Boulevard, Anaheim, California 92803.

UNIVERSITY OF PITTSBURGH SCHOOL OF LAW, Pittsburgh, Pennsylvania

Enrollment: The student body consists of 525 students.

Admission: Application for admission may be filed after September 1 and may be made after completion of six semesters of college work.

Tuition and Fees: $525 a semester for Pennsylvania residents and $1,020 a semester for nonresidents.

For applications write to: Director of Admissions, School of Law 1417 Cathedral of Learning, Pittsburgh, Pennsylvania 15213. Al other correspondence should be directed to: The Dean, School of Law, University of Pittsburgh, Pittsburgh, Pennsylvania 15219.

UNIVERSITY OF PUGET SOUND SCHOOL OF LAW, Tacoma, Washington

Enrollment: The student body numbers 385 first-year students, 130 of whom are in the evening division. Students from the state of Washington comprise approximately 74 percent of the student body with 79 percent of these coming from the Tacoma-Seattle-Olympia area.

Admission: Applications should be submitted by early winter for entry into the following summer or fall semester. Summer semester entry is for evening-division students only. No applications will be accepted for enrollment in the spring semester. Competition is keen for the spaces available. Minority-group members are encouraged to apply.

Tuition: For the day division $950 a semester; for the evening division, $700 a semester. Summer-semester tuition is $70 a credit, not to exceed $950 for the semester.

For further information and applications write to: Records and Admissions Office, University of Puget Sound School of Law, 8811 South Tacoma Way, Tacoma, Washington 98499.

UNIVERSITY OF RICHMOND, THE T.C. WILLIAMS SCHOOL OF LAW, Richmond, Virginia

Admission: First-year students may enter only at the beginning of the fall semester. Only full-time students are accepted. Applicants are encouraged to submit their applications as soon as possible after the completion of three full years of college study. All application materials should be received by the admissions office before December 1 preceding the year in which the applicants seek admission. Applications are considered roughly in the order in which they are completed with all decisions made by February.

Tuition and Fees: Approximately $2,025 for the academic year, exclusive of board and lodging.

For further information write to: Director of Admissions, University of Richmond Law School, Richmond, Virginia 23173.

RUTGERS—THE STATE UNIVERSITY SCHOOL OF LAW, Camden, New Jersey

Enrollment: Approximately 500 students are enrolled in the law school. Women students form a significant and growing proportion of the law school population. The faculty and student organizations actively seek to increase the applications and enrollment of both women and minority-group members.

Admission: About 160 students are sought for each entering class. First-year students are admitted only in September. No deadline is given for applications, but it is suggested that applicants file as early as possible.

Tuition and Fees: $920 a year for both residents and nonresidents.

For further information and application forms write to: Director of Admissions, Rutgers School of Law—Camden, 311 N. 5th Street, Camden, New Jersey 08102.

RUTGERS—THE STATE UNIVERSITY LAW SCHOOL, Newark, New Jersey

Enrollment: There are approximately 600 students in the student body of the Law School.

Admission: Admission is highly competitive; approximately 1 out of 20 applicants are admitted. Applicants are urged to take the LSAT by December, and in any event no later than February. Applications received after March 15 stand little chance of favorable consideration. First-year students are accepted for classes commencing in the fall only.

Tuition and Fees: $920 a year for both residents and nonresidents.

Send inquiries and requests for application material to: Admissions Secretary, Rutgers Law School—Newark, 180 University Avenue, Newark, New Jersey 07102.

ST. JOHN'S UNIVERSITY SCHOOL OF LAW, New York, New York

Enrollment: St. John's student body consists largely of residents of the New York–New Jersey–Connecticut metropolitan area but many other segments of the country are also represented. There are approximately 1,075 students comprising the student body.

Admission: Applications are accepted for September and February classes and should be filed as early as possible.

Tuition: Is estimated at $2,250 a year for day students and $1,600 for evening students. The tuition a semester hour is $80.

For further information and applications write to: Secretary of the School of Law, St. John's University, Grand Central and Utopia Parkways, Jamaica, New York 11439.

ST. LOUIS UNIVERSITY SCHOOL OF LAW, St. Louis, Missouri

Admission: The admission process is very selective. Careful evaluation of individual performance and potential is a most important factor. No deadline for applications is given but it would be best to get them in as early as possible. The deadline for applications for scholarships is March 1.

Tuition: $1,150 a semester.

Additional information may be obtained by writing to: Dean of Admissions, Saint Louis University School of Law, 3642 Lindell Boulevard, St. Louis, Missouri 63108.

ST. MARY'S UNIVERSITY SCHOOL OF LAW, San Antonio, Texas

Enrollment: Approximately 550 students are enrolled in the School of Law.

Admission: First-year students are admitted for the fall and summer terms. It is recommended that application for the fall term be made at least four months in advance.

Tuition: Presently $55 a semester hour. Ninety semester hours are required for the conferral of the J.D. degree.

All inquiries concerning admission should be addressed to: Chairman, Admissions Committee, School of Law, St. Mary's University, 2700 Cincinnati Avenue, San Antonio, Texas 78284.

UNIVERSITY OF SAN DIEGO SCHOOL OF LAW, San Diego, California

Enrollment: The student body numbers 877 students, of whom about 300 are evening-division students.

Admission: Applications should be submitted as early as possible in the fall preceding the desired admission date.

Tuition and Fees: For the day division approximately $1,900 for the academic year; for the evening division, $1,350.

Additional information and applications can be obtained by writing to: Records and Admissions Office, University of San Diego School of Law, Alcala Park, San Diego, California 92110.

UNIVERSITY OF SAN FRANCISCO SCHOOL OF LAW, San Francisco, California

Enrollment: The School of Law has approximately 725 students, about two-thirds of whom are enrolled in the full-time day division. For the last available year more than one-fifth were women and 19 percent were members of racial or ethnic minorities. The entering class has about 225 students in the day division and 75 in the evening division.

Admission: The school actively recruits Asian, Black, Chicano, and other minority students.

Tuition and Fees: For the day division total $2,100 a year; the evening division and summer school courses amount to $75 a credit.

Requests for catalogs, application forms, etc., should be directed to: Admissions Office, School of Law, University of San Francisco, San Francisco, California 94117.

UNIVERSITY OF SANTA CLARA SCHOOL OF LAW, Santa Clara, California

Enrollment: It is anticipated that there will be 190 students entering the School of Law in the day division and 100 in the evening division.

Admission: No deadline has been established for applications but a candidate is advised to apply early, and in any case no later than February.

Tuition and Fees: Approximately $2,175 for full-time students and $1,538 for part-time students.

Send all inquiries to: Admissions Office, School of Law, University of Santa Clara, Santa Clara, California 95053.

SETON HALL UNIVERSITY SCHOOL OF LAW, Newark, New Jersey

Enrollment: This law school is one of the largest in the country and has both a day and evening division. The main campus is located in South Orange, six miles from the School of Law. The student body consists of approximately 960 full-time and part-time students. There has been a noticeable increase in women students during the past several years.

Admission: Students are advised to file applications prior to February of the year of enrollment.

Tuition and Fees: Projected at $65 a credit hour or approximately $1800 for a day student, plus fees of $15 to $20 a semester.

All correspondence should be directed to: Admissions Office, Seton Hall University School of Law, 1095 Raymond Boulevard, Newark, New Jersey 07102.

UNIVERSITY OF SOUTH CAROLINA LAW CENTER, Columbia, South Carolina

Enrollment: There are approximately 895 students in the Law School with 383 in the entering class.

Admission: First-year students may enter the Law Center only at the beginning of the fall semester. Only full-time students are enrolled.

Tuition and Fees: For South Carolina residents are approximately $285 a semester; for nonresidents $640 a semester.

Inquiries concerning the Law Center should be addressed to: Director of Admissions, University of South Carolina Law Center, Columbia, South Carolina 29208.

UNIVERSITY OF SOUTH DAKOTA SCHOOL OF LAW, Vermillion, South Dakota

Admission: Applications should be submitted as early as possible, and must be completed by March 15.

Tuition: For South Dakota residents is $25 a credit hour; for nonresidents $50 a credit hour, according to the last available figures.

Send all inquiries, including applications, to: Office of the Dean, School of Law, University of South Dakota, Vermillion, South Dakota 57069.

SOUTH TEXAS COLLEGE OF LAW, Houston, Texas

Enrollment: The school is coeducation and nondenominational, having a diverse student body.

Admission: Beginning and transfer students are admitted for the fall, spring, and summer terms.

Tuition: $40 a credit hour for both residents and nonresidents, according to the last available figures.

Inquiries and application requests should be addressed to: Dean, South Texas College of Law, 1220 Polk Avenue, Houston, Texas 77002.

UNIVERSITY OF SOUTHERN CALIFORNIA LAW SCHOOL, Los Angeles, California

Enrollment: The entering class is limited to 160 full-time students, divided into two sections for purposes of instruction.

Admission: Students should apply by April 1 for admission the following September. Early application is encouraged.

Tuition: The last available information was $1,420 a semester. A rise in tuition may be anticipated.

Address any inquiries to: Admissions Officer or Financial Aid Officer, Law Center, University of Southern California, University Park, Los Angeles, California 90007.

SOUTHERN METHODIST UNIVERSITY SCHOOL OF LAW, Dallas, Texas

Enrollment: Approximately 625 in the J.D. (Doctor of Laws) program.

Admission: Is quite selective. The school, which is coeducational, welcomes students of all religions, races, creeds, and national origins. Entering students are accepted in the fall semester only. Applications should be completed by March 1.

Tuition: Approximately $2,700 a year.

For applications and information write to: Secretary of Admissions, School of Law, Southern Methodist University, Dallas, Texas 75275.

SOUTHERN UNIVERSITY SCHOOL OF LAW, Baton Rouge, Louisiana

Admission: The School of Law does not prescribe any prelegal courses, but strongly recommends a foundation in such courses as English, public speaking, sociology, political science, history, economics, psychology, logics, mathematics and analytical courses, and science. Students are admitted only in the fall semester. Completed application forms, together with all data and information requested, should be filed with the admissions office during the fall semester of the year prior to the year in which admission is sought.

Tuition: Free to all residents of Louisiana. For nonresidents tuition is $300 a semester. A general fee of $135 a semester is charged to all students.

Address correspondence to: Office of Admissions, Southern University School of Law, Baton Rouge, Louisiana 70813.

SOUTHWESTERN UNIVERSITY SCHOOL OF LAW, Los Angeles, California

Admission: Applications must be received at least three months prior to the start of each fall semester. Selection of students is made on a competitive basis without reference to race, religion, color, sex, or national origin.

Tuition and Fees: $50 a unit and incidental fees are approximately $50 a year for day and evening students.

Inquiries or requests for catalogs or applications should be addressed to: Southwestern University School of Law, 675 South Westmorland Avenue, Los Angeles, California 90005.

STANFORD UNIVERSITY SCHOOL OF LAW, Stanford, California

Admission: There are almost 4,000 applications for the 155 places in the class admitted in September. Applications should be completed preferably by January 1.

Tuition: Approximately $3,135 a year and expected to rise.

For information and applications write to: Admissions Secretary, Stanford Law School, Stanford, California 94305.

STETSON UNIVERSITY COLLEGE OF LAW, St. Petersburg, Florida

Enrollment: About two-thirds of the students are from Florida. Women constitute only a small percentage of the student body but their numbers are increasing. Total enrollment averages about 425.

Admission: Students are admitted at the beginning of either the fall or spring semester and at the beginning of the summer session. The college prescribes no particular major as a prerequisite for admission, being less interested in the undergraduate courses a student takes than in his ability to read and comprehend rapidly

and accurately, to think precisely and logically, and to communicate
his ideas clearly and correctly.

Tuition: $1,200 a semester and $600 a summer session.

Inquiries should be addressed to: Director of Admissions, Stetson
College of Law, St. Petersburg, Florida 33707.

SUFFOLK UNIVERSITY LAW SCHOOL, Boston, Massachusetts

Enrollment: Is approximately 2,000 students, divided equally between the day and evening divisions. The entering class comprises
approximately 300 day and 300 evening students.

Admission: Is highly competitive. An extensive moot-court program provides students with the opportunity to practice oral ad-
vocacy and legal-brief writing in each year of study, and this program is compulsory for first-year students.

Tuition and Fees: About $1,510 a year for the day division and
$1,135 a year for the evening division.

For application materials and information write to: Director of
Admissions, Suffolk University Law School, Beacon Hill, Boston,
Massachusetts 02114.

SYRACUSE UNIVERSITY COLLEGE OF LAW, Syracuse, New York

Enrollment: About two-thirds of the 550 law students are residents of New York; the rest come from 34 other states.

Admission: Students are admitted only in August.

Tuition and Fees: Are approximately $2,880 a year.

For further information and applications write to: Admission
Office, Syracuse University College of Law, Syracuse, New York
13210.

TEMPLE UNIVERSITY SCHOOL OF LAW, Philadelphia, Pennsylvania

Enrollment: The total J.D. (Doctor of Laws) enrollment is expected to be 1,250 students.

Admission: The deadline for filing applications has been April
1, but an earlier deadline is contemplated. A nonrefundable
application fee must accompany the application and an accepted applicant is required to make a $100 admission deposit
within ten days of acceptance. There are some 11 applicants

for every available place in the entering class.

Tuition: For Pennsylvania residents approximately $550 a semester for the day program, $470 a semester for the regular evening program, and $47 a semester hour for the extended evening program. For nonresidents, the tuition is $1,100 a semester for the day program, and $920 a semester for the regular evening program, and $92 a semester hour for the extended evening program.

Application forms and other information may be obtained by writing to: Director of Admissions, Law School Admissions Office, Temple University Law Center, S.E. Corner of Broad and Montgomery Streets, Philadelphia, Pennsylvania 19122.

UNIVERSITY OF TENNESSEE COLLEGE OF LAW, Knoxville, Tennessee

Enrollment: Preference is accorded to residents of Tennessee and no particular program of prelaw study is specified.

Admission: Applications should be filed as soon after October 1 as possible, and should be completed no later than March 15. A $10 application fee should accompany all applications.

Tuition and Fees: No tuition is required for Tennessee residents, only maintenance fees total about $384 for an academic year of three quarters. Nonresident tuition is an additional $240 a quarter.

Inquiries and application forms can be obtained by writing to: Assistant Dean, College of Law, The University of Tennessee, Knoxville, Tennessee 37916.

UNIVERSITY OF TEXAS SCHOOL OF LAW, Austin, Texas

Enrollment: There are approximately 1,500 students in the law school. Fifteen percent of the places in the entering class are filled by out-of-state residents.

Admission: Applications must be submitted by March 1 and all applicants must register no later with the Law School Data Assembly Service than February 1. The admissions process is necessarily very selective.

Tuition and Fees: For Texas residents total $260 for the nine-month term, and $1,260 for out-of-state residents.

For further information and applications write to: Admissions Office, School of Law, 2500 Red River Street, Austin, Texas 78705.

TEXAS SOUTHERN UNIVERSITY SCHOOL OF LAW, Houston, Texas

Enrollment: The total enrollment is about 300 with about half from out-of-state.

Admission: New students are admitted only in the fall semester The deadline for submission of applications and all supporting documents is March 1, for students planning to enroll the following fall

Tuition and Fees: For resident students approximately $135 a semester and nonresidents $675 a semester. Books and materials amount to approximately $200 a year.

For information and applications write to: James Bullock, Office of Admissions, Texas Southern University School of Law, Houston Texas 77004.

TEXAS TECH UNIVERSITY SCHOOL OF LAW, Lubbock, Texas

Enrollment: The student body numbers about 430, including 30 women, with an anticipated growth.

Admission: Applications should be filed by March 1 to receive consideration.

Tuition and fees: Consult the current law-school catalog. For this information and applications send correspondence to: Office of the Dean, School of Law, Texas Tech University, Box 4030, Lubbock, Texas 79409.

UNIVERSITY OF TOLEDO COLLEGE OF LAW, Toledo, Ohio

Enrollment: The college seeks a student body of diverse backgrounds economically, ethnically, socially, and geographically, with a variety of undergraduate majors.

Admission: Applicants filing after April 1 for the full-time program and after July 1 for the part-time program may find that the classes have been filled.

Tuition and Fees: Ohio residents will pay approximately $1,050 an academic year; nonresidents, $2,205.

All correspondence regarding admission should be sent to: Office of Admissions, University of Toledo College of Law, Toledo, Ohio 43606.

TULANE UNIVERSITY SCHOOL OF LAW, New Orleans, Louisiana

Enrollment: The school is prepared to train students from any part of the U.S. for practice in their respective states. Approximately 50 percent of the freshman class comes from outside Louisiana.

Admission: Those applicants whose undergraduate average and LSAT are above average are given early admission between January 1 and March 1. Thereafter the most qualified applicants are accepted until the class is completed, usually about the middle of May. Only full-time students are accepted. Tulane also conducts a summer school.

Tuition: $2,600 for the academic year.

Send to: Admissions Office, Tulane University School of Law, New Orleans, Louisiana 70118, for further information or application.

THE UNIVERSITY OF TULSA COLLEGE OF LAW, Tulsa Oklahoma

Enrollment: The entering class is limited to about 150 full-time students and represents about two-thirds of the states, with a majority coming from the Southwest.

Admission: Beginning students are admitted only in the fall session. The deadline for applications is May 1 and it is recommended that applications be filed as early as possible.

Tuition and Fees: Since this is a private institution, tuition and fees are the same for resident and nonresident students. Tuition is approximately $52 a credit hour.

The College of Law placement committee has established contacts with legal departments of federal, state, and local government agencies; with numerous corporate counsel offices principally in oil and oil-related companies; and with law firms, most of which are located in Oklahoma. For further information and application write to: Office of the Dean, College of Law, The University of Tulsa, 3120 East Fourth Place, Tulsa, Oklahoma 74104.

UNIVERSITY OF UTAH COLLEGE OF LAW, Salt Lake City, Utah

Enrollment: Students are primarily residents of the West, with a majority from the state of Utah.

Admission: Is selective. Entering students are accepted only in the fall semester. Applications and other credentials and fees must be submitted by April 1.

Tuition: Resident tuition is approximately $550 for the two regular semesters; for nonresidents, approximately $1100.

For further information and application write to: Office of the

Dean, University of Utah College of Law, Salt Lake City, Utah
84112.

VALPARAISO UNIVERSITY SCHOOL OF LAW, Valparaiso, Indiana
   Enrollment: The School of Law has an enrollment of 350 students
and is limited to 100 students in the first-year class.
   Admission: Early applications are highly recommended.
   Tuition and Fees: Approximately $2,190 for the academic year.
   For additional information write to: Office of the Dean, Val-
paraiso University School of Law, Valparaiso, Indiana 46383.

VANDERBILT UNIVERSITY SCHOOL OF LAW, Nashville, Tennessee
   Enrollment: The student body is composed of students from 151
undergraduate schools and 42 states. The relative proportion of
women has increased noticeably in recent years.
   Admission: The entering class is limited to approximately 150
students and is chosen from roughly 1,500 applicants. Therefore
submission of applications at an early date is recommended.
   Tuition: Approximately $2,600 an academic year, payable in two
equal installments.
   For further information and application write to: Admissions
Office, School of Law, Vanderbilt University, Nashville, Tennessee
37240.

VILLANOVA UNIVERSITY SCHOOL OF LAW, Villanova, Pennsylvania
   Enrollment: The student body approximates 600 students from
some 140 colleges and universities. About 13 percent are women,
who constitute 20 percent of the most recent first-year
class.
   Admission: Applications should be filed from November through
February preceding the fall term of intended enrollment. No distinctions are made on the basis of sex, race, color, or creed.
   Tuition and Fees: Approximately $2,075 an academic year.
   Application forms and more detailed information can be obtained
by writing to: Registrar, School of Law, Villanova University, Villanova, Pennsylvania 19085.

UNIVERSITY OF VIRGINIA SCHOOL OF LAW, Charlottesville, Virginia

Enrollment: Approximately 915 full-time students are enrolled, and of this number, 83 are women. Virginia residents comprise approximately 55 percent.

Admission: Students are admitted only in September and only for full-time study. Application deadline is February 1; any received after that date will be processed but the late applicant is at a definite disadvantage.

Tuition and Fees: Approximately $800 for an academic year for Virginia residents and $1,920 for nonresidents.

Inquiries concerning the School of Law should be addressed to: Admissions Office, University of Virginia School of Law, Charlottesville, Virginia 22901.

WAKE FOREST UNIVERSITY SCHOOL OF LAW, Winston-Salem, North Carolina

Enrollment: Approximately two-thirds of the 400 students in the student body come from North Carolina. There are usually a number of women in each class.

Admission: Applications for the September class should not be filed prior to the preceding September or later than February 1 of the year in which the applicant desires to enter. Early application is encouraged.

Tuition and Fees: Are approximately $1,700. Tuition for the summer session is based on one-half the tuition for a semester (without fees). No differentiation is made between resident and nonresident students.

For further information write to: Dean, Wake Forest University School of Law, P.O. Box 7206, Winston-Salem, North Carolina 27109.

WASHBURN UNIVERSITY OF TOPEKA SCHOOL OF LAW, Topeka, Kansas

Enrollment: Student body, approximately 517; first-year class, 220.

Admission: Deadline for applications is March 15.

Tuition: For residents and nonresidents is approximately $31.50 a credit hour.

For further information write to: Admissions Office, Washburn University of Topeka School of Law, Topeka, Kansas 66621.

UNIVERSITY OF WASHINGTON SCHOOL OF LAW, Seattle, Washington

Enrollment: Over 31 percent of the students in the student body are women. Total enrollment was 451 for last available year, with 156 in the first-year class.

Admission: Deadline for applications is February 1 for admission the succeeding September.

Tuition: Approximately $624 for Washington residents, and $1,641 for out-of-state residents, a year.

For further information write to: Admissions Office, School of Law, University of Washington, Seattle, Washington 98195.

WASHINGTON UNIVERSITY SCHOOL OF LAW, St. Louis, Missouri

Enrollment: Approximately 15 percent of the school's 530 students are women; over 5 percent are from minority groups.

Admission: Applications are received any time after September 1 for the following fall. There is no deadline for applications, but late applicants may be denied admission because all places in the entering class are filled.

Tuition: $2,600, payable $1,300 each semester.

For further information and application write to: School of Law, Washington University, St. Louis, Missouri 63130.

WASHINGTON AND LEE UNIVERSITY SCHOOL OF LAW, Lexington, Virginia

Enrollment: The student body is limited to 250 so that each student may benefit from small classes and close personal relationships.

Admission: Students are admitted only in September on a full-time basis. There is no application deadline but applicants are advised to submit applications by February 1.

Tuition: Approximately $1,050 a semester.

Address inquiries for further information to: Office of the Dean, School of Law, Washington and Lee University, Lexington, Virginia 24450.

WAYNE STATE UNIVERSITY LAW SCHOOL, Detroit, Michigan

Enrollment: The student body of 1,001 is divided into 704 day students and 297 evening students. In addition, there are 99 graduate students. The first-year class numbers about 300. It is divided into three sections, with one class divided into small groups. More than three-quarters of the students are residents of Michigan. The last three years have shown a dramatic increase in the number of both women and minority group students.

Admission: The deadline for applications is April 15. Beginning law students may enter only in September.

Tuition: Michigan residents approximately $910; nonresidents approximately $1,945.

For further information write to: Director of Admissions, Wayne State University Law School, 468 West Ferry Avenue, Detroit, Michigan 48202.

WEST VIRGINIA UNIVERSITY COLLEGE OF LAW, Morgantown, West Virginia

Enrollment: Only full-time students are enrolled. Entering classes are limited to 100 students.

Admission: Applications are accepted beginning in September of the year preceding enrollment and must be completed by March 1. New students are admitted only in the fall semester. Hence, students should take the LSAT no later than the February administration, with the October or December test dates preferred for early consideration.

Tuition and Fees: for West Virginia residents $322 for the last available year; for nonresidents, $972.

Any inquiries should be addressed to: Admissions Officer, College of Law, West Virginia University, 1530 University Avenue, Morgantown, West Virginia 26505.

WILLAMETTE UNIVERSITY COLLEGE OF LAW, Salem, Oregon

Enrollment: The student body consists of approximately 385 students. The entering class in recent years has numbered approximately 140. Enrollment of women and minority students is substantial and increasing.

Admission: Is highly selective with more than eight applicants for each position. Applications may be filed after September 1 and before January 1.

Tuition: For full-time students approximately $1,110 a semester; the tuition for each semester hour over 18 is $50. No distinction is made between residents and nonresidents.

For further information and application write to: Office of the Dean of Admissions, College of Law, Willamette University, Salem, Oregon 97301.

COLLEGE OF WILLIAM AND MARY, MARSHALL-WYTHE SCHOOL OF LAW, Williamsburg, Virginia

Enrollment: The student body consists of approximately 460 full-time students with 150 first-year students, of which 18 were women.

Admission: The deadline for applications is March 1, which is also the deadline for taking the LSAT and completing the registration process.

Tuition and Fees: Approximately $756 for Virginia residents and $1,926 for nonresidents.

Address all correspondence to: Marshall-Whythe School of Law, Admissions Office, College of William and Mary, Williamsburg, Virginia 23185.

WILLIAM MITCHELL COLLEGE OF LAW, St. Paul, Minnesota

Enrollment: There are approximately 250 freshmen who enroll each fall, with 5 percent women.

Admission: There is no deadline for applications but it is recommended that these be filed as early as possible.

Tuition: Approximately $950 for an academic year.

For forther information write to: Registrar, William Mitchell College of Law, St. Paul, Minnesota 55105.

UNIVERSITY OF WISCONSIN LAW SCHOOL, Madison, Wisconsin

Enrollment: About three-quarters of the student body are from Wisconsin. The increasing population of women in the school was up to almost 16 percent for the last available year.

Admission: Students are admitted only in August and for ful·

time study only. Application deadline is February 15. Since this is Wisconsin's only state-supported law school, some preference is given to residents.

Tuition: Wisconsin residents approximately $652 an academic year; nonresidents $2,376.

For further information and application write to: Admissions Office, University of Wisconsin Law School, Madison, Wisconsin 53706.

UNIVERSITY OF WYOMING COLLEGE OF LAW, Laramie, Wyoming
Enrollment: About three-quarters of the students are residents of Wyoming. Women law students are especially welcome and the college participates in programs designed to help members of minority races, especially those of American Indian and Spanish descent.

Admission: Students are admitted only for the fall semester. The college begins to receive applications in September for the class entering the following August. The deadline for applications is March 1.

Tuition and Fees: For Wyoming residents for the last available year were $205.25 a semester; for nonresidents, $688.25.

For further information and application write to: Office of the Associate Dean, University of Wyoming College of Law, Box 3035, University Station, Laramie, Wyoming 82070.

YALE UNIVERSITY LAW SCHOOL, New Haven, Connecticut
Enrollment: The student body consists of approximately 550 J.D. Doctor of Laws) candidates and approximately 40 graduate stu- ents. The class of 1975, with 168 students, includes 141 men and ´ women. There are 20 students of minority background in the ss. There are representatives of 80 different colleges and univer- ?s in this class.

Admissions: All necessary papers should be sent directly to: n of Admissions, Yale Law School. The deadline for applica- s is March 1. First-year students are admitted only in the fall ster and only for full-time study. Applicants in the fall must the LSAT no later than December of the preceding year in to meet the March 1 deadline.

Tuition: Approximately $3,300. Approximately 60 percent of the student body now receive some form of financial assistance.

For further information and application write to: Office of Admissions, Yale Law School, New Haven, Connecticut 06520.

INDEX